JULIE
and
JULIA

JULIE
and
JULIA

365 days, 524 recipes, 1 Tiny Apartment
Kitchen: How One Girl Risked Her
Marriage, Her Job, and Her Sanity
to Master the Art of Living

JULIE POWELL

Little, Brown and Company
New York   Boston

Little, Brown and Company
Time Warner Book Group
1271 Avenue of the Americas, New York, NY 10020

The excerpt from Paul Child's letter to his brother, Charles,
quoted on page 3 and the excerpt from Julia Child's letter to Simone Beck
quoted on page 189 are both taken from the Julia Child papers
held in the Radcliffe Institute's Schlesinger Library at Harvard University.
Both excerpts also appear in Noël Riley Fitch's biography
of Julia Child, *Appetite for Life*.

ISBN 10: 0-7394-6701-8
ISBN 13: 978-0-7394-6701-5

Book design by Jo Anne Metsch

Printed in the United States of America

For Julia, without whom I could not have done this,
and for Eric, without whom I could not do at all

CONTENTS

AUTHOR'S NOTE

For the sake of discretion, many identifying details, individuals, and events throughout this book have been altered. Only myself, my husband, and certain widely known public figures, including Julia and Paul Child, are identified by real names.

Also, sometimes I just made stuff up.

Case in point: the scenes from the lives of Paul Child and Julia McWilliams Child depicted throughout are purely works of imagination, inspired by events described in the journals and letters of Paul Child, the letters of Julia McWilliams, and the biography of Julia Child, *Appetite for Life,* by Noël Riley Fitch. I thank Ms. Riley Fitch for her fine work, and the Schlesinger Library at Harvard University for generously making Mrs. Child's archives available to the public.

—*Julie Powell*

JULIE
and
JULIA

■▪■▪■▪■

Thursday, October 6, 1949
Paris

At seven o'clock on a dreary evening in the Left Bank, Julia began roasting pigeons for the second time in her life.

She'd roasted them the first time that morning during her first-ever cooking lesson, in a cramped basement kitchen at the Cordon Bleu cooking school at 129, rue du Faubourg St.-Honoré. Now she was roasting some more in the rented flat she shared with her husband, Paul, in the kitchen at the top of a narrow stairway in what used to be the servant quarters before the old house got divided up into apartments. The stove and counters were too short for her, like everything else in the world. Even so, she liked her kitchen at the top of the stairs better than the one at school — liked the light and air up there, liked the dumbwaiter that would carry her birds down to the dining room, liked that she could cook while her husband sat beside her at the kitchen table, keeping her company. She supposed she would get used to the counters soon enough — when you go through life as a six-foot-two-inch-tall woman, you get used to getting used to things.

Paul was there now, snapping pictures of his wife from time to time, and finishing up a letter to his brother, Charlie. "If you could see Julie stuffing pepper and lard up the asshole of a dead pigeon," *he wrote, "you'd realize how profoundly affected she's been already."**

But he hadn't seen anything yet. His wife, Julia Child, had decided to learn to cook. She was thirty-seven years old.

---

*Excerpted from a letter from Paul Child to his brother, Charles, 1949.

♦ 3 ♦

▗▖▗▖▗▖▗▖▗▖▗▖

The Road to Hell Is
Paved with Leeks and Potatoes

As far as I know, the only evidence supporting the theory that Julia Child first made Potage Parmentier during a bad bout of ennui is her own recipe for it. She writes that Potage Parmentier — which is just a Frenchie way of saying potato soup — "smells good, tastes good, and is simplicity itself to make." It is the first recipe in the first book she ever wrote. She concedes that you can add carrots or broccoli or green beans if you want, but that seems beside the point, if what you're looking for is simplicity itself.

Simplicity itself. It sounds like poetry, doesn't it? It sounds like just what the doctor ordered.

It wasn't what my doctor ordered, though. My doctor — my gynecologist, to be specific — ordered a baby.

"There are the hormonal issues in your case, with the PCOS, you know about that already. And you are pushing thirty, after all. Look at it this way — there will never be a better time."

This was not the first time I'd heard this. It had been happening for a couple of years now, ever since I'd sold some of my eggs for $7,500 in order to pay off credit card debt. Actually, that was the second time I'd "donated"— a funny way of putting it, since when you wake up from the anesthesia less a few dozen ova and get dressed, there's a check for thousands of dollars with *your* name on it waiting at the receptionist's desk. The first time was five years ago, when I was twenty-four, impecunious and fancy-free. I hadn't planned on doing it twice, but three years later I got a call from a doctor with an unidentifiable European accent who asked me if I'd be interested in flying down to Florida for a second go-round, because "our clients were very satisfied with the results of your initial donation." Egg donation is still a new-enough technology that our slowly evolving legal and etiquette systems have not yet quite caught up; nobody knows if egg dona-tors are going to be getting sued for child support ten years down the line or what. So discussions on the subject tend to be knotted with imprecise pronouns and euphemisms. The upshot of this phone call, though, was that there was a little me running around Tampa or somewhere, and the little me's parents were happy enough with him or her that they wanted a matched set. The honest part of me wanted to shout, "Wait, no — when they start hitting puberty you'll regret this!" But $7,500 is a lot of money.

Anyway, it was not until the second harvesting (they actually call it "harvesting"; fertility clinics, it turns out, use a lot of vaguely apocalyptic terms) that I found out I had polycystic ovar-ian syndrome, which sounds absolutely terrifying, but apparently just meant that I was going to get hairy and fat and I'd have to take all kinds of drugs to conceive. Which means, I guess, that I haven't heard my last of crypto-religious obstetric jargon.

So. Ever since I was diagnosed with this PCOS, two years ago, doctors have been obsessing over my childbearing prospects. I've even been given the Pushing Thirty speech by my avuncular, white-haired *orthopedist* (what kind of twenty-nine-year-old has a herniated disk, I ask you?).

At least my gynecologist had some kind of business in my private parts. Maybe that's why I heroically did not start bawling immediately when he said this, as he was wiping off his speculum. Once he left, however, I did fling one of my navy faille pumps at the place where his head had been just a moment before. The heel hit the door with a thud, leaving a black scuff mark, then dropped onto the counter, where it knocked over a glass jar of cotton swabs. I scooped up all the Q-tips from the counter and the floor and started to stuff them back into the jar before realizing I'd probably gotten them all contaminated, so then I shoved them into a pile next to an apothecary jar full of fresh needles and squeezed myself back into the vintage forties suit I'd been so proud of that morning when Nate from work told me it made my waist look small while subtly eyeing my cleavage, but which on the ride from lower Manhattan to the Upper East Side on an un-air-conditioned 6 train had gotten sweatstained and rumpled. Then I slunk out of the room, fifteen-buck co-pay already in hand, the better to make my escape before anyone discovered I'd trashed the place.

As soon as I got belowground, I knew there was a problem. Even before I reached the turnstiles, I heard a low, subterranean rumble echoing off the tiled walls, and noticed more than the usual number of aimless-looking people milling about. A tangy whiff of disgruntlement wafted on the fetid air. Every once in a great while the "announcement system" would come on and "announce" something, but none of these spatterings of word salad resulted in the arrival of a train, not for a long, long time. Along with everyone else, I leaned out over the platform edge, hoping to see the pale yellow of a train's headlight glinting off the track, but the tunnel was black. I smelled like a rained-upon, nervous sheep. My feet, in their navy heels with the bows on the toe, were killing me, as was my back, and the platform was so crammed with people that before long I began to worry someone was going to fall off the edge onto the tracks — possibly me, or maybe the person I was going to push during my imminent psychotic break.

But then, magically, the crowd veered away. For a split second I thought the stink coming off my suit had reached a deadly new level, but the wary, amused looks on the faces of those edging away weren't focused on me. I followed their gaze to a plug of a woman, her head of salt-and-pepper hair shorn into the sort of crew cut they give to the mentally disabled, who had plopped down on the concrete directly behind me. I could see the whorls of her cowlick like a fingerprint, feel the tingle of invaded personal space against my shins. The woman was muttering to herself fiercely. Commuters had vacated a swath of platform all around the loon as instinctually as a herd of wildebeests evading a lioness. I was the only one stuck in the dangerous blank circle, the lost calf, the old worn-out cripple who couldn't keep up.

The loon started smacking her forehead with the heel of her palm. "Fuck!" she yelled. "Fuck! FUCK!"

I couldn't decide whether it would be safer to edge back into the crowd or freeze where I was. My breathing grew shallow as I turned my eyes blankly out across the tracks to the uptown platform, that old subway chameleon trick.

The loon placed both palms down on the concrete in front of her and — CRACK! — smacked her forehead hard on the ground.

This was a little much even for the surrounding crowd of New Yorkers, who of course all knew that loons and subways go together like peanut butter and chocolate. The sickening noise of skull on concrete seemed to echo in the damp air — as if she was using her specially evolved resonant brainpan as an instrument to call the crazies out from every far-underground branch of the city. Everybody flinched, glancing around nervously. With a squeak I hopped back into the multitude. The loon had a smudgy black abrasion right in the middle of her forehead, like the scuff mark my shoe had left on my gynecologist's door, but she just kept screeching. The train pulled in, and I connived to wiggle into the car the loon wasn't going into.

It was only once I was in the car, squeezed in shoulder to shoulder, the lot of us hanging by one hand from the overhead bar like slaughtered cows on the trundling train, that it came to me — as if some omnipotent God of City Dwellers were whispering the truth in my ear — that the only two reasons I hadn't joined right in with the loon with the gray crew cut, beating my head and screaming "Fuck!" in primal syncopation, were (1) I'd be embarrassed and (2) I didn't want to get my cute vintage suit any dirtier than it already was. Performance anxiety and a dry-cleaning bill; those were the only things keeping me from stark raving lunacy.

That's when I started to cry. When a tear dropped onto the pages of the *New York Post* that the guy sitting beneath me was reading, he just blew air noisily through his nose and turned to the sports pages.

When I got off the subway, after what seemed like years, I called Eric from a pay phone at the corner of Bay Ridge and Fourth Avenue.

"Hey. Did you get anything for dinner?"

Eric made that little sucking-in-through-his-teeth sound he always makes when he thinks he's about to get in trouble. "Was I supposed to?"

"Well, I *told* you I'd be late because of my doctor's appointment —"

"Right, right, sorry. I just, I didn't . . . You want me to order something in, or —"

"Don't worry about it. I'll pick up something or other."

"But I'm going to start packing just as soon as the *NewsHour*'s done, promise!"

It was nearly eight o'clock, and the only market open in Bay Ridge was the Korean deli on the corner of Seventieth and Third. I must have looked a sight, standing around in the produce aisle in my bedraggled suit, my face tracked with mascara, staring like a catatonic. I couldn't think of a thing that I wanted to eat. I grabbed some potatoes, a bunch of leeks, some Hotel Bar butter.

I felt dazed and somehow will-less, as if I was following a shopping list someone else had made. I paid, walked out of the shop,
and headed for the bus stop, but just missed the B69. There
wouldn't be another for a half hour at least, at this time of night,
so I started the ten-block walk home, carrying a plastic bag bristling with spiky dark leek bouquets.

It wasn't until almost fifteen minutes later, as I was walking
past the Catholic boys' school on Shore Road one block over
from our apartment building, that I realized that I'd managed,
unconsciously, to buy exactly the ingredients for Julia Child's
Potage Parmentier.

When I was a kid, my dad used to love to tell the story about finding five-year-old Julie curled up in the back of his copper-colored
Datsun ZX immersed in a crumpled back issue of the *Atlantic
Monthly*. He told that one to all the guys at his office, and to the
friends he and my mom went out to dinner with, and to all of
the family who weren't born again and likely to disapprove. (Of
the *Atlantic*, not Z-cars.)

I think the point behind this was that I'd been singled out as an
early entrant to the ranks of the intellectually superior. And since
I was awful at ballet and tap dancing, after all, always the last one
to make it up the rope in gym class, a girl neither waifish nor
charming in owlish red-rimmed glasses, I took my ego-petting
where I could get it. But the not-very-highbrow truth of the matter was that the reading was how I got my ya-yas out.

For the sake of my bookish reputation I upgraded to Tolstoy
and Steinbeck before I understood them, but my dark secret was
that really, I preferred the junk. *The Dragonriders of Pern, Flowers
in the Attic, The Clan of the Cave Bear*. This stuff was like my stash
of *Playboy*s under the mattress. I waited until my camp counselor
left the cabin to steal the V. C. Andrews she stashed behind her
box of Tampax. I nicked my mom's Jean Auel, and had already

gotten halfway through before she found out, so she could only wince and suppose there was some educational value, but no *Valley of Horses* for you, young lady.

Then adolescence set in well and proper, and reading for kicks got shoved in the backseat with the old *Atlantic*s. It had been a long time since I'd done anything with the delicious, licentious cluelessness that I used to read those books — hell, sex now wasn't as exciting as reading about sex used to be. I guess nowadays your average fourteen-year-old Texan possesses exhaustive knowledge of the sexual uses of tongue studs, but I doubt the information excites her any more than my revelations about Neanderthal sex.

You know what a fourteen-year-old Texan doesn't know shit about? French food.

A couple of weeks after my twenty-ninth birthday, in the spring of 2002, I went back to Texas to visit my parents. Actually, Eric kind of made me go.

"You have to get out of here," he said. The kitchen drawer that broke two weeks after we moved in, and was never satisfactorily rehabilitated, had just careened off its tracks yet again, flinging Pottery Barn silverware in all directions. I was sobbing, forks and knives glittering at my feet. Eric was holding me in one of those tight hugs like a half nelson, which he does whenever he's trying to comfort me when what he really wants to do is smack me.

"Will you come with me?" I didn't look up from the snot stain I was impressing upon his shirt.

"I'm too busy at the office right now. Besides, I think it's better if you go by yourself. Hang out with your mom. Buy some clothes. Sleep in."

"I have work, though."

"Julie, you're a temp. What's temping for if you can't run off and take a break sometimes? That's why you're doing it, right?"

I didn't like to think about why I was temping. My voice went high and cracked. "Well, I can't afford it."

"We *can* afford it. Or we can ask your parents to pay." He grabbed my chin and lifted it up to his face. "Julie. Seriously? Go. Because I can't live with you like this anymore."

So I went — my mom bought me the ticket for a late birthday present. A week later I flew into Austin, early enough to grab lunch at Poke-Jo's.

And then, right in the middle of my brisket sandwich and okra, less than a month after I turned twenty-nine, Mom dropped the Pushing Thirty bomb for the very first time.

"Jesus, Mom!"

"What?" My mother has this bright, smiling, hard tone that she always uses when she wants me to face facts. She was using it now. "All I'm saying is here you are, miserable, running away from New York, getting into a bad place with Eric, and for what? You're getting older, you're not taking advantage of the city, why do this to yourself?"

This was exactly the one thing I had come to Austin to *not* talk about. I should have known my mother would dig in like a goddamned rat terrier.

I had gone to New York like everybody else goes to New York — just as the essential first step for a potato destined for soup is to have its skin peeled off, the essential starting point for an aspiring actor is to move to New York. I preferred jobs that did not require auditions, which, since I neither looked like Renée Zellweger nor was a terribly good actor, proved to be a problem. Mostly what I'd done was temp, for (to name a few): the photocopier contractor for the UN; the Asian American businesses underwriting department at AIG; the vice president of a broadband technology outfit with an amazing office looking out onto the Brooklyn Bridge, which folded about two weeks after I got there; and an investment firm specializing in the money matters of nunneries. Recently, I'd started work at a government agency downtown. It looked like they were going to offer to bring me on permanently — eventually all the temp employers offered to let you go perm — and for the first time, I was considering, in a despairing sort of way, doing it. It was enough to make me suicidal even before my mom started telling me I was getting old. Mom should have known this, but instead of apologizing for her cruelty she just popped another piece of fried okra into her mouth and said, "Let's go shopping — your clothes are just awful!"

The next morning I lingered at my parents' kitchen table long after they'd both left for work, wrapped up in a well-worn gray flannel robe I'd forgotten I had, sipping coffee. I'd finished the *Times* crossword and all the sections except for Business and Circuits, but didn't yet have enough caffeine in my system to contemplate getting dressed. (I'd overindulged in margaritas the night before, not at all an unusual occurrence when visiting the folks in Austin.) The pantry door stood ajar, and my aimless gaze rested on the bookshelves inside, the familiar ranks of spines lined up there. When I got up to fill my cup one last time, I made a detour and took one of the books — *Mastering the Art of French Cooking, Vol. 1*, my mom's old 1967 edition, a book that had known my family's kitchen longer than I had. I sat back down at the table at which I'd eaten a thousand childhood afternoon snacks and began flipping through, just for the hell of it.

When I was a kid, I used to look at *MtAoFC* quite a lot. Partly it was just my obsession with anything between two covers, but there was something else, too. Because this book has the power to shock. *MtAoFC* is still capable of striking deep if obscure zones of discomfort. Find the most pale, pierced and kohl-eyed, proudly pervy hipster you can and ask her to cook Pâté de Canard en Croûte, aided only by the helpful illustrations on pages 571 through 575. I promise you, she'll be fleeing back to Williamsburg, where no one's going to make her bone a whole duck, faster than you can say, "trucker hats are *soooo* five minutes ago."

But why? What is it about this book? It's just an old cookbook, for God's sake. Yet vegetarians, Atkinsers, and South Beach bums flare their nostrils at the stink of apostasy between its covers. Self-proclaimed foodies spare a smile of fond condescension before returning to their Chez Panisse cookbooks. By all rights, I should feel this way too. I am, after all, that ultimate synthesis of urban flakiness and suburban self-righteousness, the New York actress.

Well, actually, I guess I can't say that, since I've never had a real acting job. And to tell the truth — it's time I faced facts here — I never really even tried. But if I'm not a New York actress, what am I? I'm a person who takes a subway from the outer boroughs to a lower Manhattan office every morning, who spends her days answering phones and doing copying, who is too disconsolate when she gets back to her apartment at night to do anything but sit on the couch and stare vacantly at reality TV shows until she falls asleep.

Oh God. It really was true, wasn't it? I really was a secretary.

When I looked up from *MtAoFC* for the first time, half an hour after I opened it, I realized that deep down, I'd been resigned to being a secretary for months — maybe even years.

That was the bad news. The good news was that the buzzing in my head and queasy but somehow exhilarating squeeze deep in my belly were reminding me that I might still, after all, be something else.

Do you know *Mastering the Art of French Cooking?* You must, at least, know *of* it — it's a cultural landmark, for Pete's sake. Even if you just think of it as the book by that lady who looks like Dan Aykroyd and bleeds a lot, you know *of* it. But do you know the book itself? Try to get your hands on one of the early hardback editions — they're not exactly rare. For a while there, every American housewife who could boil water had a copy, or so I've heard.

It's not lushly illustrated; there are no shiny soft-core images of the glossy-haired author sinking her teeth into a juicy strawberry or smiling stonily before a perfectly rustic tart with carving knife in hand, like some chilly blonde kitchen dominatrix. The dishes are hopelessly dated — the cooking times outrageously long, the use of butter and cream beyond the pale, and not a single reference to pancetta or sea salt or wasabi. This book hasn't been on the must-have list for enterprising gourmands in decades. But as I held it in my hands that morning, opened its cover spangled with tomato-colored fleurs-de-lys, skimmed through its yellowed pages, I felt like I'd at last found something *important.* Why? I bent again over the book's pages, searching for the cause of this strange feeling. It wasn't the food exactly. If you looked hard enough, the food started to feel almost beside the point. No, there was something deeper here, some code within the words, perhaps some secret embedded in the paper itself.

I have never looked to religion for comfort — belief is just not in my genes. But reading *Mastering the Art of French Cooking* — childishly simple and dauntingly complex, incantatory and comforting — I thought this was what prayer must feel like. Sustenance bound up with anticipation and want. Reading *MtAoFC* was like reading pornographic Bible verses.

So naturally when I flew back to New York that May, I had Mom's copy of the book stashed in my bag.

The thing you learn with Potage Parmentier is that "simple" is not exactly the same as "easy." It had never occurred to me that there was a difference until Eric and I sat down on our couch the night of my appointment at the gynecologist's, three months after stealing my mother's forty-year-old cookbook, and took our first slurps of Julia Child's potato soup.

Certainly I had made *easier* dinners. Unwrapping a cellophane-swathed hunk of London broil and tossing it under the broiler was one method that came immediately to mind. Ordering pizza and getting drunk on Stoli gimlets while waiting for it to arrive, that was another favorite. Potage Parmentier didn't even hold a candle, in the easy department.

First you peel a couple of potatoes and slice them up. Slice some leeks, rinse them a couple of times to get rid of the grit — leeks are muddy little suckers. Throw these two ingredients in a pot with some water and some salt. Simmer it for forty-five minutes or so, then either "mash the vegetables in the soup with a fork" or pass them through a food mill. I didn't have a food mill, and I wasn't about to mash up vegetables with a *fork*. What I had was a potato ricer.

Well, technically it was Eric's potato ricer. Before we were married, years ago, before Atkins hit, mashed potatoes used to be Eric's specialty. For a while, before we learned the value of Brooklyn storage space, we'd had this tradition where I'd get him arcane kitchen gadgets, the not-very-funny joke being that he didn't actually cook at all, except for the mashed potatoes. The ricer is the only survivor from this period. It was his Christmas present the year we were in the railroad apartment on Eleventh between Seventh and Eighth — this was before we got priced out of Park Slope entirely. I'd sewn stockings for the both of us out of felt — his is red with white trim, mine white with red — from a pattern in the *Martha Stewart Living* holiday issue that year. We still have them, even though I can't sew and they're totally kattywhompus: the stitching uneven, the decorative cuffs bunched and crooked. They're also way too small for things like ricers. I stuffed it in anyway. Hanging on the mantel of the nonfunctional fireplace in the bedroom, the stocking looked like Santa had brought Eric a Luger. I've never been much good at stocking stuffers.

Once the leeks and potatoes have simmered for an hour or so, you mash them up with a fork or a food mill or a potato ricer. All three of these options are far more of a pain in the neck than the Cuisinart — one of which space-munching behemoths we scored when we got married — but Julia Child allows as how a Cuisinart will turn soup into "something un-French and monotonous." Any suggestion that uses the construction "un-French" is up for debate, but if you make Potage Parmentier, you will see her point. If you use the ricer, the soup will have *bits* — green bits and white bits and yellow bits — instead of being utterly smooth. After you've mushed it up, just stir in a couple of hefty chunks of butter, and you're done. JC says sprinkle with parsley but you don't have to. It looks pretty enough as it is, and it smells glorious, which is funny when you think about it. There's not a thing in it but leeks, potatoes, butter, water, pepper, and salt.

One interesting thing to meditate on while you're making this soup is potatoes. There's something about peeling a potato. Not to say that it's *fun,* exactly. But there's something about scraping off the skin, and rinsing off the dirt, and chopping it into cubes before immersing the cubes in cold water because they'll turn pink if you let them sit out in the air. Something about knowing exactly what you're doing, and why. Potatoes have been potatoes for a long, long time, and people have treated them in just this way, toward the end of making just such a soup. There is clarity in the act of peeling a potato, a winnowing down to one sure, true way. And even if afterward you do push it through some gadget you got at Crate and Barrel, the peeling is still a part of what you do, the first thing.

I was supposed to have spent my twenties (a) hammering away for ninety hours a week at some high-paying, ethically dubious job, drinking heavily, and having explosive sex with a rich array of twenty-something men; (b) awaking at noon every day in my Williamsburg loft to work on my painting/poetry/knitting/performance art, easily shaking off the effects of stylish drugs and tragically hip clubs and explosive sex with a rich array of twenty-something men (and women if I could manage it); or (c) pursuing higher education, sweating bullets over an obscure dissertation and punctuating my intellectual throes with some pot and explosive sex with a rich array of professors and undergrads. These were the models, for someone like me.

But I did none of these things. Instead, I got married. I didn't mean to, exactly. It just kind of happened.

Eric and I were high school sweethearts. Wait, it gets worse. We were in a high school *play* together. Our courtship was straight out of one of the ickier films from the John Hughes oeuvre, *Some Kind of Wonderful,* maybe — all kinds of misunderstandings and jealous boyfriends and angst-ridden stage kisses. In other words, the sort of too-typical high school romance that people of our generation are meant to get over and cover up later on. But we didn't. Somehow we never got around to the breaking-up part. At the age of twenty-four, when we were still sleeping together and reasonably satisfied with the whole toilet-seat-and-toothpaste-cap situation, we went ahead and got married.

Please understand — I love my husband like a pig loves shit. Maybe even more. But in the circles I run in, being married for more than five years before reaching the age of thirty ranks real high on the list of most socially damaging traits, right below watching NASCAR and listening to Shania Twain. I'm used to getting questions like "Is he the only person you've ever had sex with?" or, even more insultingly, "Are *you* the only person *he's* ever had sex with?"

All this to say that sometimes I get a little defensive. Even with Isabel, who I've known since kindergarten, and Sally, my freshman-year roommate, and Gwen, who comes over to eat at our apartment every weekend and *adores* Eric. I would confess to none of them the thing I sometimes think, which is: "Eric can be a little pushy." I couldn't hack the hastily smothered expressions of dismay and smug I-told-you-so eyebrows; I know my friends would imagine something between the *The Stepford Wives* and a domestic abuse PSA narrated by J-Lo. But I mean neither shoving matches nor domineering at dinner parties. I just mean that he *pushes.* He can't be satisfied with telling me I'm the most gorgeous and talented woman on the planet and that he would die without me, while mixing me a dry Stoli gimlet. No, he has to *encourage*. He has to *make suggestions*. It can be most annoying.

So I made this soup, this Potage Parmentier, from a recipe in a forty-year-old cookbook I'd stolen from my mother the previous spring. And it was good — inexplicably good. We ate it sitting on the couch, bowls perched on knees, the silence broken only by the occasional snort of laughter as we watched a pert blonde high school student dust vampires on the television. In almost no time we were slurping the dregs of our third servings. (It turns out that one reason we're so good together is that each of us eats more and faster than anyone either of us has ever met; also, we both recognize the genius of *Buffy the Vampire Slayer*.) Earlier that evening, after the gynecologist appointment, when I was standing in the Korean deli staring at produce, I'd been thinking, "I'm twenty-nine, I'm never going to have kids or a real job, my husband will leave me and I'll die alone in an outer-borough hovel with twenty cats and it'll take two weeks for the stench to reach the hall." But now, three bowls of potato soup later, I was, to my relief, thinking of nothing much at all. I lay on my back on the couch, quietly digesting. Julia Child's soup had made me vulnerable.

Eric saw an in, and took it.

"That was good, honey."

I sighed my agreement.

"Real good. And there wasn't even any meat in it."

(Eric is a sensitive twenty-first-century sort of guy, but a Texan nevertheless, and the idea of a dinner without animal flesh gets him a little panicky.)

"You're such a good cook, Julie. Maybe you should go to culinary school."

I'd started cooking in college, basically to keep Eric in my thrall. In the years since, though, the whole thing had blown a little out of proportion. I don't know if Eric felt pride that he had introduced me to my consuming passion, or guilt that my urge to satisfy his innocent liking for escargot and rhubarb had metastasized into an unhealthy obsession. Whatever the reason, this thing about cooking school had developed into one of our habitual dead-end alleys of conversation. I was too deliciously idle after my soup to get ticked off about it, and just snorted quietly. Even that indication that he had my ear, though, was a tactical error. I knew it as soon as I'd made a sound. I squeezed my eyes shut, feigning sudden sleep or deafness.

"Seriously. You could go to the Culinary Institute! We could move out to the Hudson Valley, and you could just spend all your time learning to be a chef."

And then, no sooner than I'd cautioned myself against it, I made tactical error #2: "They won't let me in without professional experience. I'd have to go peel potatoes for two-fifty an hour for six months. You want to support me with all your big bucks while I do that?"

Giving in to the enticing prospect of emasculating my husband. Always, always a mistake.

"Maybe some other school to start, then — somewhere here in the city?"

"We can't afford it."

Eric didn't answer. He sat quietly on the edge of the couch with his hand on my shin. I thought about kicking it off, but the shin seemed a neutral enough spot. One of the cats jumped up onto my chest, sniffed my breath, then stalked off stiff-legged, her mouth open in faint disgust.

"If I wanted to learn to cook, I'd just cook my way through *Mastering the Art of French Cooking.*"

It was an odd sort of statement to make drip with sarcasm, but I managed it anyway. Eric just sat there.

"Not that it would do me any good, of course. Can't get a job out of that."

"At least we'd eat good for a while."

Now I was the one who said nothing for a moment, because of course he was right about that.

"I'd be exhausted all the time. I'd get fat. We'd have to eat brains. And eggs. I don't eat eggs, Eric. You know I don't eat eggs."

"No. You don't."

"It's a stupid idea."

Eric said nothing for a while. *Buffy* had ended and the news was on — a correspondent was standing on a flooded street in Sheeps-head Bay, saying something about a broken water main. We sat on the couch in our stuffy Bay Ridge living room, staring at the screen as if we gave a damn. All around us teetered towers of boxes, the looming reminder of our upcoming move.

When I look back on it now, it is as if I could actually hear the taut creak of a fisherman giving out just a tiny bit of line when Eric said: "You could start a blog."

I cut my eyes over to him in irritation, a massive white-skinned shark thrashing its tail.

"Julie. You *do* know what a *blog* is, don't you?"

Of course I didn't know what a blog was. It was August of 2002. Nobody knew about blogs, except for a few guys like Eric who spend their days using company computers to pursue the zeit-geist. No issue of domestic or international policy was too big, no pop-culture backwater too obscure; from the War on Terror to *Fear Factor*, it was all one big, beautiful sliding scale for Eric.

"You know, like a Web site sort of thing. Only it's easy. You don't have to know anything about anything."

"Sounds perfect for me."

"About computers, I mean."

"Are you going to make me that drink, or what?"

"Sure."

And he did. He left me alone. He was free to, now that he knew the hook was sunk.

Lulled by the calming music of ice clattering in the cocktail shaker, I began to ponder; this life we had going for ourselves, Eric and I, it felt like the opposite of Potage Parmentier. It was easy enough to keep on with the soul-sucking jobs; at least it saved having to make a choice. But how much longer could I take such an easy life? Quicksand was easy. Hell, death was easy. Maybe that's why my synapses had started snapping at the sight of potatoes and leeks in the Korean deli. Maybe that was what was plucking deep down in my belly whenever I thought of Julia Child's book. Maybe I needed to make like a potato, winnow myself down, be a part of something that was not easy, just simple.

Just then Eric emerged again from the kitchen, carrying two Stoli gimlets. He handed off one of the glasses to me, carefully, so as not to spill anything over those treacherous martini lips, and I took a sip. Eric always made the best gimlets — icy cold, very dry, with an almost-not-there shade of chartreuse lingering in their slightly oily depths.

"Okay," I said, taking another sip as Eric sat down beside me. "Tell me again about this blog thing?"

And so, late that evening, a tiny line dropped into the endless sea of cyberspace, the slenderest of lures in the blackest of waters.

The Book

Mastering the Art of French Cooking. First edition, 1961. Louisette Bertholle. Simone Beck. And, of course, Julia Child, the woman who taught America to cook, and to eat. Today we think we live in the world Alice Waters made, but beneath it all is Julia, and no one can touch her.

The Contender

Government drone by day, renegade foodie by night. Too old for theater, too young for children, and too bitter for anything else, Julie Powell was looking for a challenge. And in the Julie/Julia Project she found it. Risking her marriage, her job, and her cats' well-being, she has signed on for a deranged assignment. 365 days. 524 recipes. One girl and a crappy outerborough kitchen. How far it will go, no one can say. . . .

It wasn't much — nearly nothing, in fact. Not even so much as a recipe for potato soup. A few words strung together, is all. But together, out there, they seemed perhaps to glow, only faintly. Just enough.

Mayonnaise, like hollandaise, is a process of forcing egg yolks to absorb a fatty substance, oil in this case, and to hold it in thick and creamy suspension.

— *Mastering the Art of French Cooking,* Vol. 1

It's hard to make mayonnaise by trial and error.

— *The Joy of Sex*

Joy of Cooking

Every night when he came home from work, the first thing Dad would do was take the change out of his suit pockets and dump it into a big blue plastic cup with the arrowhead logo from my summer camp printed on it in white, which he kept in the cabinet just to the right of his sink in the master bath. Mom had a cabinet just like it to the left of her sink. She kept her makeup carousel and jewelry in hers, and old scarves she hadn't worn since she got out of high school. In his, Dad kept change and his watch, his mouthwash and Mennen hairspray and spare handkerchiefs. And the book.

I found it on a Tuesday afternoon, when I was looking around for quarters. I was eleven years old, and on Tuesdays and Thursdays I took acting classes at a place up on North Burnet, behind the Nighthawk café. I always brought fifty cents with me so I could get a Coke from the machine out back afterward. Usually I got my change from the big jar on the shelf over the washing machine, but Mom had just taken that to the bank, so I was raiding Dad's cabinet instead.

It was just a plain black clothbound book at the very rear of the deep cabinet, kept spine down so the title was hidden. The paper cover had been taken off. I'd noticed it before, but thought there must be a very good reason my father hid it so carefully. Probably, I'd told myself, it was something really boring. Probably it was about phone bills or something. But I was all alone in the house that afternoon, and it suddenly occurred to me, why would Dad hide a *boring* book?

The minute I eased the book out of its niche and saw the gold embossed title, I knew I should just put it back, right away. But by then, of course, it was too late.

The first pages were a series of large color paintings on thick shiny paper, like in an art book. Except that the pictures were of a man and a woman, naked and having *sex*. And not like movie sex either. I'd seen plenty of movie sex — we had Cinemax and during slumber parties we'd sneak into the living room late at night to catch *Friday After Dark*. But this woman had hair under her armpits, and the man had hair, well, *everywhere,* and you could actually see his *penis,* going *into* her. It was *hard-core,* like the tapes I was too embarrassed to sneak a peek at that Isabel's dad stashed behind the regular movies. The man and woman in the pictures weren't even all that good-looking. They were *old.* Actually, they looked kind of like my parents — but that made me feel weird, so I pushed the thought out of my mind.

After the color pictures came a long written part, with black-and-white drawings and entries like in a dictionary. That's what the book was, I realized — a sex *dictionary.* Lots of the entries were French. Others were simple words, like *boots* and *railways,* but I couldn't understand why they'd even be in a book like this. That was the worst part — did *boot* mean something entirely different from what I'd thought? Every time I begged my mom for a pair of purple zip-up go-go boots to go with my Miss Piggy sweater, was I inadvertently saying something dirty?

The front door of the house was right next to the door to my parents' room. When I heard my mom's key in the lock I only barely had time to lunge for the cabinet and put the book back before she found me.

"You ready, Jules? What're you doing?"

"I was just getting some change for my Coke."

I thought, *She knows!*, but she just said, "Well, let's go — you're going to be late," and walked right back out the front door.

All through class I worried — had I put it back wrong? I remembered how in the book *1984* the main character laid a hair across the top of his journal, so he'd know if anyone had moved it. I knew Dad had read *1984* — he was the one who gave me my copy. The acting teacher had assigned me a scene with Caleb, who looked just like Jason Bateman on *It's Your Move*, but I couldn't look at him without thinking about those pictures in the book. I kept forgetting my lines, and I *never* forgot lines — I was the best memorizer in the class. After class, I sipped my Coke while I waited for Mom to pick me up, but I could barely taste it — my whole mouth was tingling like I'd been chewing cinnamon gum. When she got there, though, she acted normal. We came home and Dad was doing the crossword in his chair as usual.

It was a very, very wrong thing to do, reading that book at my age. I knew it. I was betraying my parents. I was being bad. Each time I found myself sneaking back into my parents' room I whispered to myself, "Last time, last time, last time." But I knew I was lying. I'd fallen down a pit, I was begrimed with corruption, I would never again be innocent. And besides, there was so much information! The book was full of stuff I couldn't find out anywhere else — not even from Isabel, who knew more about sex than any eleven-year-old in the world, even though she was only ten. The damage was already done, so I might as well get an education out of it.

Mom was usually home when I got home from school, but sometimes she'd be out taking my brother Heathcliff to his Little League practice or a friend's house, or running errands. On those afternoons I would grab my stack of Oreos — I had a firm (well, pretty firm) rule never to eat more than ten in an afternoon — and a paper towel and creep back to my parents' bathroom. They had a small oil painting hanging on the wall, depicting a woman in a negligee. I liked the painting well enough, though I was glad they'd hung it in the bathroom. But now that I knew what was in the book in Dad's cabinet, the painting clearly seemed to hint at proclivities I'd never before imagined they had.

The book, when I took it out, smelled smoky and astringent and secret. I thought that it smelled that way because my parents used it when they were having sex, maybe with my mom dressed in a rubber vest or go-go boots or something. (It was years before I figured out the smell was just Listerine and hairspray and the still-undiscovered cigarettes Dad hid in his cabinet for an occasional smoke out on the deck, after I'd gone to bed.) I would slide down the wall under the oil painting onto the nubbly white carpet and read, resting the open book on my tented knees. I'd put the Oreos on the paper towel beside me and eat them one after the other, twisting them open, licking out the white stuff, sucking the wafers until they were chocolate ooze in my mouth, while I read about *cassolette* and *postillionage* and *gamahuche*. Some entries were just plain grody — all that stuff about smelly, unshaven armpits — while others got me aching between my legs. And then I'd hear the garage door open. I'd leap up, stuff the book back into place and shut the cabinet door, grab up any cookies I had left, and run to the kitchen so I'd be there when Mom came in, calling from the front door for help with the groceries.

If *The Joy of Sex* was my first taste of sin, *Mastering the Art of French Cooking* was my second.

For Christmas Eve dinner, Mom usually made red beans and rice — with the crimson, chili-seasoned beef and the pinto beans cooked separately, because I didn't eat beans, *ever.* This year, though, the head of Dad's firm was coming to dinner, and after some panic, Mom had decided to do something special. When I wandered into the kitchen that morning I found her already busily chopping vegetables. On the kitchen table was an old cookbook, open to page 315. Boeuf Bourguignon.

Though it had been there as long as I could remember, I'd never seen Mom take this particular thick, cream-colored tome out of the pantry. Actually, it was one of a matched pair: two fat books, both called *Mastering the Art of French Cooking,* both with a pattern of spangled floral shapes on their covers. When I asked my mom, she called the design *floordayleez.* The book my mom had out had red *floordayleez;* the one that remained in its place on the pantry shelf had blue ones.

Cookbooks were not my favorite sorts of books, and even among cookbooks, these were far from the most interesting in my mother's pantry collection. I much preferred the *Time-Life* series, two books for each world cuisine — one spiral-bound, with the actual recipes, and another, larger, with history and beautiful photos. (The Viennese one, with all those towering white cakes, was my favorite. I was always pointing out one or the other of them to Mom and asking her to make it, but then she'd point out that it had coconut in it, or nuts, or jam, and I didn't eat coconut or nuts or jam, not *ever.*) But even though they weren't my favorites, I'd always liked the look of those two books standing so stoutly among my mom's Junior League books and tattered *Betty Crocker.* They seemed old-fashioned, stately, *real,* like historical books you'd buy for lots of money in an antique shop.

I still had on my nightgown. I'd pulled over it my mom's boxy blue cowl-neck sweater with the wiggly alpine stripes. Around Christmastime I liked to pretend it might snow. In quieter moments, in the bath or before I got out of bed in the morning, I would imagine the flakes drifting down outside, while I curled up on a great pile of pillows before a roaring fireplace with Jason Bateman, whose half-cocked grins seemed to suggest *Joy of Sex* stuff, only in a nice way, and with less armpit hair. Mom's cowl-neck sweater helped enormously with these daydreams.

I grabbed a piece of Marshmallow Fluff fudge out of the tin and sat down in front of the book. Mom was at the sink, scraping carrots over the disposal. "I don't see why you insist on wearing that sweater. It's seventy degrees outside."

"I'm cold."

"Don't lose my page."

"I won't." With one finger marking Mom's recipe, I flipped through the book, trying to pronounce all the French words under my breath. An old smell came off the pages, musty but not like library books. More like a dog or a forest floor, something damp and warm and living. The words, and the smell, reminded me of something — but what it was I couldn't at first figure out.

Much of what I read made no sense to me, but I could see the recipes were full of stuff I didn't like, mushrooms and olives and spinach. Something called *sweetbread,* what the heck was *that*? Was it sort of like coffee cake? Because I *hated* coffee cake. I was getting a bit bored, when my eyes fell on a drawing of some kind of animal part — a lamb's leg, the caption said. It was laid out tail up, looking almost like a person stretched out on her tummy. I flipped backward and found another drawing. This one was of a pair of graceful hands with neat round fingernails, pressing down on a piece of something smooshy. Pastry dough. The hands were demonstrating *fraisage:* "With the heel of one hand, not the palm which is too warm, rapidly press the pastry by two-spoonful bits down on the board and away from you in a firm, quick smear of about 6 inches."

It sounded weird. It also sounded kind of, well, *dirty.*

I suddenly remembered *exactly* what the book reminded me of.

Blushing, I shot a glance up at my mom, but she had finished the carrots and was on to the onions. She had no idea what I was thinking. Of course not. It wasn't like Mom could read my mind. I used to think she could, but this last year, I'd realized that if that was true, she'd never have let me watch *It's Your Move* again.

"You're not losing my place, are you?"

"I said *no.*"

Because it was the holidays, I hadn't had the chance to look at the book in Dad's cabinet for weeks. Mom and Dad were home more, for one thing, plus they were on the lookout to make sure I wasn't poking around searching for presents. I really did try not to do that, because surprises were the whole *point* of Christmas. Besides, I didn't want to find anything that would prove once and for all that Santa really didn't exist. I pretty much knew that, but I didn't want to admit it, because what would Christmas be without Santa? It could be pretty tempting to look, though, so it was better to just avoid my parents' room altogether. So, no *Joy of Sex,* not until after New Year's probably. This book, though — well, it was practically *just as good.* It had French words, too, and lots of incomprehensible stuff to meditate on. There weren't any naked hippies, but that was okay. Sometimes the naked hippies kind of freaked me out.

Maybe instead of just sitting in front of a fireplace in a sweater with Jason Bateman, I could *cook* something for him. I'd never thought of that before. Something sexy. Like — hmm . . . what about Pièce de Boeuf à la Cuillère? That sounded dirty. "Minced Braised Beef Served in a Beef Shell" — it even sounded dirty in *English.*

"What are you *doing,* anyway?"

I practically jumped out of the chrome-and-wicker kitchen chair, like I'd gotten caught masturbating at the dinner table — not that I *masturbated,* of course. I only even knew what the word meant because Isabel had told me. Ick.

"Don't sit with your feet under you like that — I just had those chairs recaned. Can you bring the book to me over here? My hands are all bacon-y."

I turned to the page I'd been saving with my index finger and carried the book over to Mom. She gave me an odd look as I set it down on the yellow counter. "I can't understand why you're so interested in this, anyway. You wouldn't eat a thing in it. You won't even eat a *cheeseburger.*"

"Cheese belongs on *pizza,* not *hamburgers.*"

Mom rolled her eyes and went back to the cooking. I stood over her shoulder and watched for a bit. She had chopped up bits of bacon and was frying them in a pan. Once they were all brown she took them out and started frying chunks of meat.

"It smells good."

"Yes, it does, doesn't it?" She was taking out the browned meat now, and throwing in carrots and onions. I didn't eat carrots, not *ever.* But the smell really was something. I wondered if Jason Bateman might be a Boeuf Bourguignon man. "Maybe tonight you can try a little," Mom said.

"Yeah. Maybe."

Of course, I didn't try it, not that Christmas Eve — my terror of carrots, mushrooms, and pearl onions proved too great to overcome, and like the other kids at the house that night, I opted for pepperoni pizza and fudge instead. In fact, it would be another eighteen years before I did taste Julia's recipe for Boeuf Bourguignon.

Boeuf Bourguignon is at once classic and comfortable, impressive and simple, so it's a perfect dish to make when your reputation is on the line. It was what Julia Child made on the very first episode of her very first television show. It was what my mother made to impress my dad's boss. And eighteen years later it would be what I made for a certain very important person who I hoped would sweep me out of my crappy secretarial job and on to wild success and fortune. Actually, I made it twice for this very important person, but I'll get more into that a little later on. For now, let's just say that Boeuf Bourguignon, like mayonnaise, requires a certain amount of trial and error (actually, I find that mayonnaise takes far more), but once you have it down it's an excellent skill to have at your disposal. If, for instance, Jason Bateman were to blow into town looking for a dinner invitation, I could now, thanks to Julia, whip him up a good French beef stew with a minimum of fuss.

I might even cook Boeuf Bourguignon for Jason Bateman while wearing my mom's blue après-ski sweater. I still have it, and possess an irrational attachment to it that has survived the twin realizations that I will never be the sort of sylphlike slip of a thing who looks good in bulky cowl-neck sweaters, and that bulky cowl-neck sweaters haven't been sexy since at least the late eighties, anyway. But for Jason Bateman, as for Boeuf Bourguignon, sometimes the old ways are best.

January 1944
Arlington, VA

After all the uncertainty, it was finally going to happen. His bag was packed, the car was on its way; he was shipping out. Soon he would be doing real work, with Lord Mountbatten in New Delhi. It was all coming to be, just as Jane Bartleman had said. Paul carefully slipped one of his journals out from the box of his papers that he'd already packed up for his brother, Charlie, to take up to Maine, and carried it to his small bed, now stripped of its sheets. He sat and turned to the pages in which he had recorded the astrologer's predictions last April.

"A new enterprise awaits. It hangs before you like fruit on a tree."

Say what you like about astrology, but you couldn't argue with the results. Paul continued skimming the pages of his small, neat handwriting.

"Doors are going to open — doors you can't even imagine exist."

As Paul stood to wedge the journal back into the box, a small sheet of paper slipped out of it and fluttered to the floor. He recognized it as he bent to retrieve it, and a sudden prickling behind his eyes surprised him. It was a letter, years old and yellowing, from Edith, written back during their years in Cambridge together.

"My Dearest Paul, your poems always move me in this way, and yet it always surprises me . . ."

She'd been gone for just a little over a year, but still the very glimpse of her handwriting brought back with awful clarity those last months, the long desolate afternoons watching his lover gasp for air that would not come to her. Reading the poem, he realized *that somewhere deep he felt that in leaving the country, he was leaving her.*

Last spring, Bartleman had predicted there would be another woman for him, one to break apart this icy loneliness. It did not seem possible, much as he craved the comfort of a woman of intelligence, of humor and balance and perception. He'd already been given his one chance at that.

Outside, a car horn. Just concentrate on your work, *Paul said to himself. He zipped up his bag and heaved it onto his shoulder.* The hell with women, and marriage. A man can't have everything.

■.■.■.■.■.■.

You Have to
Break a Few Eggs...

Most of the stupidest things I have ever done I've done in the fall. I call it my First-Day-of-School syndrome, a bone-deep hangover from a time when autumn meant something. When I was eleven, the syndrome revealed itself in the tragically self-defining sartorial decision to match a pair of purple zip-up go-go boots with a Miss Piggy sweater. In the fall of my thirtieth year, it showed itself in the concoction of a nonsensical yearlong cooking project, to commence in tandem with the biblical ordeal of a New York move.

I did mention the moving, right?

The first clue that I was descending into one of my occasional bouts of seasonal madness should have been my mom's reaction when I told her about the Project.

"Huh."

"Do you like 'The Julie/Julia Project' for a name? I think it gives it a sort of Frankenstein mad-scientist feel, what do you think? Did you get the link I sent you?"

"Yes . . . ? I did . . . ?" All her short sentences were wavering up into hesitant, high-pitched questions.

"Don't worry. It's just for a year. I'll be cooking every night and writing every morning. It'll be like a regimen."

"Mm-hm? And *why* are you doing this again?"

"What do you mean?" What an obtuse question — though, I did dimly realize, one I'd not actually asked myself. I noticed my voice had gotten a little squeaky.

"Well — I mean, maybe this isn't the best time to start a new project like this? While you're trying to move?"

"Oh — no. No, no, no, no, it'll be fine. I have to eat, don't I? Besides, it's already out there. Online, where anybody can see it. I have to go through with it now. It'll be fine. It'll be *great!*"

At my age, I guess I should know that when the timbre of my voice reaches such unendurably cheery heights, trouble is on the way. I should know it, but somehow I never remember until it's too late.

It had started so well. The night after I wrote my first-ever blog entry, I made Bifteck Sauté au Beurre and Artichauts au Naturel — the first recipes in the meat and vegetable chapters of *MtAoFC*, respectively. The steak I merely fried in a skillet with butter and oil — butter and oil because not only did I not have the beef suet that was the other option, I didn't even know what beef suet *was*. Then I just made a quick sauce out of the juices from the pan, some vermouth we'd had sitting around the house forever because Eric had discovered that drinking vermouth, even in martinis, made him sick, and a bit more butter. The artichokes I simply trimmed — chopping off the stalks and cutting the sharp pointy tops off all the leaves with a pair of scissors — before boiling them in salted water until tender. I served the artichokes with some Beurre au Citron, which I made by boiling down lemon juice with salt and pepper, then beating in a stick of butter. Three recipes altogether, in just over an hour.

"I could do this with one hand tied behind my back!" I crowed to Eric as we sat at our dining table, hemmed in by the ever burgeoning towers of packing boxes, scraping artichoke leaves dipped in lemon butter clean with our front teeth. "It's a good thing we're moving, or it would be just *too* easy. Like taking candy from a baby!"

After we'd finished our very good and buttery steaks and cleared away the large pile of scraped artichoke leaves, I sat down to write. I made a witticism or two about artichokes — "this was my first time with artichokes, and more than liking or disliking them, I am mostly just impressed with the poor starving prehistoric bastard who first thought to eat one" — then posted my few short paragraphs onto my blog.

The next day I got thirty-six hits. I know I got thirty-six hits because I went online to check twelve times that day at work. Each hit represented another person reading what *I'd* written. Just like that! At the bottom of the entry there was a spot where people could make comments, and someone I'd never even heard of said they liked how I wrote!

I was going to eat lots of French food, and write about it, *and* get compliments from total strangers about it. Eric was right. This was going to be *brilliant!*

Day 2 was Quiche Lorraine and Haricots Verts à la Anglaise.

Day 3 I had to go to New Jersey to pass out comment forms and set up folding chairs for a meeting of families of people who died in the World Trade Center attack. The meeting was organized by the governor of New Jersey, for the purpose of making sure everyone knew that if they were unhappy about anything, it was the fault of the downtown government agency I work for. The governor of New Jersey was a bit of a prick. So I didn't cook. Instead I ate pizza and wrote this impromptu piece of sparkling prose:

Wealthy Victorians served Strawberries Romanoff in December; now we demonstrate our superiority by serving our dewy organic berries only during the two-week period when they can be picked ripe off the vine at the boutique farm down the road from our Hamptons bungalow. People speak of gleaning the green markets for the freshest this, the thinnest that, the greenest or firmest or softest whatever, as if what they're doing is a selfless act of consummate care and good taste, rather than the privileged activity of someone who doesn't have to work for a living.

But Julia Child isn't about that. Julia Child wants you — that's right, *you,* the one living in the tract house in sprawling suburbia with a dead-end middle-management job and nothing but a Stop and Shop for miles around — to know how to make good pastry, and also how to make those canned green beans taste all right. She wants you to remember that you are human, and as such are entitled to that most basic of human rights, the right to eat well and enjoy life.

And that blows heirloom tomatoes and first-press Umbrian olive oil out of the fucking water.

By the end of the first week, I'd gone on to make Filets de Poisson Bercy aux Champignons and Poulet Rôti, Champignons à la Grecque, and Carottes à la Concierge, even a Crème Brûlée — well, Crème Brûlée soup, more like. I'd written about all of it, my mistakes and my minor triumphs. People — a couple of friends, a couple of strangers, even my aunt Sukie from Waxahachie — had written in to the blog to root me on. And now I was leaving my downtown cubicle every evening with a jaunty new step, shopping list in hand, contemplating not how I wanted to rip that friggin' office phone out of the wall (or maybe the windpipe out of some bureaucrat's scrawny neck), but instead my next French meal, my next clever gibe.

Eric and I had begun the move in earnest now. On the weekend we loaded up the boxes in our living room and hauled them in our aging burgundy Bronco to our new apartment, a loft, so-called, in Long Island City, which is not on Long Island but in Queens. (Which is, yes, technically, on the water-surrounded landmass known as Long Island, but don't ever tell someone from Queens or Brooklyn that they live on Long Island. Trust me on this; it's a bad idea.) We were moving there because Eric's office had moved there, and commutes from Bay Ridge to Long Island City uncomfortably reminded us of Latin American immigrants knifed to death by bigots in subway cars en route to one of their three jobs at two in the morning. So now we would be living in a "loft." It was a step forward, a brave experiment, the urban dream. And still I was cooking — joyfully, humorously, easily. This French food stuff was a snap! I wondered why everybody had been making such a big deal out of it all these years.

And then, in the third week, we got to the eggs.

"Julie, I want you to stop."

"I can't. I can't."

"Honey, this is just something you decided to do. You can decide not to if you want. You can just *decide to stop*."

"No! Don't you get it? This is all I've got. There are people out there, *reading*. I can't just fucking STOP!"

I have been having this conversation with my mother my entire life. There was the time when I was six years old and *had* to wear my favorite sundress for the St. Valentine's Day party at school — when my mother told me it was too cold, I stood goosepimply on the front porch in my Wonder Woman Underoos for two hours to prove her wrong. Or the time that I tried out for the drill team just because I knew I wouldn't make it and then, when I did, refused to quit, and instead wound up spending eight months with a bunch of sorority girl larvae — turning bulimic and tying that stupid white cowboy hat onto my head so tightly that by the end of game nights I had to peel the leather strap out of the deep red welt it had burrowed into my throat. Or when two weeks before I got married I decided, in the midst of catering crises and maids-of-honor dress fiascos, that I *had* to make teeny-tiny sculptures of naked ladies out of Super Sculpey for two hundred guests. It's the Talking Down from the Ledge conversation. Sometimes it works. Sometimes it doesn't.

My voice grew steely and cold. "I've got to go now, Mom. I love you."

"Julie, wait." Fear on the other end of the line. Mom knew she was losing me. "Please. Honey. *Stop cooking.*"

"Bye, Mom."

I hung up the phone. My neck had a crick in it; I twisted my head around, and the tendons popped. The trek back across my living room, littered with Styrofoam peanuts, was like the Bataan Death March.

"We'll just take it easy," Eric had said. "Slow and steady wins the race," Eric had said. As a result of which, Eric and I had been moving for two and a half weeks now.

It was agony. For a week and a half we just shuttled boxes. Then, on a Saturday, we managed to get our box spring and mattress moved. We left the cats in the old place that night while we slept in the new, making the disheartening discovery that at three o'clock in the morning, our loft apartment sounded as if it was perched in the center of a monster truck rally. On Sunday we brought the cats over. En route, one threw up all over her carrier, and a second beshat herself. The third simply fell into the psychic abyss inhabited by war orphans and the sole survivors of alien invasions, and immediately upon arriving in his new abode found his way up into the drop ceiling, from where he had not returned, though we could hear him prowling around up there, and occasionally yowling. Every once in a while we'd lift up a ceiling tile and slip him a bowl of Science Diet.

Eric and I had forged through several circles of hell in the last weeks — I named them the "Last-Minute Home Repair Hell," the "Soul-Sucking Dead-End Job Hell," the "My Spouse Just Turned Twenty-nine and I Didn't Get Him Anything Hell," and the "I Have Married a Raving Schizophrenic Hell." We had bled, we had screamed, we had dropped peeled root vegetables onto the rotting floorboards of our new "fixer-upper" "loft" before picking them up and throwing them into the soup. So though we could now be said to be living in Long Island City, the word *living* seemed a rather cruelly euphemistic way of putting it. We were more like the walking dead.

The kitchen was a crime scene. Eggshells littered the floor, crackling underfoot. What looked like three days' worth of unwashed dishes were piled up in the sink, and half-unpacked boxes had been shoved to the corners of the room. Unseen down the dark throat of the trashcan, yet as conspicuous as tarpaulin-covered murder victims, were the mutilated remains of eggs. If the purplish-stained shreds of yolk clinging stickily to the walls had been blood spatters, a forensics specialist would have had a field day. But Eric wasn't standing at the stove to triangulate the shooter's position — he was poaching an egg in red wine. Two other eggs sat on a plate by the stove. These I had poached myself just before Eric's and my impromptu reenactment of that scene in *Airplane!* in which all the passengers line up and take turns slapping and shaking the hysterical woman, with Eric taking the roles of all the passengers and I the part of hysteric. These three eggs were the sole survivors of the even dozen I had begun with three hours before. One incoherent gurgle of despair escaped me, seeing those two pitiful things lying there, twisted and blue as the lips of corpses. "We're going to starve, aren't we?"

"How was your mom? Did she make you feel better?" Cool as a cucumber, Eric lifted the last egg out of the wine and laid it beside its sad blue sisters.

"I don't know. I guess. You're like Charles fucking Bronson, you know that?"

"How do you mean?"

"Oh, you know, smacking your self-destructive wife back to her senses, dispensing violent justice to foodstuffs. Thanks for doing the last egg."

"I didn't do a very good job."

"As long as it's not me not doing a good job. For once." I curled up in his arms, and soon was crying again, but gently this time, a mild aftershock.

"Babe," Eric whispered, kissing my damp hair, "I would do anything shittily for you. You know that."

"Yes. I do. And I thank you. I love you."

"You love me? Who loves *you*?"

(Remember that scene in *Superman* where Margot Kidder is falling out of the helicopter and Christopher Reeve catches her, and he says, "Don't worry, I've got you," to which she responds: "You've got me? Who's got *you*?" That's where this familiar rejoinder of Eric's comes from. He says it all the time. It's impossible to express how precious and safe it makes me feel, how held up in a pair of improbably large and blue Lycra-clad biceps — but anyone who's been with someone as long as I have been with Eric understands the power of nonsensical phraseology.)

If this had been a scene from a movie the music would have swelled, but there was no time for romance. Because making Oeufs à la Bourguignonne is about much more than just wasting a dozen eggs trying to poach them in the red wine that was the only booze we had in this hideous apartment we had been so foolish as to move into. I grabbed a bag of Wonder Bread down from on top of the fridge and took out three slices. I cut a neat white circle out of each of them with a cookie cutter, one of an enormous set that Eric's mom had given me for Christmas one year, which I had very nearly thrown out during the move. I cleared off one of the three working burners on the stove (checking burners before signing the lease being one of those smart-New-York-renter things I could never remember to do), threw a skillet on it, and began to melt half a stick of butter.

"So really, what did your mom say?"

"Wanted to know if I'd gotten the reservation at Peter Luger."

My family comes up to visit almost every fall for my father's birthday, because my father likes to spend his birthday catching a Broadway show before going to the Peter Luger Steak House in Williamsburg, Brooklyn, for a plate of creamed spinach, Steak for Six, and several dry martinis. That this year he would also get to spend his birthday helping his hysterical daughter finish moving out of her Bay Ridge apartment was just an unfortunate accident of timing.

"Are they really going to spend the night here?"

I shot my husband a look he knew well. "Yeah. Why?"

Eric shrugged, shook his head. "No reason." But he wouldn't look me in the eye.

My mother is a clean freak, my father a dirty bird, semi-reformed. Between them, they have managed to raise one child who by all accounts could not care less about basic cleanliness, but whose environs and person are always somehow above reproach, and another child who sees as irrecoverable humiliation any imputation of less than impeccable housekeeping or hygiene, and yet, regardless of near-constant near-hysteria on the subject, is almost always an utter mess. One guess which I am.

I also have a long history of trying to kill my mother by moving into highly unfashionable, and often demonstrably unhealthy, locales. It's been years, and yet she still talks about my first New York studio like it was the "hole" in a Khmer Rouge prison. And of course there is no forgetting the day she saw the one-hundred-year-old crumbling adobe building in Middle-of-Nowhere, New Mexico, that we rented the first summer we were married. She stood at the doorway, the beam of her flashlight piercing the gloom and skittering across the floor as she searched for mouse droppings or the dead bodies of larger creatures, maybe humans. Tears welled up in her wide eyes. As long as I live, I will never forget the sheer horror in my mother's voice when she whispered, "Julie, seriously — *you're going to die here.*"

I stood over the skillet, poking at the butter. "*Melt,* god-dammit." I was supposed to clarify the butter — which is done by skimming off the white scum that appears when butter melts — then get it very hot before browning the rounds of bread in it. There were a lot of things I was supposed to be doing these days that I wasn't. Instead I threw the bread in as soon as the butter liquefied. Of course the canapés — which is what I was making out of the rounds of bread — didn't brown, just grew soggy and yellow and buttery. "Fuck it. It's eleven o'clock at night and I do not give one shit about the fucking bread," I said as I took them back out again and dropped them onto two plates.

"Julie, seriously, do you *have* to talk like that?"

Now I was turning the heat up on the winey egg-poaching liquid to cook it down for sauce. "Are you fucking kidding me?"

Eric laughed nervously. "Yup. Just a little joke. Pretty funny, huh?"

"Uh-huh." I thickened the wine with cornstarch and butter. Then upon each sodden canapé I balanced an egg before spooning the sauce on top. "The eggs wore blue; the sauce wore gray," I muttered in my best Bogart impersonation, which was not very good at all — I've never been much good at impressions. In any case, the sauce was really more of a mauve color. It wasn't a good joke, and neither of us laughed.

We ate our dinner amid the unpacking detritus, in silence. The egg tasted like the cheap wine we were drinking, only buttery.

It wasn't half bad, actually.

"It's good, honey," tried Eric.

I said nothing.

"Just think, a week ago you'd never eaten an egg at all, and now you're eating *this*. How many people, in their whole lives, *ever* eat eggs poached in red wine? We're doing something hardly anybody ever does!"

I knew he was doing his best to comfort me, and so I gave him a watery smile. But he could not make the question go away, that unspoken one that hovered over our subdued table along with the gentle sounds of our mastication. "Why, Julie? Why Julia? Why *now?*"

When Julia and Paul moved to Paris in 1948, Julia was just along for the ride — and to eat, of course. She didn't really know anything about food, not yet, but she was hungry — she could put more away than anyone (other than Paul) that Paul had ever met.

Paul was saddened by how his Paris, where he had lived for so long before the war, had been tarnished. The bombed-out buildings and the heavy military presence oppressed him. But Julia had never known the city any other way, so it wasn't as bad for her. In fact, for her, life had never been better.

Their apartment on rue de l'Université was chilly, heated by a potbelly stove during a cold winter. The apartment had an odd *L* shape. Paul could lean out of the window in the living room and take a picture of Julia leaning out of the window in the bedroom, with the rooftops of Paris all around her. This eccentric, fusty apartment was where Julia learned to cook, and she loved it.

Still. Julia's mother was long dead by the time she and Paul got the Paris flat, dead long before she had married or even met Paul. Which is sad, of course. But at least she didn't have to worry about presenting her mother with a dark, smelly apartment, with a kitchen at the top of a creaky stairway, with an odd, somewhat sinister bathtub.

Actually I don't know anything about their bathtub; it might have been quite nice. It was ours that was frightening.

* * *

Our new kitchen was quite large, by New York standards anyway. It was its own separate room, with a bit of counter by the sink and full-sized appliances, lit by an industrial fluorescent fixture. The first thing we'd done once we'd moved in was to tear out three layers, nearly a hundred years' worth, of nasty tile down to the floorboards. These floorboards were dark and damp and rotting slightly — we weren't quite sure what we were going to do about that yet. But I liked the kitchen — it was why I took the apartment, why I was blinded to the faulty jalousie windows and the strange black tub and everything else that was so terribly, terribly wrong.

The bathtub was black porcelain, set up on a raised platform so you had to climb two steps to get in. If this sounds kind of sexy, in a Las Vegas kind of way, it wasn't. For one thing, the tub was rusted out and badly caulked, and the bathtub surround was of that molded plastic they used to use in less-expensive motels in the fifties, and it was cracked. The steps up to the tub were made of plywood covered in an adhesive no-slide rubber stuff painted battleship gray. Being two steps higher just brought you closer to the disintegrating drop ceiling and the hole cut into it for the dangling light fixture. The light didn't work, was more or less just a gaping black hole out of which you could not help imagining horrid beasties falling down on you while you bathed.

The apartment was long and low, with linoleum floors all painted the same battleship gray as the steps to the tub, which gave it the feeling of a submarine's interior. At the front was a large picture window framed on either side with sets of jalousies, which are the glass louvered windows you see in small towns all over the South. This also sounds nice, and it also wasn't, because Long Island City is not a small southern town.

When my mom first saw the tub, she laughed, but it was not a nice sort of laugh. When she saw the jalousies, her eyes grew wide again. "Julie, they don't even shut right. You're going to *freeze to death.*" A freight truck slammed over a large pothole right in front of the building with a room-filling crash. "That is, if you don't go deaf first."

We had dinner reservations at an Italian place in midtown. I hustled everybody out as soon as I could manage, took us all to a bar beforehand, and tried to encourage the most orgiastic atmosphere of eating and drinking possible, succeeding so well that I had some trouble holding steady enough to pour us all into cabs at the end of the night. But it wasn't enough.

By midnight we were all bedded down together in the "loft" for what would prove the longest night I have ever had. Every passing car had lost its muffler, every 7 train hit the sharp curve behind our apartment at eighty miles per hour with an unearthly screech, and every sigh or irritated rustle from the air mattress set my teeth on edge and my heart racing. I know I did eventually drift off only because I jerked awake again at five a.m. to find my mother up, in her nightgown, with her forehead pressed up against the jalousies, muttering furiously and shaking her fist at what appeared to be a two-hundred-foot crane rolling slowly past the apartment, backward, beeping loudly, presumably so that none of the bustling pedestrians overflowing the sidewalks of Long Island City at five a.m. would dart out into the middle of the street and get hit by a slow-moving two-hundred-foot crane.

The first crisis of the morning came when U-Haul, to no one's surprise, lost our truck reservation. "Exactly the kind of thing to expect in New York," as Heathcliff pointed out. (My brother's name is not, of course, really Heathcliff. Texans of Scotch-Irish descent do not name their red-headed children Heathcliff. I just think it's funny to call him that — because it pisses him off, and because "Heathcliff" does rather speak to the whole sardonic, brooding aspect.)

Heathcliff is the guy you'd want to have as your second in a duel or watching your back in a firefight, as your vice presidential running mate or your partner in any reality-TV show that might involve speaking foreign languages, jumping off tall cliffs, or eating bugs. It is impossible to imagine him screaming at service personnel on the phone or having catastrophic hissy fits on subway platforms, two activities I indulge in frequently. Because of this, and also because Eric was nursing a hangover, which I felt responsible for, it was Heathcliff I took with me to deal with the U-Haul predicament, which was resolved with remarkable ease. (If it had been Eric with me, the day would have ended with us rebuilding a diesel engine with a giant timer ticking over our heads, in front of a live studio audience, while Hindu mechanics who disapproved of my mode of dress jeered at us and pelted us with stones. Or something.)

Everything was going just swimmingly, as far as I could see. The only outstanding question was Sally.

Over the summer my friend Sally had been living with her most recent boyfriend, a Brit working on his dissertation and trying for a job at the UN. But he had recently fled back "across the pond" — as he gratingly termed it — under suspicious circumstances, and Sally was moving back into her old place, an apartment she'd been living in off and on for the past few years. Sally used to be a rabbinical student, and it turns out that one of the great advantages of being a rabbinical student in New York is that even after you drop out you still have access to all of these wonderful old prewar apartments on the Upper West Side. People are always leaving to go on a kibbutz or pursue higher education or something, and so someone's always looking for a roommate. Sally had been in and out of this particular apartment two or three times already. The only disadvantages to this arrangement were that she had to live on the Upper West Side, and that with all the comings and goings, the apartments didn't tend overly toward hominess, or furnishings for that matter. So Sally was planning to bring some movers by the Bay Ridge place in the afternoon to take the big Jennifer sofa bed, our last major piece of furniture, off our hands. But I kept trying Sally's cell, over and over, and she wasn't picking up. And then, on the way out, we heard the radio reports of five random shootings in a Maryland suburb — as it happened, the Maryland suburb Sally's parents lived in. "Oh no," I breathed.

"I'm sure they're fine," said Eric.

"I hope so. If her parents have gotten shot, I don't know what we're going to do with that fucking couch."

"*Why* are you doing this again?" Mom sighed as we took the Sixty-ninth Street exit off the Belt Parkway and drove down quiet blocks of houses with lawns and then along the great green swath of park, a majestic view — of the Verrazano Bridge (where John Travolta's friend killed himself in *Saturday Night Fever*), of New York Harbor, of Staten Island — rising up beyond.

It was the same question she had asked me about the cooking project, and the answer was the same, as well. The same, and equally inexpressible. I could not explain the soul-sick feeling I got underground late at night, when there hadn't been an R train for forty minutes and the platform was as crowded as if it were rush hour. I couldn't explain how cut off I felt, sealed in a pneumatic tube of a commute that spit me out each morning on a gray sidewalk teeming with business suits, and spit me out again at night in peaceful, isolated, hopelessly square far Brooklyn. I couldn't explain why I thought another year like the last would ruin me, maybe even ruin my marriage. I couldn't explain it because there was no explanation, I guess.

Mom was well aware of the situation that would meet her inside the apartment, mostly because of twenty-nine and a half years of history, but also because of an incident two weeks before. Basically, what happened was that our landlady in Bay Ridge, a sweet woman with a raging Brooklyn accent whose hobby was taking old photos and making them into greeting cards with off-color jokes about aging and the sex lives of married people inside, had seen the apartment. We, of course, had had no intention of that happening — at least not until I'd hired someone to clean the stove, and spackled over all the nail holes, and glued back the piece of the ceramic towel rack I'd broken off. But the landlady used her key and came into the apartment before all of that was done, and she left a message on our new answering machine. She was horrified. She was going to have to get the oven replaced. (The oven worked fine.) Please don't bother with cleaning, just get your stuff and Get Out. Basically.

My mother was treated to the subsequent hiccupping hysterical crying-jag-type phone conversation, which lasted most of an hour. So she knew that she might be faced with a problem.

It wasn't *that* bad. There wasn't a smell, or rats, or maggots. (The maggots come much, much later.) Humiliated but proud, I had, despite my landlady's edict, gone ahead and hired a woman to clean the stove. (What can I say? I was raised in proximity to a self-cleaning stove, and have never been able to square my belief in myself as a person possessed of free will with the act of getting down on my knees to stick my head in a box befogged with carcinogenic fumes and scoop out handfuls of black goo.) But if we were to conduct ourselves as responsible tenants and not trailer trash, there was a hell of a lot left to do. So for several hours we all scrubbed and painted and packed and swept. Mom even cleaned the drip pan under the fridge. I had never known there *was* a drip pan under the fridge. At last the apartment was empty but for the ugly fold-out sofa. It was 3:30 and — oh, I forgot to mention this part of the story — we had theater tickets that night. Edie Falco and Stanley Tucci in *Frankie and Johnny in the Clair de Lune*. Eighty bucks a pop.

"So — what the hell do we do with this thing?"

"You haven't heard from Sally yet?" asked Dad.

"Nope." I was trying very hard not to be angry about that — if Sally's mother had been shot through the head at a Texaco, I'd really feel like a heel being pissy about some couch.

"Well," said Mom briskly. "I think she's missed her opportunity. I say we take it to Goodwill and be done with it."

By transferring a good deal more into our decrepit 1991 Bronco than was wise, my brother, father, and Eric managed to squeeze the sofa into the U-Haul. The boys then all piled into the front of the moving truck. The plan was for them to find a Goodwill and turn in the U-Haul while Mom and I headed straight back to Long Island City in the Bronco. After we unloaded it, we'd still have plenty of time to freshen up before the play that night. So Mom and I hoisted ourselves in, started up the Bronco, and headed off.

The view from the on-ramp to the Brooklyn-Queens Expressway, just before the entrance to the Battery Tunnel, is lovely, with the sparkling harbor, the lower Manhattan skyline, picturesque Carroll Gardens unfolding below, but that is not what I will always remember about it. I'll remember instead how even in the best of times the traffic here, where the Gowanus and Prospect expressways merge, is heavy, and that the ramp is quite high off the ground, and quite steep, and that it has only one lane, and no shoulder. I will remember it as exactly the sort of spot you don't want to break down in.

Ah, well.

Long and tedious story short, Mom and I kissed our play tickets good-bye. Once we were towed off the beltway to an Atlantic Avenue gas station staffed by many very polite but none-too-helpful Sikh gentlemen, I stuffed my grease-stained mother into the back of a taxi and then waited for several hours for the tow that would get me and my incapacitated Bronco back to Queens. Mom got back to the apartment to find herself faced at the door with an upended sofa bed blocking the stairs. The search for Goodwill had been, apparently, in vain. This was the last straw for a woman without much in the way of native patience who had nevertheless gotten through this arduous day without complaint. She was exhausted, her hip hurt, she was dirty. She leaned up against the couch and wept.

Luckily, Eric had opted to stay and wait for us back at the apartment while my father and Heathcliff went to go make use of at least two of the very expensive Broadway tickets. When he heard the sofa's foot rock and bang against the wall of the entryway he came to investigate, and found my mother there, sobbing against the gray stain-resistant upholstery. He moved the couch to one side, and she was able to just squeeze past it and up the stairs, where she promptly collapsed onto the formerly white chair she had bought when she was pregnant with me, to use as a nursing chair, which she had given me when I came up to New York. "Oh my God," she moaned. "I'm never getting up again."

"Elaine," asked Eric, "is this place really that bad?"

"Yes."

"I'm sorry. It's my fault. I'm sorry I got your daughter into this."

Elaine looked around through the splayed hands she had rested on her face — at the picture window with the broken jalousies, at the rotting floorboards in the kitchen, at the odd space at the other end of the long, open room, a sort of short tail of an *L*. She looked around thoughtfully, and then gave Eric a small but warm smile. "You didn't get my daughter into anything she wouldn't have gotten into herself. Besides, we'll make it work. Now, the important question is — *do you have orange juice?*"

The Bronco and I did eventually get back to Long Island City at around 9 p.m., and after unloading the incapacitated truck and turning in the U-Haul, I came up into the apartment to find my mother bathed, with a large gin and juice in her hand, wandering around contemplating. "This back room is too cramped for a bedroom. Why don't you put the bed over here and make this space into a sort of jewelbox of a dining room? It could make a great room. I'll send you some sheers to hang, to soften it up. You'll need mirrors. And maybe a flokati rug would be good."

That night at eleven o'clock we all met at Peter Luger for Dad's birthday dinner. Dad and Heathcliff had had a great time at *Frankie and Johnny.* (Dad's a big Edie Falco fan.) They'd even managed to find a friend of Heathcliff's — well, an ex-girlfriend, actually, Heathcliff's the kind of guy who can always dig up some ex-girlfriend when he needs to — to take one of the play tickets, and she came to dinner too. We had Steak for Six and creamed spinach, and we managed to get in lots of martini toasts before my dad's birthday had officially ended. Mom started drawing on a cocktail napkin to show me how she was going to rig some special curtains at the front window to block the street noise, and chattered on about some great cheap floor covering that we could use to hide the rotted floorboards in the kitchen.

"See, now this is great," I sighed, holding up my martini to the light, good and tipsy and digesting well.

"Yeah," agreed Eric, pushing back his chair. "Now if only we had some eggs poached in red wine."

My mom glared up from her napkin, jabbing her pen at him. "Don't. Even. Joke about it."

So there it was — midnight. My father was sixty, and we lived in Long Island City, instead of just walking around it dead. Maybe it wouldn't be so bad.

April 1944
Kandy, Ceylon

"So after an hour or so we've got perhaps a vial full. Alice is up to her elbows in scales, I've got popped fish eyes all over me, in my hair, we're both holding thoroughly squashed trout or whatever they were, one in each fist, and peering sideways into the beaker to see if we've got enough of the stuff. It's a sort of cloudy pinkish color. The odor is, well, potent."

The new registrar sat with her back against the wall, squeezing her cocktail glass in one giant hand, sloshing it either for illustrative purposes or because she was drunk. Her big wide face was bright, her hair a hysterical rust-colored halo. All around her sat men and women in various states of insobriety and hilarity, some squeezing the stems of their smuggled martini glasses along with her, others nearly off their chairs laughing. Paul knew it would be best for him to join in the fun. But the racket was all too much, so instead he nursed a gin and orange at a small oilcloth-draped table in the corner and eavesdropped. The estate where they had the OSS shacked up down here in Ceylon didn't have an actual bar, but someone had obligingly, and hastily, re-outfitted the parlor with a smattering of tables and mismatched chairs for the thirsty Americans. The room was small and crowded, and in the tricky yellow light of the gas lanterns, Paul could easily make himself unnoticeable.

"'So,' I say." The registrar smacked her big mitts down on the tabletop, leaned in, cocked her eyes leftward, eyebrows flying. *"'So,' says Alice."* Her eyes darted to the right, wide at first and then narrowing in comic suspicion. All around the table, anticipatory giggles as the registrar drew out the moment nearly unbearably,

hunkering down and cutting her glance back and forth. "'Who gets the first cocktail?'"

The laughter echoed through the air like artillery fire, the registrar's most piercing of all. Paul didn't know whether to join in or duck.

"Say! I'm so hungry I'm going cross-eyed!" she shouted. The mob heigh-hoed their agreement. Paul was surprised to feel a needy grumble of his own, the first he'd had after weeks of gnawing Delhi Belly. "I know what let's do! Let's go down the hill to town. I passed a restaurant the other day that smelled delicious!"

Bateson raised a finger halfheartedly. "Now, Julie, your stomach isn't up —"

"Oh, can it, Gregory!" crowed the registrar merrily. "My stomach isn't up for any more canned potatoes, that's what it's not up for! Come on — shall we eat as the Ceylonese do?"

There was some toasting and a great scraping of chair legs as the party rose. They headed out into the darkness.

Was he intrigued by this annoyingly ebullient, oddly compelling giant of a woman? Or was he just hungry? Paul didn't know, and he didn't ponder too much, either — he just went with them.

¶¶¶¶¶¶¶

Hacking the Marrow
Out of Life

H ere's a nifty fact for you: during World War II, Julia Child worked for an undercover agency called the OSS — that stands for Office of Strategic Services, a nicely meaningless moniker, don't you think, for a very cloak-and-dagger sort of outfit? This was back when she was still just Julie McWilliams, thirty-two and single and not sure what she wanted to do with her life. She thought maybe she'd be good at espionage, though it's hard to imagine a six-foot-two-inch redheaded woman making herself inconspicuous in, say, Sri Lanka. Of course she didn't do any spying — although I suppose if she had, she wouldn't tell us, would she?

In a way I was sort of in the same boat. I too was working for a government agency — though not a particularly cloak-and-dagger one — at a historic moment. My own agency had some busy weeks ahead of it, because it happened that a lot of what the government agency did had to do with filling up the hole left when the towers fell. This is an exciting thing for a government agency to be in charge of — beats the hell out of, say, processing building permit applications or something — which is probably one reason why I caved and went permanent in May of 2002. But here it was, nearly a year after the attacks, or tragic events, or whatever you want to call it — even at the government agency, people still had a hard time with that, mostly settling for "September 11," which is at least neutral, better than "9/11," which sounds like a deodorant or something — and there were memorial ceremonies to arrange, brave new initiatives to announce, publics to garner input from, and governors and mayors to get money from.

An office competition had been held to come up with an inspirational motto for the agency. The winner got a free lunch (with the president of the agency — an odd choice, to say the least). The motto was on the stationery, the Web site, the glass front door of the office. It was a nice motto, very stirring. But I was a secretary. And when you're a secretary at a government agency in charge of filling up the hole in the ground where the towers used to be, during the weeks leading up to the first anniversary of September 11, mottoes just don't help at all.

The trouble was not an inconvenient excess of emotion — the staff was much too busy to go around feeling sad. Besides, the place was lousy with Republicans, so genuine emotion wasn't such a big commodity, anyway. Plus, the agency's office was in a building right across the street from what the world called Ground Zero but we all just called "the site"; from the windows in the conference room you could look directly into the hole. After you look at that every day for a couple of months, you just get used to it. You can get used to anything, as long as you don't mind collapsing a few mineshafts of your brain where the stuff you can't think about is skulking around. It's easy — not simple, maybe, but easy.

When I was offered a permanent position back in the spring, those yellow trucks with the giant toothed scoops were still raking delicately through neat furrows of debris, searching for bits of people. Every once in a while, when you were downtown or even when you weren't, you'd still find a torn bit of paper skittering along the gutter. Pages from legal memos, work orders, inventory sheets — all of them mashed in this odd way, like the icing on a cake that's been wrapped in cellophane, and smudged with a strange pale powder, as if they'd been dusted for prints. You always knew just where they'd come from.

The head of the agency called me into his office one day. He was a bluff sort of man, Mr. Kline, not particularly young but not old either, thick-necked, with features that were not exactly unattractive, but small and oddly close together. He probably looked a little piggy to me only because I knew he was a Republican. He was nice enough, though, and particularly so when he offered me a permanent position.

Why did I take it, after years and years of saying no? I don't know. Maybe it was because of Nate. Nate was Mr. Kline's sort of unofficial second-in-command — baby-faced, cute enough if you like the evil genius look, and two years younger than me, if you're to trust his word, which of course you can't. His offhanded compliments, casual insults — just barbed enough to leave a pleasurable sting — snide asides, and comradely sexual innuendo had drawn me in, giving me the illusion that I was working in some alternate universe's version of *The West Wing,* with President Bartlet on the other side of the political fence.

Case in point:

As I was coming out of Mr. Kline's office, having received the job offer and told him I'd think about it, I nearly ran headlong into Sarah, Vice President of Government Relations, who was rushing in. (This particular government agency was absolutely *crawling* with vice presidents, with more popping up all the time.) Sarah was an implausibly pert woman with freckles and enormous eyes as thickly lashed as those of an animé character. (She was also, as I had learned when I spent a month and a half filling in for her secretary, a raving lunatic, in my admittedly unprofessional opinion.) She stopped and grabbed my shoulders, staring into my eyes like a hypnotist. "Julie," she asked, "are you a Republican?"

I was still picking up my eyeballs and sticking them back into my head when Nate, who'd been standing right there, for all the world like he had just been waiting for me to come out of Mr. Kline's office with the job offer, gave me a little wink and smirked, "Are you kidding? Republicans don't wear vintage."

Which, when I thought about it, seemed as good a litmus test as any.

So maybe it was Nate. Or it could have been the temptation of history being made outside the window. Or maybe I was just almost thirty and afraid.

Whatever the reason, this time I had said yes, and now it was four months later, early September, and I was in my cubicle — the fourth cubicle I'd inhabited since starting work at the government agency — spinning around in my rolling office chair, digging a trench in my forehead with my fingernails while muttering robotically into a phone headset, "Yes, sir, I understand your concern that our organization is shitting on the heads of New York's Finest. Would you like to send us your comments in writing?"

As the anniversary approached, dignitaries and mourning families and reporters began streaming in and out in ever-burgeoning floods. The large room where press conferences were held was directly in front of my desk; I knew I was meant to present a professional demeanor. But frankly, I just couldn't be bothered. That was partly because I'm not very professional, but more immediately, it was because of the phone.

When Julia Child worked in Ceylon, she probably didn't even have a phone at her desk. Not a lot of international phone lines in Kandy in those days, I don't imagine. But my phone is constantly in action. It has eight lines, endlessly blinking red lights. Sometimes I'll have four or five people on hold at a time. I talk to screamers, and patient explainers, and the lonely old, who are the worst, because I can never think of a nice way to say to the housebound lady in Staten Island who is sure her idea for the memorial is being stolen by some big architect somewhere because the picture she saw in the paper looks just like the collection of crystal paperweights she keeps in her knickknack hutch, "Thank you for your input, you loon — bye now!" And then there's the mail to go through — the drawings of enormous steeples shaped like praying hands, the models built from Popsicle sticks and Styrofoam cups and cotton balls dipped in tempera paint. Each of these, of course, is carefully archived and cataloged, presumably for some distant future exhibit of wackadoo outsider art.

Sometimes, when it gets really bad, I contemplate just going ahead and bursting into tears. I figure that's just the kind of namby-pamby crap they expect from a Democrat, and maybe I'll get lucky and they'll shake their heads and let me go home with a cold compress. But I have a reputation to uphold. I am not a crier — well, not at work, anyway. I maintain more of a Weimar-era tough-cookie image, all paper cuts and ironic hysteria and dark circles under the eyes. So instead of crying, I sigh when asked to get a box of Kleenex for a grieving widow, or bang my head wearily on my desk in the middle of phone calls from some woman who can't walk anymore and hasn't been out of her apartment for a week and used to be a great hoofer and was in pictures but now can't pay her medical bills and thinks the only appropriate thing to build at Ground Zero would be a reproduction of the '39 World's Fair. Instead of crying, I make withering comments about little old men who send in poems with titles like "The Angels of 911." It passes the time. But hard-bitten cynicism leaves one feeling peevish, and too much of it can do lasting damage to your heart.

Four days after they'd arrived, I loaded my parents onto a plane back to Austin, where the living is easy. All of us, by that time, were suffering the constant nagging headaches and viselike pains around our middles that are the inevitable results of parental visits to New York. You know there's something wrong with your lifestyle when you look forward to getting back to your cleansing Julia Child regimen. The night after they left we ate Poulet Poêlé à l'Estragon, with mesclun salad out of a bag on the side, and found myself feeling very virtuous using less than a stick of butter for a dinner for three.

Heathcliff was staying on in New York for a while because he'd gotten a job. It was not clear to me exactly how this had happened. Over the last few days, he'd constantly been getting calls on one or the other of his cell phones — he had two. He never told us about any of the conversations he had on them, but after one of them he pulled me aside and asked if he could keep sleeping on our couch for a little while longer. He was going to be running a kiosk at a cosmetics convention at the Javits Center, which didn't sound at all like something Heathcliff would do, except that he was going to be selling soaps and lotions made from the milk of cashmere goats he had spent a year herding in Tuscany. *That* is Heathcliff all over.

Anyway, it seemed I had been missed, out in the virtual world. Someone named Chris posted a comment on the Poulet Poêlé à l'Estragon post, my first in most of a week: "Oh thank GOD you're back! I thought you were dead!!! I missed you SO much!" I spent fully half a day at work thrilled that I had a regular reader named Chris when I didn't even know anyone named Chris, before realizing that Chris's comment was, well, creepy. It was nice to feel appreciated, though, and after my parent- and hellish-move-induced hiatus, I came back to the Julie/Julia Project with all cylinders pumping. I started out slowly — some poached eggs, some soup. But soon I was ready for a bigger challenge. A challenge like, say, steak with beef marrow sauce.

The first obstacle in a bout with a marrowbone is simply arranging the match. Perhaps in 1961, when JC published *MtAoFC,* marrowbones hung off trees like greasy Christmas ornaments.

But I did not live in 1961, nor did I live in France, which would have made things simpler. Instead, I lived in Long Island City, and in Long Island City, marrowbones are simply not to be had.

Lower Manhattan was not much better. There were wine stores and cheese counters and cute bistros, but since most of the fashionable people who live this far downtown prefer, like vampires, sustenance they can just grab and suck down on the run, a butcher was nowhere to be found.

So I put Eric on the case. First he headed over to Astoria one evening after work. The thought was that in Astoria there would be stores patronized by good authentic immigrant people who still appreciate the value of a good hunk of bone. But the authentic immigrants seemed to have moved on; Eric had no luck. Heathcliff wasn't finishing up at the convention center until after seven that night, and I didn't get home until after nine. Dinner was roast chicken, Julia-style. I was supposed to mince up the gizzard for the accompanying sauce, but I found I didn't know what a gizzard was. I knew it was one of the things in the paper bag up the bird's bum. I knew it wasn't the liver, but among the remaining bits of innards, which was the gizzard was a mystery.

(After reading my post about this, Eric's father called me and cleared up the trouble: the gizzard is the thing like two hearts stuck together; the heart is the thing like half a gizzard.)

The next night Eric and Heathcliff tried a two-pronged approach, with my husband catching a train from work to the Upper East Side, my brother catching another to the West Village. But both Lobel's and Ottomanelli's were shuttered by the time my faithful marrowbone-retrievers got there. Butchers must really need their beauty sleep. My brother did manage to get to the Petco before it closed to buy mice with which to feed my pet snake, Zuzu. (Whenever Heathcliff is in town I take advantage of the situation by letting him take over snake-feeding duties. I figure since he's the one who *gave* me a five-foot-long ball python, back in college when he thought I needed a pet, he ought to be responsible for some of the karmic debt accrued over ten years of rodent sacrifice.) I got home just before ten and ordered pizza before I crashed on the couch. Eric had to make me wake up for long enough to take out my contacts. Waking me up when I've fallen asleep on the couch is no fun for anyone.

And then it was Wednesday, September 11, 2002. I was up at five a.m. to get to my office by seven. I spent the morning standing about. First I stood around in the back of a crowded press conference room, listening to blandly stirring politicians talk and trying to decide if Nate was looking at me or just staring into space. Then I stood outside on the concrete plaza surrounding my building. Across the street, in the hole where the towers had been, a circle of family members stood silently in the blowing construction dust. They were reading the names of everyone who died there into a microphone. In the afternoon I manned the Family Room.

The Family Room was actually a conference room that had been converted into a sort of funeral viewing area for those whose husbands and sisters and sons had never been recovered. The windows, twenty stories up, looked out into the hole; the walls were plastered baseboard to ceiling with photos and poems and flowers and remembrances. There was a sign-in book, and a couple of couches, and some toys and games for the children. The Family Room was the only place these people could go to be near those they'd lost without being assaulted by hawkers with NYFD gimme caps and Osama Bin Laden toilet paper, or tourists posing for cameras in front of the fence as if they were visiting the Hoover Dam. Until fairly recently bodies were still being found, so I suppose it made a certain kind of sense that they would want to come here, although I've never been much of a graveyard-visiting kind of person, and when I looked down there, I didn't think of God and angels and the serene faces of the dead gone over to some Other Side; I just thought of body parts.

I couldn't see how anyone who'd actually lost someone to that sucking wound could stomach it.

After the morning memorial, they all came up to the Family Room and stared into the hole some more. They brought yet more pictures and poems to affix with pushpins to the walls. They were already so full that anyone who was coming for the first time and wanted to pin something up would need help finding a spot. I helped these people, carefully moving one memento half an inch to the left, another an inch to the right, to squeeze in a snapshot that was the only photo the small Ecuadoran woman had of the son who had washed dishes at Windows on the World. It was hard for first-time visitors, not just because the walls were so packed, and not just because they hadn't started friendships with the other families that were more regular visitors, but also because if they were only coming for the first time a year after the tragic events had occurred, it was maybe because they came from another country and might not speak English, or because their relationship with the dead person they had known had been a difficult one. So I handed out Kleenex to gay German brothers and bottled water to dotty English aunts, and awkwardly patted the back of the estranged ex-husband from Belize who broke down in sobs. This was the job of the junior staff, during the anniversary of September 11 — well, some of the junior staff, anyway. The secretaries but not the city planning interns, the girls from PR but not the guys from program development. Women, in point of fact, no men at all, spent the day supplying the thumbtacks and fresh pens and water and tissues and keys for the bathroom in the hall. Maybe, being Republicans, the senior staff had some family-values sort of notion that women possess inherent delicacy and sensitivity — despite the abundant evidence to the contrary within their own organization. Or maybe they just knew that twenty-something Ivy League boys don't take kindly to being drafted for emotional shit work.

Meanwhile, the bone marrow remained a problem. It occurred to Eric that Sally was a natural to assist in this quest, but since we still didn't know for sure whether her parents had been murdered by a lunatic with a high-powered rifle, there was the risk of disaster en route to enlisting her help.

"My parents what? What?! Oh God, did I not call you?" Sally's tone was stricken.

Eric had never before inadvertently blundered into a conversation with anyone about their parents' recent hideous murder, but somewhere deep inside he had always feared, and even assumed, that one day it would come to this.

"No, no, no, everything's fine. The movers didn't show up, that's all. They were supposed to drive in from Rhode Island, but they never came. I'm so sorry, I thought I called! They're Czech, and I think they're on crank. The movers, I mean. If I get them to come again, can I still have the couch?"

It did not even occur to Eric to ask Sally why she had hired Czech moving guys who were both addicted to meth and from Rhode Island. Instead, still gasping from the unimaginable telephonic hell so narrowly averted, he told her that she could indeed still have the couch, which was still teetering on one end in the stairwell of our apartment, but only if she would help them find a marrowbone. "Sure, sounds like fun. What's a marrowbone?"

Sally and I have managed to remain close friends ever since living together our freshman year in college even though I'm the kind of person, who, when bored or unhappy, either drinks myself into oblivion or cooks very unhealthy things; Sally is the kind of person who, when bored or unhappy, goes jogging or cleans the bathroom with a toothbrush or matriculates at rabbinical school. Sally didn't yet want to talk much about the departure of her good-looking English boyfriend, but her tone, like an aural wrinkle of the nose, when she mentioned his dissertation on the prehistoric roots of feminism, and the gusto with which she agreed to join the marrow hunt, led Eric to suspect that the jig was definitely up with the Brit.

Eric took off work early, Heathcliff handed the cosmetics kiosk off to somebody or other, and Sally ventured down from the Upper West Side. They all met in front of Ottomanelli's at five minutes to six. The shop was still open, barely, but was fresh out of marrowbones. They then proceeded on their grand tour of West Village groceries, flitting from Gourmet Garages to Garden of Edens. Only after five stops' worth of flirtatious probing over meat counters (flirting by Sally, or possibly by Heathcliff, if they ran into any bubbly female butchers — but not by Eric, who was miserable at flirtation — I practically had to take him to a frat party and dose him with GHB-laced punch to seduce him) did they at last obtain their six inches of cow thighbone.

The three of them emerged from Jefferson Market with the marrowbone in its blue checkered bag held high — triumph at last! Eric felt the shudder of disaster averted. A month ago, he'd never have suspected how important a piece of cow might be to his marriage.

His giddiness was, however, somewhat squelched when Sally told him she would not be returning with him to Queens as planned, to eat the Bifteck Sauté Bercy I would be garnishing with the bone marrow of a cow. "I don't think it's a good idea," she said.

"Ah, come on," Heathcliff chimed in — not because he harbored a secret crush on her, much as I might want that to be so. I've long cherished a tiny hope that maybe the two of them would get together someday. Which, if you knew Heathcliff and Sally, you would immediately see was an epically bad idea. There must be something wrong with me.

"I just don't think I can face the subway ride back. Tell Julie I'm sorry."

She was far from the first dinner guest we had lost to the irresistible urge not to go to the outer boroughs to eat French food in a grotty "loft" apartment, but every time it happened it was both a disappointment and an obscure sort of humiliation. Socially speaking, we might as well have lived in Jersey.

Meanwhile, I had straightened up the Family Room after the last mourner left, and gone home. Even as my friends scoured the streets of the West Village for my bit of bone, I was separating the cloves of two heads of garlic for Purée de Pommes de Terre à l'Ail, or garlic mashed potatoes with a garlic sauce. Which is fantastic but sure does make for some dishes.

(Have you ever seen pictures of Julia's kitchen? It's lined in pegboard, the whole thing, with rows on rows of pots, the outline of each one drawn on with marker so she always knew which pot went where. Her husband, Paul, did that for her, or maybe he did it for his own sanity. He was always very methodical. Such a setup might come in handy for me from time to time — say, for instance, when realizing at the very moment I'm meant to add boiling milk to the rapidly darkening roux that I have not in fact put the milk on to boil. At times like these it might be convenient to be able to have the smallest saucepan immediately to hand, rather than scrabbling around under the counter with one hand while frantically stirring the roux with the other. But I will never have such a setup, because the very last thing in this world I am is methodical.)

The making of Purée de Pommes de Terre à l'Ail is exacting and not quick, but even so, and even given my late start, I was still finished before the bone retrieval party, or what was left of it, returned. I was getting a little nervous. To pass the time, I went online to check e-mail.

My friend Isabel lives in the Texas hill country with her husband, Martin, and her mother, who's a professional animal communicator. Isabel is, well — hell, I can't explain Isabel. Just take a look for yourself:

Nancy has just shared with me a BRILLIANT, weirdly prescient and Truman-Capote-mixed-in-with-Burroughs-ian dream in which I was choreographing a TV Easter special with a cast of deranged chipmunks. And it reminded me of a dream I had last weekend, which I'm pretty sure is precognitive, I've been rereading my *Dreaming into Truth,* and this has all the signs.

Now, I have never met Nancy, do not understand (nor much want to) how a dream about chipmunks dancing could possibly be construed as pertaining to Truman Capote, William S. Burroughs, or precognition, and have never heard of a book called *Dreaming into Truth.* Also, you should realize that Isabel sent this to her entire mailing list, several dozen people at least. This is what she's always like. In an age of brevity, Isabel is unembarrassedly prolix. This would read somewhat more amusingly if you knew her voice, for Isabel has a voice like a genius third grader who's skipped her Ritalin — swooping from low guttural imitations of people you've never heard of into high-pitched trills and back again, unpredictably. Sometimes eardrum-splittingly. Her voice, I think for the first time right at this instant, is not unlike Julia's:

I'm walking on cobblestones beside a river. I pass a sidewalk café, and sitting at one of the tables is Richard Hell.

(Oh, also? I have no idea who Richard Hell is. Not a clue.)

He's drinking iced tea and wearing an old argyle sweater with leather pants and very thick purple eyeliner, which looks really sexy somehow. So I say, "Remember me? It's Isabel. I just wanted to tell you that I finished *Find It Now* and it was wonderful." His book is called *Go Now,* but in the dream I called it *Find It Now,* not because I had misremembered the name of the book but because in the dream that WAS the name of the book. And Richard says, "Have some real English tea." But when I reach out to take a cup I realize I'm holding a bright pink dildo. It's teeny-tiny, it fits in the palm of my hand. I know it will only get big in the bath, like a sponge but hard.

Next thing I know I'm knocking on an apartment door painted a sort of queer faded crimson, with the number 524 on it. My friend Julie — you know Julie, she's the one who's doing that cooking blog I sent you all a link to? — opens the door, and her hair is all wild, and her husband Eric is in the background throwing rounds of pizza dough in the air, singing beautifully. Julie asks me in to eat, but I hand her the dildo and say, "Thanks for the dildo you gave me, but I can't use it."

Julie asks why, looking very shocked, and I say, "I don't take baths anymore, only showers." To which Julie says, with this totally un-Julie-like primness:

"Well, that's your problem, isn't it?"

Now, this is embarrassing, and my aunt Sukie is going to just die when she reads this, but Isabel didn't make up the thing about me sending her the dildo. We'd been having an e-mail exchange — a *private* e-mail exchange, I might add — about Isabel's sex life, which I guess was less than totally satisfying, which, well, whose isn't? And it's not like I'm some kind of dildo maven, but I did spend some time in San Francisco once. I guess I wanted to look hiply pro-sex or something, because sometimes when you're friends with Isabel it's nice to know more about something than she does. So I sort of talked up the joys of sex toys — gleaned from several years of Web surfing, rather than much in the way of actual experience. And I guess I talked a pretty good game, because Isabel wound up sort of enthralled with the concept. Then it was almost like I couldn't *not* send her a dildo for her birthday. So I did.

God, I hope her husband isn't on her mailing list.

I was not at all sure how to respond to this missive, so I went offline again without answering and went back to the kitchen. Deciding to assume that Eric, Heathcliff, and Sally's late arrival

JULIE and JULIA

was a good sign, I opened the Book to the page on extracting marrow.

"Stand the bone on one end and split it with a cleaver," wrote Julia, sounding ever so confident and blithe. I could think of one possible wrinkle right off the bat, which was that I had no cleaver. A few other vague misgivings were floating around in the old brainpan as well.

At that moment the door swung open. Eric and Heathcliff strode through like Arctic explorers in from the cold. Eric bore his plastic bag before him like a prized ice core sample. He was no doubt expecting a thankful kiss, at the very least — perhaps a good deal more. "Who's the man?" he bellowed.

"You got it, did you?"

"I sure as hell did!" He cackled, even did a little dance. Heathcliff grinned a one-sided grin, and graciously did not roll his eyes.

"Did you have to trade Sally in for it?"

"What?"

Heathcliff explained, "She couldn't make it. Didn't want to deal with the subway."

I sighed. I hadn't kissed Eric hello, and he was beginning to fear his hopes for a show of gratitude would be dashed. "Well, maybe it's for the best anyway."

"How do you mean?"

"It's time to extract the beef marrow." The look I gave the two of them was slightly stricken. "Not sure she'd want to be around for this."

My largest knife was a carving one with a serrated edge, probably nine inches long with a blade about an inch and a half at its widest point. I'd always thought it a rather grand, daunting sort of a knife, but after one whack I could see it was not nearly tool enough for the job. "Julia must have the strength of ten secretaries," I muttered. "She should have been a crusader — she'd have been hell at dispatching infidels. 'Split it with a cleaver,' my ass."

For a moment Eric and Heathcliff stood over the bone in silence. Eric rested his chin in his hand thoughtfully; Heathcliff
scratched the back of his head.

A few years ago, Heathcliff lived in New York for a while. The
plan was that he would crash on our couch for a few weeks while
looking for a place — he wound up staying there an entire year.
This sounds like the worst kind of horror, a married couple with a
brother-in-law lodged permanently in the living room, but it actually worked out pretty well. We cooked together a lot — Heathcliff
makes a mean spinach, sausage, and cream pasta — and watched
a ton of movies, and had a hell of a good time, actually. On the
downside, Eric and I had sex like a dozen times that entire year.
(But I don't think we can really put all the blame for that at
Heathcliff's feet.) On the upside, I had lots of opportunities to sit
back while my husband and my brother worked out various domestic puzzles, which was fun and saved me having to do it besides. Watching them sussing out the marrow situation got me
feeling a little nostalgic, actually.

"Do you have a jigsaw?" Heathcliff asked.

For twenty minutes the two of them went back and forth with
the saw Eric had dug out of the hall closet, until both of them
were dripping with sweat. They managed to cut into the thing
about an inch. The oozy pink stuff on the blade of the saw was,
though exactly what we were looking for, truly horrifying. The
boys were looking a little green.

"Hell, give it to me."

I threw the bone into some simmering water on the stove.
This felt wrong, like Julia would not approve, but I just didn't
know what else to do. I scooped the bone out of the pot after a
few minutes and went after it again, this time with my very
smallest knife, a paring one, about three inches long and narrow
enough to fit into the round tunnel running down the middle of
the bone. Slowly, painfully, I wormed my way into the interior.

I clawed the stuff out bit by painful pink bit, until my knife was sunk into the leg bone up past the hilt. It made dreadful scraping noises — I felt like I could feel it in the center of *my* bones. A passing metaphor to explorers of the deep wilds of Africa does not seem out of place here — there was a definite *Heart of Darkness* quality to this. How much more interior can you get, after all, than the interior of bones? It's the center of the center of things. If marrow were a geological formation, it would be magma roiling under the earth's mantle. If it were a plant, it would be a delicate moss that grows only in the highest crags of Mount Everest, blooming with tiny white flowers for three days in the Nepalese spring. If it were a memory, it would be your first one, your most painful and repressed one, the one that has made you who you are.

So there I was, scooping out the center of the center of things, thinking mostly that it was some nasty shit. Pink, as I think I've mentioned. Very wet. Not liquid, but not really solid, either — gluey clots of stuff that plopped down onto the cutting board with a sickening sound.

The boys looked on, mesmerized. "Someday," Eric said, swallowing hard, "our ship is going to come in. We are going to move out of New York, and we are going to have our house in the country, like we've always wanted."

I thought he was just trying to talk me into my happy place, but he had a point, and when he finished swallowing his bile, he made it.

"When this happens, we need to get ourselves a rescue cow. We will buy it from a slaughterhouse. And then we will treat it *very well*."

"Yes," agreed Heathcliff. "Damned straight."

It's true. I am a fanatical eater of flesh. But bone marrow, it struck me, was something I had no right to see, not like this, raw and quivering on my cutting board. Unbidden, the word *violate* popped into my head. "It's like bone rape. Oh God, did I just say that out loud?"

We got maybe a tablespoon and a half out of the bone and decided it would have to be enough. Eric and Heathcliff had to go into the living room and find a football game to rid themselves of the horrid vision. Muttering "Shake it *off,* goddammit," I went ahead and began sautéing the steaks.

But once you've got your head in a place like that, it can be hard to crawl out again. Reading about "the moment you observe a little pearling of red juice beginning to ooze at the surface of the steak" didn't help at all in that department, though it did make for an excellently prepared steak. The sight of the pink stuff on my cutting board was still making me feel sick, but I thought I detected another, more buried sensation as well. A dark sort of thrill.

When the steaks were done, I put them on a plate and stirred the marrow and some parsley into the buttery pan juices. The vestigial heat from the juices is supposedly sufficient to lightly cook the marrow. Besides, Eric assured me, there was no way you could get mad cow from marrow, and even if you could, cooking it would make no difference — something to do with prions or something — but it sure looked scary, so I decided to leave it on the heat just a bit anyway. Then I dolloped a spoonful of the marrow sauce onto each steak, plopped down some garlic mashed potatoes and Tomates Grillées au Four — just whole tomatoes brushed with olive oil and roasted in the oven for a few minutes — and dinner was served.

If I had thought the beef marrow might be a hell of a lot of work for not much difference, I needn't have worried. The taste of marrow is rich, meaty, intense in a nearly too-much way. In my increasingly depraved state, I could think of nothing at first but that it *tasted like really good sex.* But there was something more than that, even. (Though who could ask for more than that? I could make my first million selling dirty-sex steak.) What it really tastes like is life, well lived. Of course the cow I got marrow from had a fairly crappy life — lots of crowds and overmedication and bland food that might or might not have been a relative. But deep in his or her bones, there was the capacity for feral joy. I could taste it.

One theory on cannibals, of course, is that they eat parts of their slain enemies to benefit from that person's greatest assets — their strength, their courage. Then there's that thing they do in Germany. You heard about that, didn't you? Some man over there agreed to let another man cut off his penis, cook it, *then feed it to him* — now, what in hell was that all about? What did he think the taste of his stir-fried cock would tell him about himself? Was he seeking to wring one last drop of pleasure out of the thing? (Goodness, that's an unnecessarily vivid metaphor.) But somehow — I said this over dinner — this steak with beef marrow sauce, it didn't seem all that different. "It's like eating life. It's almost like eating *my own* life, you know?"

"No, not really. But it's a hell of a good steak, sis."

If I tried to say something like that to anybody at the downtown government agency I would get nothing but blank looks and a subsequent internal investigation. Especially on the first anniversary of the tragic events, some might think that a discussion of spiritual cannibalism might be seen as being in poor taste. Sally, the only sex maniac former rabbinical student we know, might understand, if only she could withstand the trauma of a subway ride to the outer boroughs. Julia might, too.

As I lay in bed early on the morning of September 12, dreading the approaching moment when I would have to throw off the covers and go to work, I thought about Julia's job for her government agency. The OSS existed before the invention of cubicles and all that that implies, so Julia didn't have to work in a cubicle. She didn't have to answer the phone, and she didn't have to comfort crying people, and she didn't have to ride the subway to get home. She got to handle information substantially more top-secret than that bureaucrats are assholes, and that a not-insignificant minority of the American people are blindingly

stupid, shithouse crazy, and/or really terrible memorial designers. In all these things she was better off, in her secretarial days,
than me.

But she didn't have her Paul yet, either, I thought as I curled up
against Eric's back for one last rest. And (as I tasted one last,
gentle, beefy burp) she didn't yet have beef marrow, either. So I
guessed I had a few things up on her as well.

June 1944
Kandy, Ceylon

One bare, glaring twenty-five-watt bulb was not sufficient for this close work at noontime on a bright day; at dusk on a rainy one it was close to impossible. Paul pinched the bridge of his nose hard between his thumb and forefinger, then pushed the heels of his palms into his eye sockets. His bowels were in rebellion yet again, and he ought to be in bed, but these jobs weren't going to get done by themselves — when you are the Presentation Division, you get no sick days.

He stared absently out his window. Through the curtains of warm rain he could watch the small elephants being herded out of the botanical gardens for their evening meal. The animals' slow, gentle pace, their small swishing tails and comically long Theda Bara eyelashes always cheered him, and the gardens were beautiful in any weather. On the wall of the cadjan hut where he worked, an emerald-green lizard perched, making a sound like a spatula rasping across the bottom of a cast-iron pan. Paul dug his fingers down into his sock to scratch uselessly at his damned athlete's foot, then returned to his drafting table, setting his mind to get one last board done, at least.

But then, just as he'd gotten himself settled and his head back into his work, the one light he had went out. Of course.

"Dammit." He reached up and gingerly unscrewed the bare bulb, shook it for the light rattle of a sprung filament, but there was none. He replaced it, got up, and went to peek out his door. The lights were out everywhere. He'd suspected as much. This late in the day, they'd probably not come on again.

To think he'd once thought work with the OSS would be dashing and exciting. Well, perhaps he could at least organize some *concepts for the boards he'd have to start first thing tomorrow. He began to shut his door again.*

"Paul! Just what are you thinking of doing, alone in there in the dark?"

It was Julie, of course, no mistaking that voice, but at first he did not see from where she was speaking to him. He peered into the dishwater dimness of the hallway but saw no one. "Paul! Behind you!"

She and Jane had their faces pressed to the flimsy shutters of his one window and were grinning like a couple of twelve-year-old kids. Jane wiggled a summoning finger at him, and Julie cried, "Come with us to watch the elephants get washed. Don't tell us you don't want to!"

"Need to get this work done, I'm afraid. I'm already late with them, they need finished boards by tomorrow at the latest."

"Balls to that! If they want to get work out of you they ought to get you some light, I say."

Jane cocked her eyebrow at Paul in a way that would have been more seductive if it hadn't been so obvious she meant it to be. "See what a bad influence you've been on our little Julia? She's got the mouth of a sailor these days."

Paul sighed. The girls had a point, didn't they? Balls to that, indeed. He set his pen down. "I'll be right out."

DAY 40, RECIPE 49

▪▪▪▪▪▪

. . . To Make an Omelette

W hy don't you just call someone to take the damned thing away?"

I was sitting in the living room with my right ankle — swollen to twice its usual circumference and turning an unsettling shade of yellowish-green — propped up on an ottoman. Eric was in the kitchen, getting me some ice; Heathcliff was standing over me with his arms crossed.

"I told Sally she could have it. She's going through a rough patch."

"Yeah, well, you can't get into your apartment without major injury. I'd say that's pretty rough."

I shrugged.

"Now who was it she broke up with? A David?"

"Of course."

In the ten years I have known her, Sally has dated at least a dozen Davids. It's kind of creepy.

Eric came out of the kitchen with some ice in a Ziploc freezer bag. "What do you want me to do about dinner?"

"I'll cook. I've got the artichokes to do. Anyway, I'm really behind."

"You shouldn't be putting weight on that foot. Hold the ice on."

But I was already getting up and hopping back toward the kitchen. "I only did six recipes last week. And the week before that with the folks in town I didn't do any at all. My readers *need me!*"

I had meant that last to be construed as a joke, even though it wasn't, really. Eric was having none of it. "Your *readers?* Come *on,* Julie."

"What?"

"I think the dozen people who click onto your Web site while they take their coffee breaks will manage to carry on if they don't get to read about you sautéing thorny vegetables in butter for one more day."

"Oh, fuck off."

Eric and I glared at one another with a poisonous good humor meant to suggest this whole argument thing was just a big loving put-on. Heathcliff smirked, eyes sliding between us, taken in not at all.

My brother has house-sat for a mobster in Crete. He's been mugged by policemen in Hungary. He's chewed coca leaves offered to him by a waiter in Peru. He left an island off the coast of Sicily once because he was the only redhead the people there had ever seen, and the old ladies kept crossing themselves whenever they saw him. What's more, the woman he lives with off and on, when he isn't getting his wallet stolen in Budapest or herding goats in Italy or selling soap in New York, is the kind of person who can just decide of an evening to whip up an apple pie from scratch. Together they make ice cream for the pie by putting milk and cream and sugar and vanilla in a coffee can set inside an old potato chip tin filled with ice, then sitting catty-corner on their kitchen floor and rolling the tin back and forth between them. Clearly, he's got laid-back domestic bliss down just as pat as brave adventuresomeness.

When I snap at Eric in front of Heathcliff, then, it's a humiliating acknowledgment of my relative failure on both these fronts. But it's not only that. It's also a searing reminder that I will *inevitably* turn out just like my mother, either a martyr or a nag or irrational or just grumpy about my bad joints. Hopping around the kitchen on a swollen ankle while bitching meanly at a spouse, for example, is exactly something my mother would do. I would have soothed the irritation provoked by this realization with a healthy vodka tonic if only Eric hadn't dropped the bottle of Stoli he'd bought on the way home on the subway platform, smashing it. Getting mad about that would be another very Mom-like thing to do, so I just gritted my teeth and set about preparing the very strange meal I'd planned for the night, Omelettes Gratinées à la Tomate and Quartiers de Fonds d'Artichauts au Beurre — tomato-filled omelettes *gratinéed* with cream and cheese, and artichoke hearts, quartered and buttered.

Chris — the one who wrote the halfway creepy thing about missing me so much when I didn't post and thinking I was dead — found it mind-boggling that before the Julie / Julia Project began, I had never eaten an egg. She asked, "How can you have gotten through life without eating a single egg? How is that POSSIBLE???!!!!!"

Of course, it wasn't *exactly* true that I hadn't eaten an egg. I had eaten them in cakes. I had even eaten them scrambled once or twice, albeit in the Texas fashion, with jalapenos and a pound of cheese. But the goal of my egg-eating had always been to make sure the egg did not look, smell, or taste anything like one, and as a result my history in this department was, I suppose, unusual. Chris wasn't the only person shocked. People I'd never heard of chimed in with their awe and dismay. I didn't really get it. Surely this is not such a bizarre hang-up as hating, say, croutons, like certain spouses I could name.

Luckily, eggs made the Julia Child way often taste like cream sauce. Take Oeufs en Cocotte, for example. These are eggs baked with some butter and cream in ramekins set in a shallow pan of water. They are tremendous. In fact the only thing better than Oeufs en Cocotte is Oeufs en Cocotte with Sauce au Cari on top when you've woken up with a killer hangover, after one of those nights when somebody decided at midnight to buy a pack of cigarettes after all, and the girls wind up smoking and drinking and dancing around the living room to the music the boy is downloading from iTunes onto his new, ludicrously hip and stylish G3 PowerBook until three in the morning. On mornings like this, Oeufs en Cocotte with Sauce au Cari, a cup of coffee, and an enormous glass of water is like a meal fed to you by the veiled daughters of a wandering Bedouin tribe after one of their number comes upon you splayed out in the sands of the endless deserts of Araby, moments from death — it's that good.

Still, I think it was the omelette section that really turned me around on eggs.

The diagrams in *MtAoFC* are always exciting. You can pretend you're mastering something really daunting, like lithography or cold fusion or something. Or maybe there's another analogy in here somewhere:

Grasp the handle of the pan with both hands, thumbs on top, and immediately begin jerking the pan vigorously and roughly toward you at an even, 20-degree angle over the heat, one jerk per second.

It is the sharp pull of the pan toward you which throws the eggs against the lip of the pan, then back over its bottom surface. You must have the courage to be rough or the eggs will not loosen themselves from the bottom of the pan. After several jerks, the eggs will begin to thicken.

It's not just me, is it? Surely you too think immediately of some ancient and probably very painful Japanese sex practice you vaguely remember reading about when you were in college?

Okay, maybe it's just me.

JC writes, "A simple-minded but perfect way to master the movement is to practice outdoors with half a cupful of dried beans." I can just picture her chortling to herself as she wrote this, thinking of all those early-sixties American housewives in their sweater sets and Mary Tyler Moore flip hairdos scattering beans all over their manicured lawns. Because simple-minded is my middle name, I followed her advice, only instead of a lawn, my pinto beans got scattered all over the grimy sidewalks of Jackson Avenue. Drivers of semis honked at me; prostitutes stared. A minivan from Virginia pulled up in front of me. The driver, seeing that she had spotted someone of good sense and breeding in the person of Julie throwing beans out of a pan onto the sidewalk, asked me for directions to New Jersey.

"Lady, you are hell and gone from fucking New Jersey."

My manners are not always the best, I'll admit, and unsuccessfully flipping dried beans in a skillet in front of God and everybody does not do much to improve them.

(When I write about this incident, my high school boyfriend Henry, who I broke up with to go out with Eric, and who didn't really forgive me for that for about ten years, writes, "Now your neighborhood has a crazy bean lady. That is so cool. . . ." Also, somebody I don't know from Adam takes the trouble to lament the fact that I use the word *f**king* so much; people who object to my choice of language always use lots of asterisks.)

Accomplishing this technique with actual eggs can make you feel quite giddy — it's like managing to tie a cherry stem into a knot with your tongue. The first time I managed it — sort of, anyway — was on a Sunday morning, for Eric and his friend from work, Tori. I didn't know Tori all that well — she was an artist, she spent her days in an office with my husband, and she was pretty. For all I knew she could tie cherry stems into perfect bows with her tongue and flip omelettes like a whirling dervish to boot. So I was a little nervous.

When cooking omelettes the Julia way, everything goes so fast. It's just silly to try to decipher the drawings and their captions — which besides being generally intimidating are also written for the right-handed among us, necessitating some synapse-switching on my part — while actually cooking. I couldn't get the first one to flip at all; it just crumpled against the far lip of the pan, cracking up some at the stress points. But once I flipped it onto a plate it sort of covered up the filling — mushrooms cooked down with cream and Madeira, good, good stuff — and looked more or less like something one might call an omelette. So that one I decided to call a qualified success. The second, though, could not qualify as a success under any circumstances; first it stuck, and then when I flipped harder, the eggs sloshed all over the stovetop. Another flip sent a large portion of the semi-congealed thing to the floor. I gave up, flipped its raggedy ass onto a plate, and called it mine. On the third, with increasingly terrified jerking motions, I managed to get a start on the rolling thing Julia describes, a bit. I managed not to spill anything more onto the stovetop, at least, and it stayed in one piece. I guess you can't ask for any more than that. We ate our *omelettes roulées* with some prosecco Tori brought. I do love an excuse to drink before noon.

Anyway, by the time I limped into the kitchen to make a dinner of artichoke hearts and tomato omelettes for my husband, my brother, and me, I'd gotten pretty comfortable with the whole egg-flipping thing. The omelettes came out more or less omelette-looking, no harm done to the stovetop, and soon enough dinner was served. All should have been well, but somewhere along the way, with the lack of liquor and the embarrassing marital bickering, I'd gotten my hackles up, I guess.

Sally's couch was what started it. Discussion of why it was still teetering in the foyer had led naturally enough to talk of her love life, always an interesting conversation.

"It's not like the guy's some great catch. He's cute, I guess — if you like the type." Sally's type is muscular, loud, handsome, funny, and arrogant; mine is thin, quiet, dark, funny, and shy. In our years of friendship we have never once been attracted to the same man. "But he's a total fraud. He basically told her that she had to apply and go with him to Oxford so he wouldn't be *ashamed* of her. *Him,* ashamed of *her.* That ass isn't worthy to lick her Manolos." Sally was the only person I knew who actually owned Manolos — she'd bought them on eBay, and they made her feel deliciously sexy. And when Sally felt deliciously sexy, every man within a three-block radius thought her deliciously sexy as well — it was like a pheromone thing, she couldn't help it.

Heathcliff poked at his artichokes somewhat warily, as if they might still have some fight in them. But while it's true that when you attack artichokes, artichokes can fight back, the benefits of evolution had not saved these particular specimens — sprained ankle or no, I had been more than a match for them. I'd broken off their stems and snapped off their leaves, sliced and pared them down to tender yellow disks with spiky purple centers like tropical flowers, floating in a bowl of water doused with vinegar to keep their color up, simmered them, and mercilessly scooped out those tough, colorful petals, the artichokes' last defense, until they were nothing more than accommodating delivery systems for butter. "So if he was such an asshole, what's the problem?"

"The problem is, she wants somebody. Or thinks she does. If she doesn't want to hear that she keeps picking assholes, what am I supposed to say?"

I've been with Eric the entire time I've known Sally, and in all this time Sally has never dated a boy for more than six months. This is a state of affairs that cuts both ways. Sometimes she'll present us with a flurry of boys all at once: Cuban food with one on Wednesday, a Ben Stiller movie with another on Friday, brunch on Sunday with a third, the two of them freshly showered and flushed from one last morning round. She'll have a cheerful, leering glint in her eye, and when the boy gets up to use the restroom, she'll lean across the table with a grin and whisper, "What do you think? He's cute, isn't he?" These periodic springtimes of Sally's erotic life can sometimes knock me for a loop. One thing that must be said about marrying your high school sweetheart is, one does rather miss out on the polyamorous lifestyle. But it's always a kick seeing Sally so confident, proud, with these guys' dicks in one hand, the world on a string in the other.

But then some high school friend gets pregnant, or Sally's mother gives her insufferably well-adjusted little sister who's getting married a homemade family cookbook of well-loved recipes, then refuses to give one to Sally because "It's only for the wives in the family." Then Sally starts bringing only one boy around, one of the original three or another one altogether, and this time there's a slightly desperate appeal in her eye, and when she asks, "He's cute, isn't he?" it's more like a plea for reassurance than a prideful acknowledgment of her catch. She starts asking other leading questions: "You know," she'll say, her eyes wide with worry, "he only wants to have sex like three times a week. That's a bad sign, right?" Or she might just say, "What do *you* think I should do?"

Sally's looking for my usual "married friend" advice: "Relationships have ups and downs," "stay the course," etc. But I don't want to give it. I usually don't like the guy, anyway, and I don't like who Sally is when she asks me. What I like, when it comes down to it, is the gleeful, sex-crazed, willfully neurotic Sally. The Sally who doesn't care about being married like her dull sister, who knows that not one of the boys she brings over for us to meet is one whit good enough for her — not smart enough, not kind enough, with no gift to match her percolating laugh, her voice that can spread its champagne bubbles throughout a room of strangers.

Eric skated his last artichoke quarter heartily around on the plate he had balanced on my swelling foot — which in turn was resting on his lap — sopping up the last bits of melted butter. "It's not like Sally's some kind of saint."

Just as he plopped the last khaki green, dripping triangle into his mouth I smacked him, hard, on the shoulder; quite a trick, since I had to reach across the entire length of my outstretched leg to do it. "Don't be a jerk."

"Come on. You know I love Sally. But she's — *prickly.*"

It's true that none of my girlfriends are much for compliance. Gwen once got into an actual *fistfight* on the subway after telling a bunch of squealing high school girls to shut the hell up. (One of the girls gave her a scratch across the cheek from her three-inch fake nails — it didn't heal for weeks.) Isabel's singularly raucous baby voice and willfully obscure sense of humor have been known to actually make men break out in hives. And Sally is the most challenging of all of them. If she were a movie star, she'd be Rosalind Russell in *His Girl Friday;* if she were a vegetable, she'd be an artichoke. As it is, she's Sally, tough cookie extraordinaire and a hell of a person to try to set up on a blind date.

"You know," added Heathcliff, "maybe Sally just isn't the marrying kind. *Ow!* What?"

Maybe if the men in my life weren't always making smart-ass comments, they wouldn't have to worry about bruises so much.

When we were kids, Heathcliff used to have a toy, a twisty piece of blown glass with two bulbs on either end, connected by a twining bit of pipe. It looked rather like some kitchen gadget Julia might have picked up on her travels abroad, except that it was filled with a mysterious red liquid. The idea was that you held the bulb with the liquid in it in your palm, and the heat from your body would be enough to make it boil up to the other bulb. Only it didn't work for me. When I held the empty bulb, the red liquid in the other bulb seemed to be pulled *back* to my palm, as if whichever law of physics or chemistry made this toy work didn't apply to me. This was just one of many ominous clues to the puzzle of What Kind of Freak Was I, Anyway? Another was the way I lost things — car keys, eyeglasses, retainers, twenty-dollar bills — at a rate that went way beyond plain flightiness, into the paranormal realm. Or how later, when I was a teenager, driving home alone after some late sexually fraught night out, I'd burn out the streetlights — they'd extinguish in front of me as I drove down the highway, one after another after another.

When I started cooking, in college, I quickly learned that I possess an eerie inability to make anything that requires setting, fermenting, jelling or rising. Bread, mayonnaise, vodka Jell-O shots, it doesn't matter. If a liquid and a solid are meant to mix together and become something else, something airy or puffy or creamy, I'm hopeless.

Also, I kill every plant I touch.

I didn't read comic books growing up, and so didn't know about the X-Men until Eric explained them to me as an adult. If I had, I would have realized much sooner that I'm a mutant — I'm thinking something like Magneto crossed with Rogue, with a bit of Lucille Ball mixed in. Perhaps it's all connected somehow to my hormonal trouble — the unwelcome genetic gift that is one more thing my perfect brother, being male, will never have to worry over. That gift worth a fortune to the electrolysis technician and someday, I assume, to the obstetrician who'll be writing up the scrips for the drugs I'll need to use to get pregnant, if indeed I'll be able to get pregnant at all. The shock of panic that shoots through me when I think about this proves that (a) there is such a thing as a biological clock, (b) I have one, and (c) it's ticking.

All my life, it has been as if tiny explosions were going off all around me, small revolutions, conspirators in my own body setting off booby traps. So when Heathcliff spoke the words "not the marrying kind," I recognized the rumble of the bomb it set off deep in the underground garage of my gut.

"What does that even mean? 'Not the marrying kind'?"

Heathcliff and Eric were now both rubbing their sore arms. "What's so bad about that? Marriage isn't for everybody!"

Of course not. Marriage is no more for everyone than heterosexuality or French cooking. But the queasy spasm that tore through me when he said it was real, and it didn't go away.

"You're not just born one way or the other."

"Oh, I don't know. Maybe you are."

Heathcliff has never been short on women, much like Sally's never been short on men, yet he has always remained essentially a bachelor. He lives lightly on the land, has few possessions, keeps a distance — a kind of redheaded Last of the Mohicans. Usually it doesn't bother me.

"So, what, you think you're *beyond* the whole marriage thing?"

"What?" He raised his eyebrows, sardonically baffled as only Heathcliff can manage.

"Don't look at me like that."

"Like what?"

"Like you're better than me, that's what like." Suddenly, my blood was pounding in my ears, and I realized I was getting ready to say something I would regret. I was going to Tell.

When I was in fourth grade and Heathcliff was in first our parents separated. Our father went to live in some condo in far south Austin, and for most of a year we'd see him only twice a week — once when he came to take us out for burgers and video games, and once when he picked up our mother for their marriage counseling sessions. They worked it out, and Dad moved back in, and everyone lived happily, if occasionally grouchily and resentfully, ever after. All of this was old family history. But there was one thing I knew that Heathcliff didn't.

It happened in Dad's ZX. My father was driving, my mother

was in the passenger seat, I was in the back, and my mother was crying.

"Are you okay, Mommy?" I asked.

"No, honey, I'm not okay."

"Does your head hurt?" (Mom had sinus trouble — her head often hurt.)

"No. My heart hurts."

This was new. "Why does your heart hurt?"

"Because your father is in love with another woman!"

My mom and I have always shared a gift for the cutting melodramatic statement; I was dimly aware even in the dreadful moment that I had just backed her up on a hell of an alley oop. Even as I began to sniffle in the backseat, somewhere deep I thought to memorize those lines — I knew the value of a good sob story.

The whole thing was so exciting and dramatic that it wasn't until days later that the knowledge of this Other Woman began to weigh on me. But once it did, it only got heavier and heavier. I started staring at women at the mall or on the street, wondering if one was Her. I began to get tired easily. The circles under my eyes got so bad that teachers would send me home from school (although, to be honest, I might have been taking some advantage here of my inherited histrionic streak). When my mother asked me please, please, please not to tell what I knew to Heathcliff, I promised. Why spread this kind of misery around?

Well, apparently the promise stuck, because when I finally broke it that night over our artichokes and tomato omelettes — blurting out to Heathcliff, as if in revenge, that when he was in first grade his father had slept with another woman, and that his parents stayed together anyway, not because they were "the marrying kind," but because they worked like hell and loved each other more than they'd hurt each other — I began to shake, and a lump of dread, small but heavier than iron, threatened to close up my throat entirely, as if my body judged choking to death a better fate than telling a secret.

What did I think? That upon the instant of breaking my silence, my brother would transform into the six-year-old I had to protect, crouched in his pajamas by my parents' bottle-green glass coffee table, his bright hair still damp from his bath, his face crumpling into uncomprehending tears?

Well, he didn't. Instead, he took another bite of omelette. "I didn't know that," he said. He stuck a fork into his final bit of egg, smearing it around the plate to get at the last of the sauce. "But it only makes sense, doesn't it? It all turned out okay, so I guess it doesn't matter."

He burped. "I thought omelettes for dinner was a weird idea, but that was pretty good."

And that was that. I'd broken faith, failed to keep perhaps the only real secret I had ever been trusted with. And the ground did not swallow me up. It turned out, in fact, to be no big deal. I didn't know whether to be relieved or disappointed.

There is an entire chapter in *MtAoFC* devoted to the preparation of eggs. But in cooking my way through it, I found myself ravenously curious about something of which there was no mention: Julia's *first* egg. I mean, surely she didn't just start off blithely jerking off perfect omelettes at birth, right? Surely even the great JC required some *practice*. So what was Julia's first egg like? Was it scrambled — a traditional choice? Was it an Easter egg she boiled herself, to tide her over until the big ham dinner? Or was she older when she cooked her first egg, a young woman, embarrassed to tell anyone she'd never acquired the skill, trying to make a dozen eggs Benedict in her first New York apartment and winding up throwing out half a dozen spoiled poached eggs while her roommates' backs were turned?

Could she even have married before she mastered the egg? Julia married late, at thirty-five; perhaps she had wondered for a time if *she* was the marrying kind. That night, while Eric washed dishes and Heathcliff ate Ben & Jerry's straight out of the carton and I recovered from the discovery that revealing a decades-old secret was no biggie, really, I wondered if that could be. For some reason it comforted me to think of Julia's first egg as happening in her garret apartment in Paris, as she spun around in her cocoon, about to hatch as the new Julia, the Julia she was meant to become.

Disaster/Dinner Party,

Dinner Party/Disaster:

A Study in Duality

O n January 1, 1660, a young government worker in London started a diary. He wrote about going to church, where the preacher was saying something or other about circumcision, and about lunch afterward; he mentioned that his wife burned her hand while heating up turkey leftovers.

For the next nine years this guy wrote *every single day*. He witnessed the Great Fire of London and some disappointingly overdone roasts. He went to hundreds of plays, vowed to quit drinking then changed his mind. He ate a lot — no matter the precarious state of the union, a barrel of oysters was always appreciated — and worked a lot, and fondled whatever girls would deign to allow it. And he wrote about all of it — honestly, self-indulgently. He was often entertaining, often mind-bogglingly boring, every now and then ablaze with life — the Sid Vicious of seventeenth-century diarists. And then on May 31, 1669, he just stopped.

Some bloggers might say that Samuel Pepys was a sort of proto-blogger, but we're not a terribly measured lot, so I don't know that I'd listen to us if I were you. Sure, Pepys obsessively chronicled his interior-decorating ups and downs and the time he masturbated in the water taxi. Sure, he wrote in his pajamas. But although he carefully saved his diary, volumes and volumes of it, for the rest of his life, he never showed it to a single soul. Today, when we blog about our weight-loss problems and our knitting and our opinion of the president's IQ level, we do it on the blithe assumption that someone gives a shit — even though there's a guy stuck in Baghdad who blogs, and a Washington DC staff assistant who gets paid by Republican appointees for sex who blogs, and our own jottings must all be dreadfully dull by comparison. Nowadays anyone with a crap laptop and Internet access can sound their barbaric yawp, whatever it may be. But the surprise is that for every person who's got something to say, it seems there are at least a few people who are interested. Some of them aren't even related.

What I think is that Sam Pepys wrote down all the details of his life for nine years because the very act of writing them down made them important, or at least singular. Overseeing the painters doing his upstairs rooms was rather dull, but *writing* about it made overseeing the painters doing his upstairs rooms at least *seem* interesting. Threatening to kill his wife's dog for pissing on the new rug might have made him feel a bit sheepish and mean, but write it down and you have a hilarious domestic anecdote for the centuries. Imagine if he'd had, say, a safely anonymous pamphlet cranked out on a press and passed around on the streets of London. Wouldn't he have enjoyed occasionally overhearing some fellow in a tavern recounting to general hilarity Pepys's own yarn about the king's spaniel shitting on the royal barge?

There's a dangerous, confessional thrill to opening up your eminently fascinating life and brain to the world at large, and the Internet makes it all so much faster and more breathless and exciting. But I wonder — would we still have Sam's jack-off stories, the records of his marital spats, if he'd been a blogger rather than a diarist? It's one thing to chronicle your sexual and social missteps to satisfy your private masochistic urges, but sharing them with the world at large? Surely there are some limits, aren't there?

I wanted to make Heathcliff an orange Bavarian cream while he was in town. Orange was his favorite flavor. But my mutant jelling handicap made me hesitate. In my progress through the dessert chapter so far, my Crème Brûlée had wound up soup, and my Plombières had ranged from smooth but loose to solid but grainy. The Bavarian, unlike the Plombières, had gelatin in it. I didn't know if this boded ill or well. The prospect of serving my brother, he who effortlessly improvises ice-cream makers out of tin cans, a failed dessert had me terrifically nervous.

On the morning of the last Saturday Heathcliff would be in town, I was awakened by Eric's moans and instantly knew we were in for another of his Blanche days. Everyone has some genes to curse — Eric's was the one that occasionally made him throw up all day, spending the between times lying in bed with his arm flung over his eyes, suffering through a splitting headache. It isn't very nice to say, but I had no patience with the Blanche days, since he wouldn't talk to a doctor about them, citing instead the "Powell stomach" or "drinking too many vodka gimlets." During the Blanche days, besides moaning and retching violently, Eric also sweated and smelled bad — he was just no fun to be around. If ever I decide I'm not the marrying kind after all, I know it will be on one of Eric's Blanche days.

I was out of bed early, hoping to drown out the first of the heaves with some NPR and the burble of the coffee maker. Sally called at eight on the dot.

"Oh my God. Did I wake you up?"

"No, I'm up."

"Are you sure? God, I can't believe I woke up so early! I can't sleep these days."

"It's fine. I'm reading the paper. What's up?"

"I talked to Boris."

"Who's Boris?"

"Boris! My Croatian moving guy."

"I thought you said he was Czech."

"Yeah, I was wrong, he's Croatian. Anyway, he and his brother are going to drive up from Providence today. They're leaving at nine, so I guess they'll be in Queens by like twelve thirty or so? Can we come pick up the couch then?"

"Um, sure. I just have to go shopping, but I can be back by then."

"You sure it's not a pain in the ass?"

"Nope. I mean yep."

"Okay — I'll see you at twelve thirty, then."

By the time I got off the phone the vomiting had begun, right on schedule. I peeked into the half bath, on the floor of which Eric was now slumped. "Sally's coming over today to get the couch."

"She is?"

"Yeah. Around twelve thirty."

"Oh. Okay." His voice was full of watery determination — by twelve thirty he would not be sitting on the floor of the half bath retching up violent green bile, as God was his witness, he *would not*. I'd seen this courageous defiance before — Eric hits all the Vivien Leigh highlights on his Blanche days. It wouldn't make any difference.

"I'm going to Western Beef now, so I can be back in time."

"Are you taking the Bronco?"

"I have to, I guess."

"Be careful."

(After our moving-day disaster we'd gotten the Bronco running again with a new alternator, but I caught the guy who did

JULIE and JULIA

the replacing staring aghast after me in the one mirror the truck still possessed as I drove away, and it's true the brakes were feeling awfully soft.)

The single best thing about Western Beef on Steinway Street is its name, but there are other things to recommend it as well. For instance, it has convenient recycling vending machines, which might come in handy if I lose my shit and go off on an evil Republican bureaucrat, get fired, and have to start collecting cans for a living. It has reasonably decent produce, a bizarre and fascinating section of West Indian herbs — including some fleshy pinkish seaweed-looking stuff in a cellophane bag labeled "Virility"— and a walk-in refrigerated section. There are no nifty insulated coats like I've heard they pass out at the big Fairway on the Upper West Side, but eighteen eggs are less than two dollars, cream is sold in gallon cartons, and they've got shelves and shelves of every cheap cut of meat you could want. (And I was making Pot-au-Feu for dinner, so I wanted plenty.) What Western Beef does not have is the sugar cubes I needed for the Bavarian.

(I'll just bet sugar cubes were a lot easier to get in 1961. Now, of course, it's all sugar *packets,* not to mention those godawful powders, which always remind me of that scene in *9 to 5* when Lily Tomlin thinks she's accidentally poisoned Dabney Coleman. Talk about a movie that could give a secretary at a government agency some *ideas.* But that's neither here nor there. It's a shame about the sugar cubes, is all. Sugar cubes have such a neat white wholeness to them — when we were kids, Heathcliff and I used to leave sugar cubes out for the reindeer every Christmas Eve, on the coffee table beside Santa's plate of cookies, stacked like a tiny crystalline igloo. What are you going to do now, leave the reindeer nine packets of Sweet'N Low?)

The Key Food on Thirty-sixth Street in Astoria didn't have sugar cubes either, though I did pick up the beets and potatoes for the Salade à la d'Argenson that I had totally forgotten to get at Western Beef because I'd written them down at the last minute, on the other side of the shopping list. So I tried the Pathmark. I'd never been to the Pathmark, and let me tell you, I'm never going again. There's nothing I need that much. The sliding doors at the Pathmark open into a wide, white, empty hallway, totally devoid of any sign of life or foodstuffs. At any moment I expected to see a chiseled Aryan commandant come around the corner to usher me along: *"Ja,* please, right this way, take a cart, the food is just through here."* But I was at last funneled into not a gas chamber, but a glaring white supermarket the size of a stadium, where for the price of the existential horror felt upon witnessing families buying two carts full of RC cola and generic cheese doodles, or a lonely older man purchasing three dozen packages of ramen noodles and four cartons of no-pulp orange juice, I could procure sugar cubes.

It was a very good thing that the Bronco was running. After all this, just lugging the stuff around the teetering sofa bed and up the stairs back to the apartment was enough to get me feeling whiny and put-upon — if I'd had to haul that load home on foot, I'd have probably wound up braining Eric in his bed with a pork shoulder.

He was, of course, still racked out when I came back to the apartment. "Do you need any help, honey?" he moaned as I huffed up the stairs with my bags of meat.

"Oh, shut up and go back to sleep."

"Okay. I'll get up soon, I promise."

"Whatever."

On the way home, I had had a sudden stab of dread concerning the beet and potato salad. It had made me a little sweaty under the arms, and even more irritable than I might have been otherwise. Once I dumped the meats into the fridge, I rushed to consult my *MtAoFC,* and it was as I feared: the potatoes and beets needed to sit together for "at least 12 hours, preferably 24."

The Bavarian needed to set "3 to 4 hours or overnight."

The Pot-au-Feu you should "start cooking 5 hours before you expect to serve."

It was 10:30 in the morning, and I was already running behind. This is hardly unusual, but it pisses me off every single time.

Sam Pepys threw dinner parties as a young man — he enjoyed food as much as he enjoyed impressing people, so he was a natural. But of course he didn't actually *cook* — he had a wife and a servant for that, or he could just go around the corner to pick up some meat pies or barrels of oysters or something or other. And besides, there just were not as many things to freak out about, foodwise, in Restoration England. Life could be pretty treacherous, what with the plague and the bladder stone surgery sans anesthesia and the occasional violent overthrow of the kingdom, so food just wasn't all that high on the list of people's anxieties. Sam didn't have to worry about no-carb regimens or his father's heart condition or his neighbor's new vegan lifestyle. The chickens weren't getting shot up with antibiotics. There was no mad cow disease. Neither did he agonize over the symbolic weight of the fare — "Will the Secretary of Ships be bored to death of prawns with cheese?" At least if he did, he didn't write about it, and this is a man who wrote about being blue-balled by scullery maids.

Well, if Sam wrote about blue balls, it seems like recounting a dinner party disaster or two is the least I can do.

What happened was this: I got called up by this reporter from the *Christian Science Monitor,* of all things, who had had the totally *insane* idea to have me cook Boeuf Bourguignon for the editor of *MtAoFC.*

I won't lie to you — when I started my blog, I certainly entertained daydreams about unlikely fame and fortune. I was, after all, Out There, hanging out on the Internet like it was Schwab's drugstore, popping gum in a tight sweater, penning off-the-cuff culinary bon mots. But, as we all establish to our sorrow by the time we are about eleven, these things don't happen, not really. And anyway, it would have been almost heresy to consider the actual Julia Child and my own endeavor within the same theater of possibility. Maybe blogging Christians believe that Jesus Christ is reading their online diaries; but I didn't have the chutzpah to even contemplate the possibility that Julia, or any of her delegates, might be reading mine.

But now Judith Jones was coming to dinner. *The* Judith Jones — She Who Got It, the woman who recognized history in the onionskin manuscript of a French cookbook, the person who brought JC to the world.

I share with neither Samuel Pepys nor Julia Child a sanguine nature, and for me a dinner party with Judith Jones — "Like the Virgin Mary, only with better clothes and a corner office in midtown!" I shrieked to my nonplussed husband — was the occasion of much hysteria.

And then too there was the matter of the blog. Old Sam could write whatever he wanted because no one was ever going to read it. But I had an audience, disembodied and tiny though it might be. I wasn't much afraid of writing something that would make me look pathetic or incompetent, nor of getting myself sued. But I didn't want to look, you know, *conceited*. Because under the sheer terror, I was feeling pretty damned proud of myself. After all, I'd gotten *the* Judith Jones to accept an invitation to dinner at my house. Or the *Christian Science Monitor* reporter had, anyway. But I didn't want to seem like I was bragging or anything. On the other hand, I couldn't just not mention it. I was going to be cooking Boeuf Bourguignon, after all — *the* classic dish of French cookery, the first dish Julia Child ever cooked on *The French Chef.* People would notice if I just skipped over it. And I didn't want to seem *coy,* either.

Worst of all, though, I might jinx the whole thing.

Quite a cyber-tightrope to walk, let me tell you.

The violent flurry of interest that ensued when I let slip that Someone Important was coming to dinner took me by surprise. High-flying guesses were bandied about in my comment box — at one time or another everyone from *Iron Chef*'s Chairman Kaga to Nigella Lawson to actor-I-most-want-to-have-sex-with David Strathairn to Julia Child herself were supposed to be heading out to Long Island City on a Wednesday night to eat with me. And the guesses were made by some in an apparently near-religious state of ecstatic apprehension. "Who IS IT??????" wrote Chris, whom I was beginning to picture for some reason as a Minnesotan woman of late middle age with a pixie haircut and slight thyroid condition. "This is KILLING ME! I HAVE to KNOW!!! Pleeeeez tell us NOW, I can't STAND it!!!!"

It was oddly exhilarating, the grand ambitions all these strangers had for my dinner party. These people thought that Julie Powell, with her yearlong cooking project, was sufficiently fascinating to draw the greatest lights of food celebrity chefdom, and maybe even some minor movie stars, to her crappy outer-borough apartment. Hell, maybe it was true. Maybe my Boeuf Bourguignon, the ninety-fifth of the 524 recipes I had challenged myself to cook in one year, *was* fascinating. It must be, in fact. For while Julia Child wasn't coming to dinner, her editor was. This was just the beginning. I was going to be famous! *Famous,* I tell you!

It's a good thing there's always another disaster to poke a hole in the old self-esteem before it gets dangerously inflated.

I started my first Boeuf Bourguignon at about 9:30 on the night before the Dinner. I began by cutting up a thick piece of slab bacon into lardons. When my mom made this for Christmas Eve in 1984 in Austin, Texas, she used Oscar Mayer; she didn't have any choice. But in 2004 New York, there's no excuse — certainly not when the woman who discovered Julia Child is coming over. I simmered the lardons in water for ten minutes once they were chopped so they wouldn't make "the whole dish taste of bacon." I personally didn't see the problem with this, but I'm no Julia Child, and in a situation as fraught as this one it must be assumed that Julia's opinion is the correct one.

I browned the bacon, meat, and vegetables, each in turn, then put them all back into the pot and poured in red wine to cover it all, along with a spoonful of tomato paste, some crushed garlic, and a bay leaf. I brought it all to a simmer on the stovetop and then stuck it into the oven at 325 degrees.

This was when things began to fall apart. Because Boeuf Bourguignon is meant to cook three to four hours, and it was already after ten o'clock at night. And so I made the fateful — or maybe I should just come right out and say "very bad" — decision to drink a vodka tonic or two while I waited. After about two and a half — vodka tonics, I mean, not hours — I made fateful/very bad decision #2, which was to just set the alarm for 1:30 a.m., get up and take the stew out of the oven, then let it cool on the stovetop until morning. I reached over Eric, already racked out across the bed from his share of the vodka tonics and the jalapeno-bacon Domino's pizza we'd eaten for dinner, and grabbed the alarm clock. It was one of those NASA-designed battery-powered jobbies you always get from more distant relatives who don't really have the first idea what to get you for Christmas. I sat down on the edge of the bed to set it, but I couldn't figure the damned thing out. In the course of fiddling with it, I found that if I lay prone with my cheek resting on my husband's naked bum, I was in a good anchored position from which I could focus my eyes better on all the tiny, tiny buttons and the nearly illegible script describing a needlessly baroque clock-setting procedure. The buttons were so very small, though. The method so very unclear. I fiddled and fiddled and fiddled.

And next thing I knew it was four o'clock in the morning. My neck ached from being cushioned on Eric's ass, my contacts had adhered to my eyeballs. The Boeuf Bourguignon, needless to say, was toast.

The nice thing about waking up at four on the morning of the most important dinner party of your life to a thoroughly destroyed French beef stew inside your oven is that you will definitely not be going to work. Once the situation became clear, I felt free to sleep a few more hours before calling in sick and heading out to the grocery store to replenish supplies for the second Boeuf Bourguignon. And the second time I made Boeuf Bourguignon, I'll have you know, it turned out perfectly. Sometimes it just takes some trial and error, that's all.

And so I wrote my day's post and cooked my second Boeuf Bourguignon, all while recovering from what I had told my boss was a stomach flu but was in fact something somewhat less innocent, and by a miracle something more than minor, the meal was well in hand by 5:30 or so. I was just contemplating taking a shower — in my house the ultimate expression of hostessing confidence — when the phone rang.

It wasn't even Judith who called. I've never spoken to Judith — and now it looks like I never will.

"I'm *so* sorry," moaned the journalist. He was distraught. "I know how much you were looking forward to this. She just doesn't want to venture out to Queens in this weather."

Of course, since this journalist was a freelance one, and young, I wasn't the only one who'd lost an opportunity at career advancement. I held it together valiantly, for his sake. "Well, she is ninety, after all, and it is sleeting. Maybe next time. You should come over still, though. There's all this food, we'll never eat it all."

"Oh — you sure you wouldn't mind? I'd love to — that would be great!"

I'm such a good Southern girl at heart, I didn't even start wailing disconsolately until I was in the shower.

The peas that night were lovely, the conversation wide-ranging. And the Bourguignon rocked, so it's really Judith who lost out, isn't it?

Samuel Pepys wrote of a dinner disaster of his own: ". . . and thither came W. Bowyer and dined with us; but strange to see how he could not endure onyons in sauce to lamb, but was overcome with the sight of it, and so was forced to make his dinner of an egg or two." It seems that guests have always disappointed. But when someone turned up his nose at Pepys's sauce, did some benevolent stranger comfort him by saying, "W. Bowyer can suck it!" Nope.

This, I learned the next day after informing my readers of my cruel jinxing, was one thing I had up on Samuel Pepys. That felt good.

Let's just hope Judith Jones isn't a big blog reader.

There are dinner parties ruined by guests, and there are dinner parties ruined by hosts, and then there are dinner parties when everyone contributes to the disaster. I feared that the Pot-au-Feu and Bavarian night was turning into one of the latter.

Sally called again at noon.

"You're going to kill me."

"What."

"The Croatian movers? They're leaving Providence at nine *p.m.*"

"Your movers are driving in from Rhode Island at nine o'clock at night on a Saturday?"

"I told you — they're on crank."

"So, what — they're going to come move the sofa bed at half past midnight?"

"Is that okay? I'm *so* sorry about this."

"No, it's fine. Hell, I'll probably still be cooking."

"How is that cooking thing of yours going, by the way? You're crazy, you know."

"*I'm* crazy?"

Sally's laugh burbled. "Fair enough."

"Why don't you come over and eat dinner with us? You can see the new place. I've got entirely too much food for the three of us."

"That would be fun. Oh, and hey! I can bring over this guy I met. I think you'll really like him. He's got red hair, and a motorcycle, and his name is — wait for it! — David."

"You're not serious. Sally, it's really getting eerie, with you and the Davids."

"Yeah, I know. You know what else? He's a *sex maniac*. He's why I haven't been sleeping. So, would that be okay?"

"Sure. The more the merrier."

"Okay. I'll see you around eight? Should I bring wine?"

"Sure. Call if you get lost."

The water was boiling now. I threw in potatoes, let them cook until tender, boiled the beets while I was peeling and slicing the potatoes, peeled and diced the beets, tossed the potatoes and beets together with some minced shallots and a vinaigrette of olive oil and vinegar with some salt and pepper and mustard. So that was done. It was nearly one o'clock. I started mooshing up the sugar cubes with a fork. Which is oddly difficult, actually. When you press the tines down onto the cube, it just flies out from under them, so that the sugar cube goes flying and the fork smacks down on the bottom of the bowl with a scraping clang that puts your teeth on edge.

In the middle of all this, the phone rang again.

"Hey."

"Hey. How's the soap selling?"

"Oh, pretty good." Heathcliff sounds just like our father on the phone sometimes. "Hey, would it be okay if I invited Brian over for dinner?" Brian was one of Heathcliff's oldest friends — they'd been buddies since first grade — a chubby, smiling supergenius with big dorky glasses. Remember Nate, the evil genius at the government agency I work for? Well, Brian is like a Nate for the forces of good. Heathcliff had told me he was in New York, getting some kind of higher mathematics degree at Columbia, but I hadn't seen him, not for years and years.

"Sure. Sally's coming over — she wants us to meet her new guy."

"Sally has a new guy? That was fast."

"Yup." I tried to detect some hint of forlorn loss in my brother's voice, but no dice.

"Okay, so we'll be over there around seven or eight. Should we pick up some booze?"

"Sounds good."

"All right. Later."

The orangey sugar cubes at last mooshed, I proceeded to zest and squeeze oranges, soften gelatin, separate eggs — doing it just the way Meryl Streep does in *The Hours,* by gently juggling them back and forth in my hands, letting the white slip through my fingers into a bowl waiting below. Felt like the way Julia would do it — very cook-y. I was feeling very cook-y in general, actually, cool and collected, until I got to "forming the ribbon." This sounds like some ancient Asian euphemism for kinky water sports, but it was really just what I was supposed to do with the egg yolks and sugar. The yolks are supposed to "turn a pale, creamy yellow, and thicken enough so that when a bit is lifted in the beater, it will fall back into the bowl forming a slowly dissolving ribbon." But you are not to "beat beyond this point or the egg yolks may become granular."

Granular? *Scary.*

I beat and beat and beat, guessed rather blindly at the right consistency, then beat in some boiling milk and poured the mixture into a saucepan. I was supposed to heat this stuff up to 170 degrees. I was not to heat it *over* 170 degrees, or the eggs would "scramble." (*Terrifying.*) Judging by sight and hovering fingers the precise temperature of hot milk is an inexact science, to say the least, but I did my best. Then I took it off the heat and stirred in the orange juice with gelatin. I beat the egg whites up to stiff peaks and folded them into the egg yolk–orange juice–gelatin mixture, along with some kirsch and rum — I was supposed to use orange liqueur, but I didn't have orange liqueur, and I figured in a pinch booze was booze. I stuck the whole thing into the refrigerator. I was having my doubts about all this.

Don't know much about gelatin, but I know a little something about foul moods. And if only Bavarois à l'Orange was a foul mood, I could tell you for sure how to set it like a damned rock. Just make it take a shower in our apartment on a cold day. When it has to wash its hair.

"Aaah! Goddammit!"

"Honey? You okay?" Eric warbled weakly from the bed, where he was still racked out.

"The hot water's gone!"

"What?"

"No. Fucking. Hot. WATER!"

I finished the shower mewling, then hurried out, hair still slightly bubbly with shampoo, and rubbed myself roughly with a towel for warmth. I pulled on a hideous old plaid flannel robe I'd bought for Eric back when we were in college, when I thought flannel was quaint and New England-y, then, shivering, hurried back into the kitchen, beat some chilled whipping cream until stiffish, stirred it into the custard in the fridge, poured the mess into the Bundt cake pan that was the only moldlike accoutrement I possessed, and stuck the thing back in the fridge. Not feeling so cool and collected now — perhaps that was why I folded the whipping cream into the custard too early, before the custard was halfway set. This was not going to turn out at all. Oh well. A little dessert soup never hurt anybody.

I was just getting ready to start the Pot-au-Feu when the phone rang again. "Hi, Julie. It's Gwen."

(Gwen always announced herself on the phone as if she wasn't entirely sure I was going to remember her.)

"Hey, honey."

"What're you doin' tonight?"

"I'm eating Pot-au-Feu with Heathcliff and his friend Brian and Sally and her new boy. Eric's having one of his days, we'll see whether he gets up for it."

"Sally's got a new boy already? Damn, that girl moves fast."

"Yup."

"I need to get her to give me some pointers."

"You and me both."

"I need me a man, dude."

"Yeah. You wanna come over?"

"Sure. Should I bring booze?"

"Sure. Around eight?"

"Around eight it is."

After I hung up, before I commenced to hacking away at meat for the Pot-au-Feu, I went over to Eric, still prone in bed.

"You feeling better?"

"Mm-hm." This without lifting his forearm from over his eyes.

"We've got some people coming for dinner."

"Oh?" He tried to sound happy about it.

"Gwen and Heathcliff's friend Brian and Sally and her new boy."

"Sally has a new boy?"

"They're coming at around eight. And the Croatian movers are coming at twelve thirty tonight to get the couch."

"You're kidding."

"Nope."

"I thought they were coming at noon?"

"That was a misunderstanding."

"I thought they were Czech."

"Sally misspoke."

"Okay. What time is it now?"

"Two."

"Okay."

Eric set to dispatching his headache with renewed, if utterly motionless, gusto, while I went to get started on the Pot-au-Feu.

First, the meat. I spent the better part of half an hour working the thick, large-pored pig skin off the enormous pork shoulder I'd bought, but when I finally pulled it off, I was rewarded with a hearteningly grisly prop. "Look, Eric!" I leaned out of the kitchen door into the bedroom, holding the ragged pig flesh to my bosom. *"It puts the lotion on its skin or else it gets the hose again."*

"Hm? What?" He didn't remove the arms flung over his eyes.

"Eric! You have to look! *It puts the lotion —* "

"What is that?"

"It's the skin from the pork shoulder."

"No, what you were saying, about the lotion?"

You know that dejection that comes upon you when you realize that the person you're talking to might as well be from Jupiter, for all the chance you have of making them get what you're saying? I hate that. "You haven't seen *Silence of the Lambs?* How can that *be?*"

"Hey, we should put that on our Netflix!"

It was the most animated I'd seen him all day. Not that that's saying much.

After the skin was off I hacked the shoulder meat into two pieces, wrapped up the piece with the bone in it for the freezer and set the other aside for the pot, tying it up with kitchen twine first until it vaguely approximated something that had not been torn to pieces by rabid dogs. Then I clipped the chicken in half down the middle with kitchen shears. I tied up one half of that with string as well. (I was halving the recipe, which was making for some rather odd butchering assignments.)

Trussed chickens always look like sex-crime victims, pale and flabby and hogtied. It turns out that this goes double for trussed half-chickens.

The great thing about Pot-au-Feu is that, although it takes

donkeys' years to cook, there's nothing much to it. I stuck all the meat into my biggest pot, poured some chicken broth over it, and brought it up to a simmer. Julia has this sort of uncharacteristically persnickety, unnervingly Martha-esque suggestion of tying a long piece of string to each piece of meat and tying the other end to the handle of the pot, so you can easily check the doneness of the meat. I did it, but I didn't like it.

I took a break to check my e-mail. While I waited through the horrendous dial-up screech for the "You've Got Mail" bleep, I contemplated how much more bearable my life would be if only I could afford broadband.

Just as soon as I'd gotten a connection, the phone rang, cutting it off. It was Sally.

"I just realized I'm not going to Bay Ridge. How do we get to you?"

One dial-up screech later, the phone rang again. It was Gwen.

"Hey. How do I get to your new apartment, anyway?"

By the time I finished with her, it was time to go into the kitchen and add to the Pot-au-Feu the vegetables — carrots, turnips, onions, and leeks. (These Julia wanted me to tie up into bundles with cheesecloth, but no. Just . . . no.) But oh, the Bavarian! I was supposed to be stirring the goddamned Bavarian, and I'd totally forgotten! I raced to the refrigerator, but it was too late. The Bavarian was set, hard as a rock. Not soup, at least, though it did look funny, sort of puckered. "Damn," I said.

"What was that, honey?"

"Nothing, goddammit!"

In the way these days happen, between poking at the meat and checking on the e-mails and worrying over the dessert, it was seven o'clock at night before I knew it. Eric dragged himself out of bed and into the shower, and came out looking like a man who might just not die in the next five minutes. As I was dumping some sliced kielbasa into the Pot-au-Feu pot, Heathcliff came in with two bottles of Italian wine and his friend Brian.

"Brian? Oh my God, Brian!" I gave him a hug, more to prove to myself the reality of him than anything else. Because Brian had turned into an Adonis. A deep-voiced, super-genius, string theory–spouting, hugely muscled, fabulous gay Adonis. I would not have recognized him; at least, not unless he smiled at me. When he smiled, he was five again. He had a smile you couldn't stay mad at, a smile that made you think he would never be unhappy as long as he lived. All maturity had done was inject a dose of sexual charisma right into the impishness. A good, good smile.

Everybody else would be here soon. But, oh Christ, I'd forgotten to make the mayonnaise for the beet and potato salad! Maybe the fact that the Bavarian seemed to have set into something other than broth had me cocky, but I decided to beat it by hand. I had never made my own mayonnaise before, but there are nine different recipes for it in *MtAoFC,* so I figure I ought to get started on them. Anyway, how hard could it be?

Heathcliff, Brian, and Eric all looked on as I beat some egg yolks and then, trembling, began to whisk in the olive oil, pouring it from a Pyrex measuring cup with a spout. I whisked and whisked and whisked, adding one drop of oil at a time just like JC said, most of the time, anyway. It was hard to avoid the occasional nervous, sloshing tremor, given my history with setting jelling things. When I'd gotten it sort of thick, I beat in hot water, as an "anti-curdling agent," and it thinned right out again. Well, anyway, it tasted fine — like olive oil, mostly. I mixed it in with the beets and potatoes, which were by now violently pink. Then the mayonnaise was violently pink as well.

Gwen and Sally and her boy David came all in a rush. Gwen immediately set about mixing everybody vodka tonics, a skill at which she was expert, while I bustled around with dishes and forks and scooped up the Pot-au-Feu. I tried to be neat about it, heaping some of each vegetable in each corner of a large square platter, with a pile of mixed meats in the middle. But there are some dishes you oughtn't try to make pretty, and a boiled dinner is one of them. My efforts resulted only in a medieval pile of flesh — the prim separation of vegetables just highlighted the essential barbarity of the food.

No, boiled dinners are not made to be looked at, they're made to be eaten. Once we had all served ourselves, everything looked, smelled, and tasted as it should. We all got meat dribbles down our fronts, which has a way of putting people at their ease.

The potato and beet salad really was quite an unnerving shade of pink.

"Maybe we just weren't meant to eat pink food, as a species I mean," considered Brian as he gingerly took a small serving. "I'm feeling some pretty primordial fear here."

"What about cotton candy?" countered Gwen, who was piling the salad on her plate with more abandon.

"Okay — no pink moist foods then, maybe."

"Strawberry ice cream?" Sally's boy David bravely suggested, though he too was looking a little green.

"No pink moist savory foods."

But then everyone tasted and agreed that primordial fears were made to be gotten over.

"Amazing, beets. Isn't everyone supposed to hate beets?" asked Eric, who looked considerably pinker himself, and was taking seconds.

"Like Brussels sprouts, right."

"I love Brussels sprouts!"

"Me too!"

"Sure, sure — but that doesn't change the fact that Brussels sprouts are *supposed* to be disgusting."

"I used to eat jarred beets when I was a baby," I said. I hadn't thought about this in years. "Mom thought I was nuts. Then of course I stopped eating them, because who eats beets, right? But you know the thing about beets? They're really beautiful. Once you cook them and peel them and slice them, they're gorgeous inside, marbled and crimson. Who knew, right?"

Later, as everyone fell deeper into their cups and began on second and third helpings, I felt a little pang, watching my friends eat around our table, sitting on ottomans and packing boxes around a table in a badly lit, crappy Long Island City apartment. There was Sally with her new boy, who was broodingly handsome and funny and couldn't keep his hands off her. There was Brian, most unlikely beauty, grinning ear to ear as he explained superstrings to Eric, who looked like he'd never been sick a day in his life. There was Heathcliff, tomorrow headed back to his girlfriend in Arizona, and who knew where the day after that, flirting amiably with Gwen in the way of friends who will never be a couple, and there was Gwen pushing back her plate with a husky laugh, lighting her first cigarette. "Hey," she said, pointing up at the ceiling. "Do I hear something crawling around in your ceiling?"

"Oh, that's just the cat."

"Which one? Cooper?"

"Yeah."

"Crazy."

I felt like a Jane Austen heroine all of a sudden (except, of course, that Jane Austen heroines never cook), confusedly looking on at all the people she loves, their myriad unpredictable couplings and uncouplings. There would be no marriages at the end of this Austen novel, though, no happy endings, no endings at all. Just jokes and friendships and romances and delicious declarations of independence. And I realized that, for this night at least, I didn't much care if anyone was the marrying kind or not — not even me. Who could tell? We none of us knew for sure *what* kind we were, exactly, but as long as we were the kind that could sit around eating together and having a lovely time, that was enough.

Which just goes to show, I guess, that dinner parties are like everything else — not as fragile as we think they are.

The Bavarois à l'Orange turned out, well, *oddly*. When I shook it out of its Bundt pan mold I saw it had separated into layers — the top one light and mousse-y, the bottom one a deeper orange, Jell-O-like. But when I sliced it and placed it on plates for everyone, it actually looked very pretty, almost like I'd planned it that way. Instead of a union of airy cream and gelatin, I had made two separate layers, idiosyncratic but complementary interpretations of orange. It was not the way Julia had intended it. But perhaps for all that, it was just the thing.

■▀■▀■▀

May 1945
Kunming, China

"Thank God the food is an improvement, is all I have to say."

"Well, you're right about that. I just loved our meal last Sunday, didn't you?"

"Wonderful." Paul sat on his bunk, attempting to finish up his letter to Charlie by candlelight, as the lights were out again. Ceylon or China, some things, it seemed, never changed.

Julie was perched in the chair by his small desk with one of her long legs hitched up on the seat, sipping from a juice glass of Chinese gin and reading the copy of Tropic of Cancer he'd lent her. She gave a deep sigh and stretched. It seemed to Paul she'd grown quieter in the year he'd known her, more thoughtful. It was a pleasure spending time with her on these quiet nights. Though of course her laugh could still blow out the windows. "There's quite a forest of cocks here, isn't there?" she remarked.

"I suppose so." Julia's self-consciousness about sex grated on him slightly, but he would never say so. It wasn't her fault, anyway; she was just inexperienced, and young for her age.

"Still, it's astonishing. Thank you for lending it to me."

"Of course," he murmured distractedly. He was struggling over a passage in his letter; Charlie had written to him of some of Bartleman's further predictions concerning Paul's romantic life, this grand future he could expect to fall into his lap at any time. The mingling of nearly mad hope and increasing cynicism put up such a buzz in his head that he couldn't think straight.

"Paulski, when shall we try that restaurant Janie mentioned? Ho-Teh-Foo, she called it. Oh, if I could have some Peking duck right this instant!"

"*Perhaps I can get a half day one of these Sunday afternoons soon.*"

"*Lovely. And a trip to one of the monasteries, don't you think? Now that the weather is getting so nice.*" With a contented sigh, she returned to her book, bending over it to make out the words in the dim light.

Paul wrote, in a scrambled hand, of how much he needed love. Years later he would read it again, and when he did, he would write angrily in the margins, bemoaning his obtuseness, at the years wasted by his blindness to what was right there in front of him, reading Tropic of Cancer.

But for the moment, he just licked the gummy airmail adhesive and sealed the envelope shut.

DAY 108, RECIPE 154

The Law of Diminishing Returns

> *Hey. You there?*
< *Yup.*
> *I've got a problem.*
< *You've got a problem?! I've got a live one on the line over here!*

It was turning out to be just one of those days. Between the purchase orders and the Republicans and the insane phone calls, I was beginning to think the bell jar had come down around my cubicle for good, until I heard that beautiful, beautiful popping sound, and up jumped the talk window in the center of my screen. It was Gwen, who had introduced me to instant messaging. God bless her.

> *What's she saying?*
< *It's a guy, actually. He wants to build a football stadium on Ground Zero. With a special box for the victims' families. Classy, right?*
> *Jesus.*

You cannot imagine how it eases the suffering of serving a mind-numbing public, when you can snidely judge said public via IM at the same time.

> < So what's up?
> > Remember I told you about this guy Mitch from the LA office?

Gwen works at a production company in Tribeca that makes music videos and commercials. This sounds like a cool job, and in some ways it is. She's always going to film shoots and to hear bands way too hip for me ever to have heard of, and one time she got to call Jimmy Fallon a "fucking retard," to his face, which must have felt pretty good. On the other hand, she too spends her whole day answering phones, and running out into the rain to the Garden of Eden when someone in the office becomes outraged that the only soy sauce in the fridge is "*Kikkoman,* for Christ's sake? You must be *kidding* me!" Her boss is a neurotic, closeted coke fiend, a nice enough guy, though he does have a tendency to do things like bend over Gwen while she's at her desk and bite her shoulder, then say, "Gosh, I haven't gotten myself into a harassment suit, have I?" That isn't what gets her bothered, though. What gets her bothered is Mitch.

Like Gwen said, Mitch works in the LA office, in some kind of higher-up position. I didn't know anything about him, really, except that he apparently gave *very* good IM. So Gwen had hinted.

> < Sure. What about him?
> > It's getting really bad. He's coming out here. For a "business trip," so-called.
> < Yay! That's great!
> > Yeah . . . except . . .

< *Oh God. What?*
> *Well. He's older than me. 35.*

Gwen wasn't *trying* to make me feel like an ancient hag, she
really wasn't. She's only twenty-four. Sometimes it's like talking
to a third grader who wonders if she can have the change when
you get your senior citizen discount at the movies. I try not to
take offense.

< *Not exactly pushing up the daisies or anything . . .*
> *Yeah, well, there's something else.*
< *What?*
  What??!!!
> *Well, it turns out he's married.*

Jesus. Is that all?
I suppose Gwen meant this news to be earth-shattering. But
it's a funny thing about instant messaging, how it somehow tele-
scopes everything said through it, so that every event becomes
reassuringly distant and compellingly lurid at the same time. Besides, this guy was from LA. Didn't everybody sleep around in
LA? I thought that was the whole attraction, that and the swim-
ming pools and movie stars.
Still, I didn't want to come off like a complete heel here. Gwen
really liked this guy. She was disappointed.

< *What a jerk. When did you find out?*
> *Oh, I've known all along.*

Oh well. So much for shielding my friend's delicate sensibilities.

> *But if he comes to town, I'll really have to have sex with*
  him, Julie. Will you hate me if I have sex with him?

< WTF?! Why would I hate you??
> For being a skanky adulteress?

When did I become poster child for the sanctity of marriage? Just because I've been hitched longer than Gwen has been able to vote, all my single friends seem to think I'm some kind of moral authority. I don't *do* sanctity. Gwen, of all people, should know that.

< Shut up and let him worry about the state of his marriage. I say, if he wants to send someone not his wife lewd instant messages, that's his lookout.

I know, I know. I'm a terrible friend and a traitor to the institution of matrimony. I would be the world's worst advice columnist. I have nothing to offer in my defense but the insistence that I did do nearly a full minute of soul-searching before offering this bit of highly questionable guidance. I asked myself what I would do if Eric was given the same recommendation by one of his friends. This was slightly hard to envision, because I couldn't imagine Eric (a) being tempted into infidelity, (b) daring to tell anyone he was being tempted into infidelity, or (c) having a friend of the sort who would offer this kind of advice. Still, I did my best. I felt not a flicker of anguish. The most I felt was the barest hint of envy. How come nobody ever sent *me* lewdly suggestive instant messages?

> Well. It probably won't happen anyway.

Yeah, right. Now Gwen was going to go out with this guy, make wild jungle love with him because I told her she could, and then not tell me about it because she thought she'd make me feel bad, me the old married lady with her married-lady sex.

Great. Just great.

* * *

Another thing Sam might have served at one of his dinner parties, besides oysters and lamb in onyon sauce, is Oeufs en Gelée. Oeufs en Gelée is poached egg in aspic. Technically, if I am to trust Julia's word — and when it comes to aspic, I suppose I must — "aspic" usually refers to the finished dish, and *gelée* refers to the jelly itself that the eggs, or whatever, get immersed in. In the case of Oeufs en Gelée, my very first aspic, the gel in the *gelée* comes from calves' feet — which I imagine is just how Sam would have made it. Or would have *had* it made, rather. I simply can't see Sam making *gelée* out of calves' feet himself. For one thing, as it turns out, making *gelée* out of calves' feet makes your kitchen smell like a tannery. The *gelée* also, in my admittedly limited experience, *tastes* like a tannery.

What you do is, you simmer these calves' feet that you've soaked and scrubbed and otherwise attempted to make somewhat less toxic, along with some salt pork rind, in a (homemade, of course) beef broth for a good long time, until all the gelatinous properties of the feet and skin and whatnot have leached into the broth, and at that point the broth should, when chilled, transform into a very solid jelly, capable of holding a poached egg (or chicken livers, or some braised beef, or whatever) securely in its rubbery maw.

I think I can safely say that no one — not me, not the blog readers, certainly not Eric — considered eggs in aspic when making the decision to embark upon this culinary journey. And it's a good thing, because eggs in aspic is enough to quail the sturdiest heart.

The crosses of tarragon over the snowy-white poached egg centers were like the negative images of chalk marks on the doors of quarantined houses. But we sallied forth, Eric and Gwen and I, and with a single tap of our forks cracked open our Oeufs en Gelée. I suspect the aspic was not quite so solid as it should have been, for it slipped off and puddled on our plates with almost indecent eagerness — like silk lingerie, if silk lingerie was repulsive. When the (cold, runny) poached eggs were cut, their innards inundated the aspic remains. The resulting scene of carnage was not, let us say, that which *Gourmet* magazine covers are made of.

Also, it tasted slightly of hoof.

Chris was the first to protest this post concerning my very first aspic. "Can't you just SKIP the aspics?!!! I don't know if I can take any more of that!!!" Now, Chris had become known around the Julie/Julia Project as a bit of a hysteric. But in regard to the aspic, she had many fellows.

Isabel suggested that rather than eating the aspic, I might want to unmold it and preserve it in polyurethane. RainyDay2 reminded me, "When Julia was MtAoFCing, aspic was da' bomb. Coating anything with the stuff somehow made it chichi (at the time, anything French, 'à la mode de whatever' and poodles were cool, too . . .). Why bother?"

Stevoleno seconded the motion, and the blog readers — I was beginning to think of them as my "bleaders" — then carried it nearly unanimously: No More Aspic, Please.

It was not as if I began this project in pursuit of the perfect Oeuf en Gelée. Certainly not. To tell the truth, I couldn't remember exactly why I *had* begun. When I thought back to the days Before the Project, I remembered crying on subways, I remembered cubicles, I remembered doctor's appointments and something looming, something with a zero at the end of it. I remembered the feeling of wandering down an endless hallway lined with locked doors. Then I turned a knob that gave under my fingers, everything went dark, and when I came to again, I was chortling away at midnight at a stove in a bright kitchen, sticky with butter and sweat. I wasn't a different person, exactly, just the same person plunked down into some alternate, Julia Child–centric universe. I didn't remember the moment of transition — I expect that wormholes do funny things to the memory — but there was no question I was in a different place. The old universe had been subjugated under the tyranny of entropy. There, I was just a secretary-shaped confederation of atoms, fighting the inevitability of mediocrity and decay. But here, in the Juliaverse, the laws of thermodynamics had been turned on their heads. Here, energy was never lost, merely converted from one form to another. Here, I took butter and cream and meat and eggs and I made delicious sustenance. Here, I took my anger and despair and rage and transformed it with my alchemy into hope and ecstatic mania. Here, I took a crap laptop and some words that popped into my head at seven in the morning, and I turned them into something people wanted, maybe even needed.

I couldn't figure out the origin of the forces acting on me. It couldn't be this arbitrary challenge I'd set for myself; I'd never risen to a challenge in my life. Surely it couldn't be Julia Child. A year ago at this time, Julia meant even less to me than Dan Aykroyd, and that's saying something. She seemed the polestar of my existence now, it was true, but surely not even Julia could be the driving force of a whole universe. For a while, until the great Aspic Mandate, I satisfied myself by simply working to fulfill the needs of my bleaders. That was enough to get me through the days without questioning the odd new circumstances I found myself in. It's strange how easy it is to get used to things.

But then the No Aspic verdict was passed down. Lingering with me along the edges of the great dark moorlands of Aspic — nine recipes in all — the bleaders had given me a free pass:

"Dinnae ga on the moooors."

They meant it as a kindness. And yet I found myself thrown into a terrible confusion. My bleaders would stay with me if I did not make the aspics; in fact their loyalty was being severely tested by the prospect of endless posts on boiled calves' feet and the casting of various foodstuffs in cold jelly. But I knew I had to do it. I was being pulled relentlessly forward, not by my own will (who has the *will* to make aspic?), and not by the people who needed me (for I was beginning to feel that, in this alternate universe, these bleaders were people who needed me, for reasons for the present obscure) but by some other implacable gravitational force, over the horizon or buried in the center of the earth. It frightened me, but there was no resisting.

The Oeufs en Gelée that provoked this flurry of bleader revolt and subsequent existential turmoil were served as a so-called appetizer for a Thanksgiving supper that, thank God, went uphill from there. Preparing them was the work of several days — not so much because that's how long Oeufs en Gelée requires as because before each step I had to gird my loins all over again. First I made the initial *gelée* itself, which aforementioned odor succeeded in chasing me out of the kitchen and putting me off any cooking whatsoever for at least twenty-four hours. Then I had to let the stuff cool, skim off the fat, and clarify it, which is one crazy hell of a process. First you combine beaten egg whites with the stock and stir it gently over low heat while it comes to a bare simmer and the whites get white, then you balance the stockpot on one edge of the burner so only one side of the stock at a time bubbles. Turn the pot in quarter circles every five minutes until the pot's hit the points of the compass. You ladle the stock out into a colander lined with cheesecloth, and, the theory goes, the egg whites get left behind in the colander, taking all those cloudy, impure bits out with it.

This sounds like something our friend Sam might attempt when he found himself with some extra lead on hand and his coffers a little light on gold, but it actually worked. Still, for all that mumbo-jumbo-type work, I want at the very least something that doesn't smell like processed livestock. It pissed me off so much I had to go buy some vintage clothes on eBay to get over it.

Then there were the eggs to poach. I am still pretty far from an egg-poaching expert, and these eggs weren't going to be napped in cheese sauce — they were going to be out there in front of God and everybody, clothed only in a crystalline coating of calves' foot jelly, and they had to be pretty. So that took a while, too.

After that there's the composition of the Oeufs en Gelée proper. This is a matter of layering. You start by pouring a thin layer of the *gelée,* warmed back up to liquidity on the stove, into each of four ramekins. That's the idea, anyway. Actually, I used small clear Pyrex dishes I'd been given for Christmas one year — *mise en place* bowls, if you want to get all hoity-toity about it. I'd've used my real ramekins, but one of the four I had had been hijacked by Eric, who was using it to hold his shaving soap, because Eric shaves with old-fashioned shaving soap and a brush, because *GQ* told him to and when it comes to shaving, Eric is *GQ*'s servant. Only actually, now *I'm* using the shaving soap in the ramekin for my legs, because Eric's gotten too good for the buck-fifty Duane Reade shaving soap and has graduated to fancy Kiehl's stuff.

Anyway, after I'd poured in that first layer in each of the dishes, I put them into the refrigerator to set, then got a tiny pot of water boiling and dumped in some tarragon leaves, just for a few seconds, before draining them, drying them, and setting them, too, in the refrigerator. Once the leaves were cool and the jelly was almost set, I began laying the leaves in their X pattern on top of the jelly. Fiddling with damp tarragon left me so intensely irritated that when I was done I had to stick the ramekin/ *mise en place* bowls back in the fridge and go watch both the episode where Xander is possessed by a demon *and* the one where Giles regresses to his outrageously sexy teen self and has sex with Buffy's mom, just to get over it.

I woke up at six a.m. on Thanksgiving morning to finish putting the little bastards together. I rewarmed the aspic and placed a cold poached egg on top of each tarragon X in each chilled ramekin. The least attractive side of the egg is supposed to face up. This was largely academic in the case of my eggs. Then I poured over more liquid aspic and set the eggs in the refrigerator for their final chilling. By then it was eight a.m., and though I still had a whole Thanksgiving meal left to cook, roast goose and cabbage and onions and green beans and soufflé, I felt giddy with relief. The rest of the day would be a picnic, a Victorian one with parasols and white georgette dresses and games of whist and servants to carry all the baskets, compared to fucking eggs in aspic.

And it really was a cakewalk. Or at least it all went as smoothly as could be expected. Or maybe not, but between all the Pepsi One and having my first aspic done, by six o'clock, when Gwen arrived, I was flying anyway. Famished, but flying.

Gwen is not so much polite as she is considerate. So while she had the good sense not to eat any more than the token bite that proved indubitably that Oeufs en Gelée was not something she would ever again in this life sample, she also had the good grace to say, "Julie, this isn't your fault — it's just the recipe." The soul of kindness, that Gwen. I wanted to believe her, but when I nodded my head as if to agree, I could hear a familiar voice in my head, yodeling on about how *frightfully elegant* an aspic might be, and I felt ashamed.

The good thing about starting your Thanksgiving feast with Oeufs en Gelée is that everything afterward is going to taste pretty goddamned great by comparison, and by the time we'd gotten through the gorgeously crisp and moist goose, the prunes stuffed with duck liver mousse, the cabbage with chestnuts, the green beans, and the creamed onions, aspic was largely forgotten, and we didn't even mind much that I had begun the Thanksgiving preparations with the absolutely *insane* idea that I would make chocolate soufflé for dessert once we were finished with dinner. This, of course, being the delusion of a diseased mind. Then, having fed the aspic to the cats, who didn't mind it at all, we moved to the couch for the annual holiday screening of *True Romance,* a tradition begun the year that my brother was living with us in Bay Ridge, when we decided to make a drinking game out of it and take a sip every time someone said the word *fuck*. (That's not part of the tradition anymore; if you've seen the movie you know why.) Doped up on fat calories and wine, Eric drifted off to sleep about twenty minutes into the film, right in the middle of Gary Oldman's very boisterous death scene, but Gwen and I made it all the way to James Gandolfini's equally impressive death scene, and got so drunk together that Gwen had to spend the night on the couch, and eat some Oeufs en Cocotte the next morning to recover.

If there are two kinds of friends in the world, those who inspire in you all that is great and good and those who'd prefer to get right down on their haunches and help out with the mud pies, Gwen definitely falls into the latter category. I call her the devil on my shoulder. Sally encourages me to find my inner greatness, to love myself and treat my body like a temple. She wishes I'd quit drinking so much and wants me to go to therapy. I probably should spend more time with her. But especially during the tough times, the days of aspic and freezing rain, I found myself craving not betterment and hope and an exercise partner so much as a fresh bottle of booze, a pack of Marlboros, and someone content to eat butter sauce and watch reruns on TV with me. It's lucky for me, though perhaps too bad for Gwen, that I'm just a solitary outer-borough secretary with a taste for vodka and cigarettes, rather than, I don't know, a bi-curious stripper with a small coke habit — I get the feeling that with such a wealth of potential disaster to work with, Gwen would truly come into her gift as some sort of Shakespearean corrupter of innocence.

I don't want to give the wrong impression. It's not as if Gwen is some uncontainable libertine, Falstaff personified as an impressively bitter, petite blonde with fashion sense (and I say this as a person with nearly depthless reserves of bitterness). Really what she is is *accommodating*. If I want to get drunk and eat my-

self silly and watch four episodes of *Buffy* and smoke so many cigarettes that I feel like an ashtray the next morning, well then, so
does she, by God. Probably if she was hanging out with Sally, the
two of them would be applying to graduate school and taking
Bikram yoga classes together. But she's hanging out with me.

I suppose that, knowing the thoroughly questionable advice I
gave her about the whole Mitch Thing, one could argue the question of who exactly is the bad influence on whom, here. But I'm
sticking to my guns on this one.

December descended. One day I was taking an appointment for
Bonnie in her Outlook and it came to me that I was officially
more than one quarter of the way through the Project. I realized
I didn't even know how many recipes I'd done. I rushed home
that night to count up all the small black checks I had been making beside each recipe as I went along, like a trail of bread crumbs.
(Along with the actual trail of bread crumbs, and other foodstuffs, that had begun to lodge themselves near the spine, and
glue the pages together.) It was as I feared.

"Eric, I'm not going to make it."

"Make what?"

"'Make what'? My deadline! What's *wrong* with you?"

I was bent over the Book, which lay open on the island in the
kitchen, with a pen in hand with which I'd made a bunch of hash
marks in the margin of the *Times* sports section. A couple of
salmon steaks I'd bought for a shocking amount of money at the
Turkish grocery near my office sat on the counter, waiting to be
broiled and napped in Sauce à la Moutarde, which is a sort of fake
(Julia calls it "mock," but let's call a spade a spade, shall we?) hollandaise sauce, with some mustard stirred in for interest. Slumped
beside the fish was a bag of slightly wilted Belgian endive, which
I was just going to be braising in butter. Not exactly a demanding
menu. Not exactly Foies de Volaille en Aspic, just to cite one

example of how I could be living my life more aggressively and bravely and generally being a better person.

The *NewsHour* was turned up in the living room. A daunting stack of dishes teetered in the sink, but Eric had his laptop on his lap at one of the kitchen stools and was playing FreeCell. Badly.

"I'll have turned myself into a whale for nothing. I'll have wasted a year of my life! Dammit. Goddammit! GOD. DAMN. IT!"

Over the years, Eric has developed the defensive tactic of selective hearing. I've seen this kind of evolution before — my father has the same skill. The benefits of this are obvious — much less time wasted in attending to every fleeting hysterical fit his wife indulges in. I, however, have in response mastered a technique of incremental amplification that has proven most effective in breaking down his defenses. And once he is roused to a reaction, he is at a distinct disadvantage, as he has not heard much of my rant and therefore cannot accurately judge what piece of it he should best respond to in order to defuse it. Plus, because he was the one not listening to me, I gain the moral high ground. Darwinism at work, my friends.

"You won't waste it. I won't let you."

"So you *do* think I'm fat, then. Is it that bad?" (See?)

"What? No! You're going to make it. How many recipes have you made?"

"One hundred and thirty-six. One thirty-eight after tonight."

"See? You're more than a quarter of the way done. You're golden!"

"No, no, no. I have aspics. I have to *bone a whole duck.* Can you even *conceive* of boning a duck? Of course you can't. Your brain's too consumed with the *NewsHour* and FreeCell to waste time on something just because it's of all-consuming importance to your *wife.*"

Our cat Maxine took the opportunity of my distraction to steal a seat on *MtAoFC*, which promptly tipped off the edge of the counter, tumbling rubenesque cat and book both to the floor.

Max dashed off in irked humiliation; the spine of the book had ripped loose from the back cover. By the time I'd picked it up again and found the page for Sauce à la Moutarde, Eric was gone, taking his iBook with him, leaving behind a whiff of hurt fury. My moral high ground had evaporated into mist.

I didn't want to do this anymore. The Salmon à la Moutarde matched with braised endive was a disaster — somehow the endive made the salmon taste fishier, and the salmon made the endive taste more bitter. Eric and I hadn't had sex for a month, and we sure weren't going to end the drought tonight. But I couldn't stop. Living in a universe where the laws of thermodynamics have run amok can be pretty great for a while, but eventually it can leave you careening out of control.

Gwen had known Mitch as a business associate for most of a year, through phone conversation, but it wasn't until after he met her in person when he came to town for a commercial shoot that The Thing started up. She was the one who buzzed him into the office that morning.

"The famous Gwen, I presume?" he said, smiling, as he strode up to her desk, sliding off a pair of gloves with the languor of an adept hit man.

"Um, yeah?"

"At last we meet. Mitch from the LA office." He held out his hand.

Mitch wasn't a terribly big man, nor in fact a terribly good-looking one, when you got down to it, though his dark hair was stylishly mussed and he was wearing an overcoat so expensive-looking and luxurious that Gwen found herself wanting to touch it. Quite a coat indeed for an Angeleno who only wore it the two times a year he was in New York during the winter. When Gwen said, "Oh! Hi! Nice to meet you!" it came out louder, and squeakier, than she had meant it to.

"Phil said you looked like a young Renée Zellweger." Gwen, who maintains a long-standing abhorrence for Renée Zellweger that I've never quite understood, had heard this several times before from Phil the shoulder-biter; she just grimaced. Mitch continued, "He's an asshole. You're clearly a dead ringer for Maggie Gyllenhaal."

"Oh, come *on.*" She was starting to blush.

"Listen, I don't go around telling women they look like movie stars. I'm serious — I've worked with Maggie. You could be her twin." He leaned over the reception desk to get a better look at her. "Maggie's teeny-tiny, elfin twin."

Gwen knew she was grinning like a fool, but she couldn't figure out what to do about it.

"Oh well; can't expect Phil to be an astute judge of women, I don't guess." His large dark eyes were laughing at her, and he seemed to take up a bigger space in the narrow office than could be justified by his small frame. "Is the man in, actually?"

He gave her a wave and a wink when he walked out of Phil's office as the both of them headed out to the set, but that was pretty much the sum of their sparkling repartee. So although Gwen had felt a passing, annoyingly Bridget-y sort of a jones for him, she did not think much of it.

Until she got the first IM three days later.

> *Well, my mini-Maggie, I didn't have the opportunity to get you drunk and have my way with you. A mistake I do not mean to duplicate on my next New York trip.*

Gwen never had a chance.

As far as I understand, phone sex has always been a marginal activity, indulged in by a relatively small and specific, and generally lonely and unhappy, demographic. But the birth of the Internet bestowed the joys of anonymous noncontact sex upon the general populace. You can now find, with the click of a mouse, dozens upon dozens of sites dedicated to the notion that the hip and young, of every sex and all persuasions, *choose* cybersex, not out of hunger, but as one of many modes of satisfaction available to them in an ever-larger world. Now, I'm no sociologist, so forgive me if I'm making a faux pas here, but I'd be willing to bet that among these cutting-edge consumers of gratification, phone sex still does not pop up too often on the menu of options. I think that there's a very simple reason why, which is that the written word is sexy.

Probably Eric and I are together to this day because of the sexiness of prose. When we were living in different states, back in college, we had our share of fraught, whispered, two a.m. phone calls, sure. But it was the letters that really kept the fire going. The entire tortured process — finding the envelope in the mailbox, carrying it in my backpack all day unopened until I was alone in bed at night, huddling over the pages to parse the cramped handwriting and violent scratch-outs, scrawling my reply, sweating out my anxiety until the next letter arrived — kept me in a haze my entire freshman year. It's an absolute miracle I didn't fail my first semester.

So I can understand exactly what Gwen was going through as she and Mitch began their agonizing IM back-and-forth. If you've ever done anything like this — and I suspect that if you're a single office worker under the age of, say, forty, you almost can't have avoided it — you'll know what makes it almost impossible to resist is the combination of craft and spontaneity, joined by the particularly lethal instant gratification that the twenty-first century does so very well. In response to your coworker's impromptu admission of lust, you will construct a riposte of baroquely balanced daring and aloofness, deliberating over every pronoun and abbreviation. All thought of work duties will cease as you immerse yourself in this literary puzzle, but painstaking though you may be, you will feel remorse from the moment you click the Send button, for a joke too juvenile or pretentious, a word too coy or vulgar. And professional concerns will not return to the forefront, because you will also be imagining him, in his own office four thousand miles away, going through the same creative spasms you just had — unless he isn't, unless (perish the thought) he doesn't plan to answer at all. You will suffer the pangs of the damned until his icon pops up on your screen again:

> *>You know what happens to cheeky monkeys like you, Maggie? They get spanked.*

And by the time he lets slip the small fact of his eight-year marriage, you are far too far gone to care.

Foies de Volailles en Aspic is marginally less agonizing than Oeufs en Gelée — or was for me anyway, mostly because one taste of the calves' feet *gelée* was enough to convince me that packaged gelatin and canned broth were the way to go for aspic when your name is Julie, not Julia. (Actually, my name is Julia too, but no one has ever called me that — I just don't possess the gravitas, I guess. A Julia is brave and Junoesque and slightly forbidding; a Julie is a seventies-era cheerleader in pigtails and hot pants. No one would ever start a joking cyber-flirtation with someone named Julia. Apparently no one much wanted to start one with me, either. But that had nothing to do with my name and a lot to do with pushing thirty and ten pounds of butter-weight.

The item being aspic-ed in Foies de Volailles en Aspic is chicken liver, first sautéed in butter with shallots, then simmered in cognac until the wine's gotten syrupy, then chilled. When they're cold, the livers are immersed in *gelée* — topped with a slice of truffle if you can afford that kind of thing and rent too; I can't — and chilled until set. Eric and Gwen and I ate these for dinner one evening, with Concombres au Buerre, also known as baked cucumbers, on the side.

"Concombres? We don't need no steenkin' concombres!"

This is what Eric said when I handed him his plate. Gwen just stared in silent terror. She had called that evening after a terrible day at work, asking if she could come to dinner, and although I'd sort of been hoping to get dressed in some outrageous lingerie and seduce my husband that night, I agreed, because since the whole Mitch Thing started, she'd been prone to depressions — thunderous, palpable depressions that made me look like a total lightweight. The poor girl must have been wondering why she'd turned to the friends she *knew* would try to cheer her up with aspic and baked cucumbers.

Eric dove in first — he chose to go with the aspic. He took a bite and shrugged. "Ehn." Thus emboldened, Gwen and I attempted tastes as well.

The verdict on Foies Volailles en Aspic? Surprisingly undisgusting, but why eat chicken livers cold with jelly on top of them, when you could eat them hot without jelly?

Our Concombres au Buerre lay on our plates, limp and pale and parsley flecked, waiting. "Okay, Eric, you first," I said.

He got a cucumber strip onto his fork and gingerly took a bite. His eyes widened, expression blank, sort of like a character on *South Park* before delivering a punch line — I couldn't tell what he was thinking.

"What?" Gwen and I asked in unison.

"Huh."

I took a bite, too. "Huh!"

"What?"

Gwen ate some of hers, and said, "Huh!"

Verdict: baked cucumbers? A fucking revelation. They don't melt away, and they actually taste like cucumbers. Only better, because I don't like cucumbers.

After dinner, I walked Gwen down to let her out while Eric was washing the dishes. "Thanks for the cucumbers. They were really good."

"No problem. You going to be able to get home all right?" I asked as I held the front door open for her.

"Sure — there's my bus now, actually." She stepped out into the cold, waving at the bus coming around the corner. It stopped and she hurried for it. Just before she got on, though, she turned around and shouted, "He's coming. Mitch. Tomorrow night."

I dimly remembered the feeling expressed by the look she shot me as she climbed aboard — half shitless terror, half stupid glee. And I felt a pang of envy.

Upstairs, I shed my sweatpants and T-shirt and sneakers and vamped through the kitchen doorway in a bra and panties set that actually matched. "Hon? Why don't you leave the dishes until tomorrow morning?"

"I guess I'm going to have to — we just ran out of hot water." He wiped off his hands, turned to me, looked me up and down, and said, "I need to check my e-mail." Then he went to the laptop, where he spent the next forty-five minutes surfing CNN.

What am I, chicken livers in aspic?

I'm a secretary at a government agency, and so I can talk with some authority about things that are a pain in the ass. Say, for instance, filling out purchase orders. But do you want to know what's *really* a pain in the ass? Poulet en Gelée à l'Estragon.

First you truss and brown in butter a whole chicken, season it with salt and tarragon, and roast it in the oven. When it's done let it cool to room temperature, then chill it. I did this on Saturday, after I'd scrubbed the toilets and cleaned the kitchen as best I could. Actually, I roasted two chickens this way, so we'd have something to eat for dinner.

The kitchen was beyond my poor powers to improve by much. Cat hair clung stickily to the stainless steel grid suspended over the window, on which my pans were hung. Greasy yellow stains wouldn't come off the walls above the stove, no matter how I scrubbed. I distracted myself from the misery of my poor house-keeping with the misery of making *gelée,* which at least wasn't my fault. This particular *gelée* was made with canned chicken broth, steeped with tarragon and flavored with port — some Australian stuff I'd gotten at the wineshop at Union Square, which tasted surprisingly good. Good enough to have two glasses, because Eric was at the office, "working," though probably he just didn't want to spend his Saturday in a filthy "loft" watching his wife work her-self into a snit making *gelée.* I couldn't blame him — I didn't want to spend my Saturday doing that either.

But I guess there are even worse things to do with your Satur-day, because he came home at seven in a surly mood. All he said about the dinner was that he didn't like tarragon, and we wound up drinking too much, watching some German movie from Net-flix, and falling asleep on the couch.

Then, to cap it all off, he woke up Sunday with one of his head-aches. He lay in bed until late in the morning. "Honey," I called to him at eleven or so, not trying very hard at all not to sound ir-ritated, "you want coffee?"

"Gah, no. I'll pick up some Gatorade on the way to the office."

"You're *not* going to the office! You can't, you're practically dead."

"I have to. I'll feel better once I get up." Then he propelled himself out of bed in a single resigned lunge, retrieved the crum-pled clothes he'd shucked on the way to the bed when we awoke at two a.m. with our contacts seared to our eyeballs and match-ing cricks in our necks, and went to the bathroom to throw up. After that was done he stared at the paper for a while, rubbing the stubble on his gray cheeks as if for comfort, and then abruptly stood up and lurched for the door. I've never under-stood that about Eric, how he can just head outside all of a sudden, with not a moment of preparation. I couldn't do that if we were evacuating under threat of radiation poisoning.

"Um, bye?"

"Sorry, honey." He came back to where I was sitting and pressed chapped lips quickly up against my cheek. "My breath stinks. I'll see you around six, I hope."

To put together Poulet en Gelée à l'Estragon, start by heating up the jelly and pouring a thin layer of it onto an oval serving dish. Except I didn't have an oval serving dish, so I used a hip-to-be-square chunky white Calvin Klein platter that we got for a wedding present. (Did you know Calvin Klein had a line of chinaware? Well, he does.) This is then supposed to chill until set, which of course entailed emptying an entire shelf of my fridge, so that I had jars of jams and half-gone limes and forgotten sour creams and wilted bags of parsley and odd pats of butter with funny smells scattered over my none-too-clean countertop. For a person like Sally or my mother, this would have been enough to kick off a refrigerator-cleaning spree, but I am not such a person.

Once the first layer of *gelée* is jelled, carve the chicken you've roasted and chilled and arrange it on the platter. I am not much of a chicken carver. My pieces came out looking rather mauled, but I was in no mood to care. Stick the platter back in the fridge while you stir a cup of the warmed jelly in a bowl set over another bowl of ice, until it cools and begins to set. Spoon it over the chicken on the platter. Julia told me that the first layer would "not adhere very well," and that was certainly the case.

Gwen called. "Hey."

"Hey. How was your big weekend?"

"Can I come over?"

"Uh-oh. That bad? Don't answer that — come on over. Eric won't be home until six. I'm making aspic."

"Oh great. The perfect ending to the perfect weekend."

Repeat the whole pouring-half-set-jelly-on-top-of-the-chicken-pieces twice more. The next two layers stick better than the first.

The chicken will begin to look polyurethaned, which I suppose is the point. Slide it back into the refrigerator to finish setting.

I was stuffing the crap I'd pulled from the refrigerator into a big black garbage bag when Gwen rang the doorbell. She must have sprung out of her door the second she hung up the phone. Not a good sign. I went downstairs to let her in.

"I brought vodka. Can we start drinking yet?"

"Oh, Gwen. What happened?"

We headed back up to the kitchen, and while I started blanching tarragon leaves — dumping them in boiling water, scooping them right out again, running cold water over them, laying them out onto paper towels to dry — Gwen parked herself on a stool and gave me the blow-by-blow, as it were.

It had all started out so well. Well, I mean once you set aside the sheer impossibility and bad judgment of it. They'd met on Thursday night in a suitably skeezy bar Mitch knew in the West Thirties. He had the situation in hand from the second she sat down beside him in the booth and he had a drink waiting for her — Scotch and soda. She'd told him she was more of a vodka tonic sort of girl, but he just said, "Not tonight you aren't." And thus the tone of the evening was set. The arrogant, dominating, sexually irresistible Mitch of the instant messages had been made flesh. One Scotch and soda later, she had her hand on his crotch, right there in the bar; two more after that and they were locked in a stall in the ladies' room, grappling to get into each other's clothes.

"Grappling in a ladies' room stall sounds pretty good to me, or maybe that's just five years of marriage getting to me." I opened up the refrigerator to get the chicken back out, passing Gwen the ice tray while I was at it. (She'd decided that 3:30 was *definitely* not too early to start drinking.) "So what's the problem?"

"Well, we went back to the apartment where he was staying, and — God, is that what we're eating for dinner?" The third layer of jelly on the chicken was almost set, and I was painstakingly and frustratingly dipping each small tarragon leaf into yet another

cup of semiset *gelée* before arranging them in little stupid-looking
X's on the chicken pieces. On the Oeufs en Gelée, tarragon *X*'s
had looked vaguely forbidding; on Poulet en Gelée à l'Estragon,
they just looked bedraggled and sad. "Afraid so."

"No offense or anything. I'm sure it's great. Can we heat it up
first or something?"

One last cup of jelly got poured over the chicken, which katty-
whompused the tarragon leaves. Screw it. I threw it back in the
fridge, mixed myself a vodka tonic — what the hell — and settled
down on the other kitchen stool. Gwen shook out a cigarette and
lit it for me, then one for herself.

"It was this absurdly fantastic loft, you could put a roller-
skating rink in there — belongs to a friend of Mitch's, I don't
know who. Not that I got much of a chance to look at it. Julie, the
sex was just — *God*. You know how when you're with a guy
who's, you know, really *big*, he's usually lousy in bed, it's always
just about worshipping his breathtaking member or whatever?
Well, Mitch is, well — you know — but he isn't like that at all. I
swear to God, I came at least ten times, no joke."

I have been with the same man since I was eighteen years old,
and yet my single friends continue to talk to me about these things
as if I have a clue. I don't know if they think I was some kind of
world-class teenage slut, or I can remember my past lives, or what.
Thank God for *Sex in the City;* I just put on my best Cynthia Nixon
commiserating-savvy-girlfriend face and nod.

"Sure sounds like a shitty weekend, all right." I couldn't help
sounding the tiniest bit bitter. Gwen has a weekend of explosive
sex, then comes over to my house depressed and *complains* about
being served aspic. This is a situation that Julia would no doubt
handle with aplomb. But Julia doesn't hate aspic as I do. And she
probably gets more sex.

"Wait, I'm getting to that part. So he asks me to leave when
we're done, he's got to get some rest because he's got a pitch meeting the next day — which is fine, whatever, it's not like I need to be

rocked to sleep in his warm embrace or anything. So Friday I go to work. He comes in and hardly even looks at me, which, you know, fine. This isn't something he wants to make public. But all day I wait for him to IM me. I'm dying to IM *him,* of course, but I resist, which I've got to say was pretty impressive of me, don't you think?"

"Very."

"So he doesn't. IM me, I mean. I hang around at the office un-til nine o'clock — not a peep."

"Ah."

"I stay at home all Saturday with my laptop on and my cell in my pocket. Finally — of course — I can't take it anymore, and at 5:30 I go ahead and send him an instant message. I just say, *Hey, you doing anything tonight?* And not ten minutes later he IMs back: *Come to the apartment.*"

"Oh! Can I have another cigarette?"

"Take as many as you want. So, of course I'm there in like twenty minutes flat, and it's the same thing all over again, just as good as the first time. Better."

"Uh-huh. I'm waiting for the shitty part."

Gwen made a sheepish face at me. "Well, now that I think about it, I guess there isn't really a shitty part, per se."

"I knew it. You just came here to criticize my aspic and mock me with your fabulous LA sex life."

"No, no, no. I mean — I was with him all night, and then at the end I got dressed and went home, he got on a plane to go back to his wife this morning — which I'm totally fine with, I don't want to marry the guy or anything. It's all good, right? We understand each other."

"And the source of your tragic ennui is?"

"Well, it all starts over now, doesn't it? Best-case scenario, we IM and IM and IM, and I totally obsess for six months or however long it is until he comes back to New York again, and the cycle continues. Only now I know what the sex is like. And it's not *that* great. I mean, it's *great,* but how could it possibly compete with what we'd been writing to each other? With the imagining of it? It *can't*. Nothing ever does, does it?"

"Jesus, Gwen. Jesus. That's pretty fucking depressing."

"Exactly. Can you get out the tonic and some ice? I feel the need for a refresher." I passed her the ice tray, then went into the refrigerator for the tonic. There squatted the tarragon chicken in aspic, wanly gleaming. Gwen had gotten me down, I guess, because the sight of it just made me want to sit down on the floor and never get up. "But that's not the worst part. The worst part is that the only thing worse than the cycle continuing would be if it didn't. If the IMs stopped, then I wouldn't even have these diminishing returns on my investment. I'd have bupkes. So I have to keep on keeping on, you know?"

Christ.

There is a law out there, if not of thermodynamics then of something equally primary and inescapable, that explains why everything from instant messaging to fabulous sex to aspic can in the end be defined as an illustration of the futility of existence. And it really, really sucks.

By the time Eric came home at six, Gwen and I were both a little drunk and a little morose. Eric, who had not yet shed his Blanche-headache, wasn't able to do much to lighten the mood. The Poulet en Gelée à l'Estragon was able to do even less.

We did try to eat it. It wasn't that it was bad, though when Eric saw it, his face went a shade or two grayer. It just tasted like cold chicken with jelly on top of it. We all chewed glumly for a bit, but it was no use.

Eric was the first to declare defeat. "Domino's?"

Gwen sighed in relief, pushed her plate away, and lit another cigarette. "Bacon and jalapenos?"

Chicken aspic and bacon-jalapeno pizza. Talk about diminishing returns.

The first one is tough, no fuckin' foolin'. The second one, the second one ain't no fucking Mardi Gras, either, but it's better than the first one because — you still feel the same thing, you know, except it's more diluted. It's better. . . . Now I do it just to watch their fuckin' expression change.

— *Virgil (James Gandolfini),*
  True Romance

If you object to steaming or splitting a live lobster, it may be killed almost instantly just before cooking if you plunge the point of a knife into the head between the eyes, or sever the spinal cord by making a small incision in the back of the shell at the juncture of the chest and tail.

— *Mastering the Art of French Cooking,*
  Vol. 1

░░░░░░░

They Shoot Lobsters,
Don't They?

Aunt Sukie grabs me by my upper arms and shakes me gently. "Oh, Sarah, Sarah, Sarah! What are we going to do with you?"

(My aunt Sukie is not senile; she does remember my name. Sarah is a nickname. Short for Sarah Bernhardt. I couldn't tell you how this came to be. I don't even know why on earth anyone would know who Sarah Bernhardt is anymore. *I* only know who she is because I've been nicknamed after her my whole life.)

"What do you mean?" I wonder if she's going to make a crack about my upper arms. I haven't seen her since the last time I was back in Texas for Christmas, and they have gotten a little meaty since then.

"I went onto the computer and I read what you're up to!"

I cringe a little at this. Aunt Sukie is a schoolteacher in Waxahachie, Texas, and one of those smart, kind people who nonetheless mystifies you by continuing to vote Republican. She also, unlike anyone in my nuclear unit, keeps a civil tongue in her head. Once Aunt Sukie handed out a high school paper I wrote

on *The Great Gatsby* to her English class — God knows how she
got her hands on the thing. But somehow I have the feeling that
she would not be giving her students links to my blog.

But she isn't thinking of my stevedore's arms or my sailor's
mouth. She leans in close and whispers, "You're worrying your
mother. Don't work so hard!"

Until the day she died, my granny said things just like this to
my mother. "You do too much!" "You'll make yourself sick!"

It used to drive my mother completely around the bend.
"*MOM!* Don't tell me what's too much! I'll *tell* you when I'm doing too much, *goddammit!*" (My mom and my granny fought
about lots of things — laundry, ice cream, black people, television. But this one, the one about my mom doing too much, was
a favorite, probably because it gave Granny the illusion she had a
maternal bone in her body, and Mom the illusion she wasn't
working herself sick.) I figure that Mom, who is terrified above
all things of turning into her mother, is reluctant to ride me too
hard on this crazy cooking project deal. So she got her brother's
wife to do it. She must have really wanted to get through to me if
she showed Aunt Sukie the blog. She had to know that my aunt
would not be thrilled with comparisons of, say, trussed poultry to
sexual fetishists.

But somehow I'm not irritated at all. Actually, it makes me feel
looked after. And kind of like the circle stays unbroken, gene-
wise. I give my aunt a hug. "I'm *fine*. Don't worry about it."

It's always nice to go back to the folks' house. There's no
mildew in the bathtub, and you can shower for as long as you
want and the water will stay hot. There's a queen-sized bed to
sleep in, no roaring semitrucks passing in the night, a hundred
channels on the television, and broadband on the computer. On
Christmas Eve we jack up the air-conditioning so we can light a
fire. There are trees — not just in little concrete boxes on the
sidewalk, but everywhere. I love it here.

I think I may not go back.

Yes, New York is a stinking, chaotic, life-sucking cesspool and Austin, Texas, is a verdant, peaceful paradise, but that's not really the problem — well, at least not the only one. No, the truth is, I'm on the lam.

Over a period of two weeks in late December of 2002, at the exhortation of Julia Child, I went on a murderous rampage. I committed gruesome, atrocious acts, and for my intended victims, no murky corner of Queens or Chinatown was safe from my diabolical reach. If news of the carnage was not widely remarked upon in the local press, it was only because my victims were not Catholic schoolgirls or Filipino nurses, but crustaceans. This distinction means that I am not a murderer in the legal sense. But I have blood on my hands, even if it is the clear blood of lobsters.

We had finally gone ahead and bought one of those sleep machines to drown out the roar of freight trucks that rumble past our apartment all night. It had a small speaker that fit under the pillow, and most nights it did the trick. But on the eve of my first crime, the lulling roar and crash of the "oceania" setting droned at me: "Lobster killer, lobster killer, lobster killer. . . ."

I was awake by dawn, worrying. It was Sunday in Long Island City — forget killing a lobster, how would I even get one, for God's sake? How much would it cost? How would I get it home? I peppered Eric with these questions, hoping that he would reply, "Oooh, you're right, that isn't going to work. Oh well — guess we'll have to save lobster for another day. Domino's? Bacon and jalapeno?"

He didn't say that. Instead he got out the yellow pages and made a phone call — the first fish market he called was open. The Bronco started, the traffic to Astoria was smooth. The fish store didn't smell fishy, and they had lobsters in a nasty-looking cloudy tank. I bought two. The stars fell into alignment, for fate had decreed these two lobsters must die.

I had been imagining lugging the lobsters home in a bucket,

but the guy just stuck them in a paper bag. He said to keep them in the refrigerator. He said they'd be good until Thursday. Ick. I brought them back to the car and set them in the backseat — what were we going to do, cradle the creatures in our laps? On the drive home the back of my neck tingled and my ears stayed pricked for the sneaking crinkle of a lobster claw venturing out of a paper bag — but the lobsters just sat there. I guess suffocating will do that to a body.

Julia gets very terse in her description of Homard Thermidor. She always seems to go all Delphic on me in my times of need. She doesn't speak to the storage of lobsters, for one thing. Neither, to be fair, does the *Joy of Cooking,* but at least that tome gives me the hint that lobsters should be lively and thrashing when they come out of the tank. Hey. My lobsters didn't thrash. *Joy* said if they were limp, they might die before you cooked them. It seemed to think that was a bad thing. I peeked into the paper bag in the refrigerator and was faced with black eyes on stalks, antennae boozily waving.

I had read up on all sorts of methods for humanely euthanizing lobsters — sticking them in the freezer, placing them in ice water then bringing it up to a boil (which is supposed to fool them into not realizing they're boiling alive), slicing their spinal cord with a knife beforehand. But all these struck me as palliatives thought up more to save boilers from emotional anguish than boilees from physical. In the end I just dumped them out of the paper bag into a pot with some boiling water and vermouth and vegetables. And then freaked the fuck out.

The pot wasn't big enough. Though the lobsters didn't shriek in horror the second I dropped them in, their momentary stillness only drew out the excruciating moment. It was like that instant when your car begins to skid out of control and before your eyes you see the burning car wreck that is your destiny. Any second the pain would awaken the creatures from their asphyxia-induced comas, I knew it, and I couldn't get the goddamned lid down! It was just too horrible. My heroic/homicidal husband had to take things in hand. I'd have expected him to collapse just like me, he's not exactly the *Field & Stream* type, but some of those pitiless West Texas sheriff genes must have hit their stride, because he managed to get those bugs subdued with a minimum of fuss.

People say lobsters make a terrible racket in the pot, trying — reasonably enough — to claw their way out of the water. I wouldn't know. I spent the next twenty minutes watching a golf game on the TV with the volume turned up to Metallica concert levels. (Those Titleist commercials nearly blew the windows out.) When I ventured back into the kitchen, the lobsters were very red, and not making any racket at all. Julia says they are done when "the long head-feelers can be pulled from the sockets fairly easily." That they could. Poor little beasties. I took them out of the pot and cooked down their liquid with the juices from some mushrooms I'd stewed. I strained the reduced juices through a sieve, presumably to get rid of any errant bits of head-feeler or whatever, then beat it into a light roux I'd made of butter and flour.

When Eric and I start our crime conglomerate, he can be in charge of death; I'll take care of dismemberment. The same no-nonsense guy who brusquely stripped two crustaceans of their mortal coils had to leave the room when I read aloud that next I was to "split the lobsters in half lengthwise, keeping the shell halves intact."

But it was no problem, really. For once, a blithely terse turn of phrase by Julia was not an indication of imminent disaster. The knife crunched right through. It is true that all within was not as clear-cut as you might think. When Julia told me to "discard sand sacks in the heads, and the intestinal tubes," I was able to make an educated guess. The sacks full of sand were sort of a dead giveaway. But when she said to "rub lobster coral and green matter through a fine sieve," I got a little lost. There was all manner of green matter — what is "green matter," though, and why won't

Julia tell me? — but the only orange stuff I found seemed to re-
side where a lobster's shit would go, so I decided not to risk it. After that was done, I pulled the rest of the meat out chunk by
chunk, cracking open the claws, using a tweezer — carefully
cleaned of all eyebrow hairs, naturally — to pull the strips of
meat out of the legs. The sieved "green matter" got beaten into
some egg yolks, cream, mustard, and cayenne, poured into the
lobster broth/roux sauce, and boiled. I sautéed the meat in some
butter, then poured in some cognac and let it boil down. Then I
stirred in the stewed mushrooms and two-thirds of the sauce. I
heaped the mixture into the four lobster half-shells, poured the
rest of the sauce over, sprinkled with Parmesan and dotted with
butter, and ran them under the broiler.

They were, I must say, delicious.

I stalked my third victim in Chinatown on a rainy evening one
week later, inconspicuous amid the bustling Christmas shoppers
picking up knockoff bags and the more obviously murderous
umbrella wielders. (Umbrella wielders in Chinatown have the
key advantage of diminutive stature. On a rainy day — and it's always a rainy day in Chinatown — one must step lively or risk losing an eye.) The creature stopped groping almost immediately
after the guy in the shop tied it up in a plastic bag, dropped the
plastic bag into a paper one, and handed it to me in exchange for
six dollars. I was nervous about getting on the train with the
thing, fearing it would thrash around and call attention to itself,
but it just sat there like a bag of groceries.

When I got home I peered down at the lobster to see how he
was doing. The inner plastic bag was sucked tight around him and
clouded up. It looked like something out of an eighties made-for-
TV movie, with some washed-up actress taking too many pills
and trying to off herself with a Macy's bag. I tore open the bag to
let in some air — so this underwater creature would breathe better? — before putting him in the freezer. Suffocating is worse than
freezing to death is better than being steamed alive? Perhaps an-

ticipation of my evening of bloodletting had addled my brain, but the philosophical intricacies of lobster murder were proving too much for me to rationally negotiate.

The second murder went much as the first — steamed in water spiked with vermouth and some celery, carrot, and onion. The rosy-red dead lobster was bisected in just the same way, its flesh removed, and again its shell was stuffed with its sautéed meat, this time napped in a cream sauce made with the lobster's cooking juices. I think I overcooked it a little.

I confessed to Eric as we sat down to our Homard aux Aromates that cutting lobsters in half was beginning to prove eerily satisfying. "I just feel like I've got a knack for this shit."

Eric looked at me, and I could see him wondering where was the finicky, soft-hearted young girl he had married. "By the end of this you'll be comfortable filleting puppies."

That chilled me. I lay low after that for a good long while, until after Christmas. I told myself it was because a transit strike was threatening, and I didn't much relish the idea of buying a lobster in a bag and then unexpectedly having to hike across the Queensboro Bridge with it, in the company of a hundred thousand grousing outer-borough shoppers and menial workers. But that wasn't really it. The reason was the next recipe, Homard à l'Américaine. For while I am sure that the argument can be made that any meat-eating person ought to take the responsibility once in her life for slaughtering an animal for food, that one ought to chop that animal up into small pieces while it's still alive, I am less certain of. And even more frightening was the thought Eric had planted in my head — what if I *liked* it?

My mother did everything short of chaining the kitchen doors shut to keep me from cooking while we were home, and while you can see how her claim that she was doing it for the sake of my sanity did hold some water, I honestly think she was more concerned that I not make her eat aspic or kill anything. "Julie, just leave it alone for a week, *goddammit*," she said, standing before the stove with her arms crossed.

"But I'll never make it! I'm on a really tight schedule! Besides, my bleaders are waiting for me to post!"

"Your *what?*"

"Mom, I just need to."

"Julie, what you *need* to do is relax. I want you to think very hard about why you're doing this. Julia Child can fucking wait!" (Yes, it's true — I come by my sailor's mouth honestly.)

For nearly a week I neither cooked nor grocery shopped. Instead, all of our various families took Eric and me out for Mexican food, for barbecue, for beignets. We ate cheese biscuits with Rice Krispies, and spiced pecans, and red beans and rice, and gumbo, and all those other things that New Yorkers would turn up their noses at, but New Yorkers don't know everything, do they? This is what Texas, and family, are for. Eric and I slept late in my childhood bedroom, which I had never realized was so blessedly quiet and cool, in an enormous, comfortable bed made up with stylish 400-thread-count bed linens that never had even a single pebble of kitty litter in them.

After five days of it, I was miserable. I spent breakfasts eyeing my mother's gorgeous stainless steel six-burner stove longingly. I took to perusing *MtAoFC* compulsively, and sneaking back to my parents' office to check the blog. Every forlorn comment from some person wondering where I was, if I'd given up, produced a throbbing pulse in the pit of my stomach, like the one I felt when I thought about my hormonal condition and how I might not be able to have a baby. In addition, someone seemed to have attached some sort of transmitting device on my medulla oblongata. I could not understand the words that seemed to emanate from the deepest recesses of my brain, but the warbling voice was unmistakably familiar. I began to question my sanity.

Luckily for me and the Project (though maybe not ultimately

so lucky for the New York lobster population), Isabel and her husband, Martin, came into town from their country house for my parents' Christmas Eve party. She was wearing a mauve fifties prom dress (back in high school Isabel and I used to hit the vintage stores together, and neither of us has lost the habit), had her hair ratted up into a bouffant, and had painted her lips brick red. Martin was carrying a bag of presents and wearing his usual invisibility suit. The first thing she said when she walked in the door was, "You've been a naughty widget. Your followers are despondent. What're we eating tonight?"

"Nothing," I sighed miserably. "At least nothing I made. Mom's not letting me cook."

"What?!"

"She got a buffet basket from Central Market."

Isabel took me by the arms. "Okay, Julie. Let me handle this."

One thing you have to say about Isabel is that she does have the gift of gab, and she could sell ice to Eskimos. She is also persistent. All night long she worked on my mother, slipping in beside her at the bar, cornering her in the kitchen. She would not be ignored.

"So, Elaine, aren't you *proud* of what Julie's doing? She's a *goddess,* in my opinion."

"Oh?"

"Abso-*lutely.* You *have* been reading the comments, right? Julie is *adored!* She's inspiring people all over the damn place!"

"Yes . . . I guess. . . ."

The truth of the matter was that my mom hadn't really thought much about the people *reading* about what I was doing. She read my posts faithfully, but she tended to think of them much as she would a hospital stat sheet, perusing them mostly for any signs of imminent crack-up.

"Well, it's no surprise to you, of course — you Foster women can do anything."

(Foster is my maiden name. Even among the handful of

---

women of my age and socioeconomic status who have in fact married, those of us who actually took our husbands' names are considered freaks of nature.)

"I suppose. But, Isabel, I do worry. She's so stubborn when she gets a notion in her head, and she's just pushing herself so *hard* with this —"

"Oh, come *on*, Elaine! When has Julie ever not managed brilliantly? Remember drill team?"

"Of *course* I remember drill team! That's exactly what I'm talking about! She lost twenty pounds and cried herself to sleep every night!"

"*Exactly*. And she ate nothing but Skittles and Coke for a year and we all thought she was killing herself but she came out of it fine, and with a mean high kick to boot. She didn't even turn into a Junior Leaguer! Hey, did you know Henry reads the blog?"

Henry was my ex-boyfriend from high school, the one who'd had such trouble forgiving me for that whole dropping-him-for-Eric thing eleven years ago. My mom always really liked Henry.

"Really?"

"Yeah. He's really proud of Julie, too."

"That's nice of him."

"Your daughter's doing a great thing. She's cooking for our sins!" (This had become Isabel's favorite new phrase. She was thinking of making T-shirts.) She popped a chipotle-grilled shrimp into her mouth. "This is pretty good. For something from a grocery store, I mean."

Heathcliff, of all people, chimed in, just before Isabel managed to undo all the good work she'd done. "You know, I don't actually think Julie's freaking out all that much. I mean for Julie. I saw her rip up like a dozen artichokes, and she didn't scream even once. It was kind of eerie, in fact."

"But I read about it! I see what she's doing! She's taking on too much!"

Heathcliff has always known how to end an argument, and he's a genius with a raised eyebrow. "Mom. You do know you sound *just* like Granny. That's like *on purpose,* right?"

So that was that. That very night my mother agreed, with many sighs and much rolling of eyes, that if I absolutely *had* to do it, maybe I could cook something for New Year's Eve.

"Thanks, Isabel."

"Well, sure. Small price to pay to keep the Project alive, right? But listen, I've got to tell you something." She grabbed my hand and pulled me out onto my parents' back deck. It was absolutely balmy out there, or seemed so to my New York–hardened skin, but Isabel shivered in her tulle dress as she pulled me over to the Adirondack chairs, looking for all the world like a woman with a secret. She pulled me down into the chairs and bent toward me to whisper.

"Remember that dream I e-mailed about, about the dildo? Well, I was right, it was *totally* precognitive."

"Um. Oh?"

"There's this guy, Jude. He plays guitar in a punk band in Bath — England, you know. I met him on the Richard Hell fan site. I've never heard his music before, but I've read his lyrics, and they're *amazing.* And then I *dreamed* about the music, like I could hear exactly what it sounded like. I bet I'm right, too."

"Uh-huh?"

"And he sent me a picture of him, *and* he's sent me some of his poems, including one he wrote just for me, which I think are *brilliant.*"

"Okay?"

"And I think I need to meet him."

Suddenly it did feel a little chilly, and I glanced around, worried suddenly that maybe Martin was lurking around in his invisibility suit, smoking a cigarette in some dark corner of the deck. "But — I mean, do you mean you're going to — ?"

"No! That's what my mother thinks, that I should just go and have sex with him and get it out of my system, but that's so *wrong,* don't you think?"

Looking at the slightly crazed gleam in Isabel's eyes, I had the uncomfortable feeling that her mother's scheme might be the most reasonable one I was going to hear.

"No, I want to meet him, and if he's as wonderful as I think he is, then I'll talk to Martin, and we'll just see what happens next."

"Isabel —"

"Hey, Isabel, we've got to go if we're going to catch your dad at the thing." Martin was standing at the door, peeking out. I could just see the spiky silhouette of his mussed hair.

"Yeah, okay, honey. Coming." Isabel gave my hand a squeeze and was gone.

I had no idea what to think about that.

And so on the eve of the New Year, I made Veau Prince Orloff for eleven cousins and aunts and uncles, who I'm sure believed their crazy Yankee-fied niece had dropped completely off the deep end.

Veau Prince Orloff is an absurd recipe. What you do is this: You roast the veal with some vegetables and bacon. You save the juices. We did this the night before, and then left the roast sitting on the counter overnight — slightly overdone, I think, as I so often do with Julia's meats, which is particularly a shame when the meat you're roasting is $15.99 a pound. Then you can wake up a few times in the early hours of the morning in a cold sweat, convinced your parents' golden retriever has gotten to the eighty-dollar veal roast. That stress should offset some of the catastrophic caloric intake you're about to experience.

On the day you're serving, you make a *soubise,* which is a bit of rice briefly boiled and then cooked slowly with some butter and a lot of sliced onions for forty-five minutes or so. The water that sweats out of the onions is sufficient to cook the rice, which is kind of neat, sort of like a chemistry experiment or something. Then you make *duxelles,* which are just minced mushrooms sautéed with shallots and butter.

Out of the veal juices and some milk you make a *velouté sauce,* which is a roux-based type of thing. You combine the *velouté* with the *soubise,* run the *soubise* through the sieve / Cuisinart, then stir in the *duxelles* and cook it all up, thinning it out with cream.

This, surprisingly, takes all morning. And produces a hell of a lot of dirty dishes, which my mother, being my mother, patiently washed. Which is as it should be, because guilt is what Christmas is for.

I sliced the veal as thinly as I could, then stacked it back together again, one slice at a time, smearing mushroom filling on each slice as I went. I stirred some cheese into the warm *velouté,* then poured it over the veal. The veal now looked like some kind of wet beige footstool. I sprinkled some more cheese on top, and some melted butter. My mother is a Texan and knows the value of cooking fats, but even she was horrified when she did a stick-of-butter count. The veal got thrown into the oven about half an hour before it was time to serve, just to warm through.

If you fed this veal to a racehorse, it would instantly drop dead of gastric torsion. Very good. Who cares if the roast is overdone, I think, when you've got that much shit on it? It goes a little oddly with San Antonio squash casserole with Velveeta and canned chiles, cornbread dressing, turkey, and pecan pie. But no matter.

We flew back to New York on January second. As I sat at the kitchen table that morning before our flight home, sipping a cup of coffee and maybe wallowing a bit in the vague dissatisfaction that the day after the first day of the new year always brings, Heathcliff came in, rubbing his eyes, his red hair kicked up by sleep. Heathcliff is not much of a morning person; I'd kind of figured I wouldn't see him again before we left.

"Hey."

"Hey. You're up early."

"Mom said we'd all go to breakfast before your flight."

"Yeah."

He flung himself into a chair, picked up the front page, peered at it sleepily. Then I must have sighed, because he looked up again and said, with a crooked grin, "What's the matter, sis?"

"I don't know. Have to go back."

"Aaah. You'll be fine. Gotta get back to your cooking."

"I've got to kill a lobster, though. I've got to chop it into bits while it's still alive. I don't know if I can handle it."

"Julie. I've watched you brain a mouse against a marble counter before feeding it to a python."

"That's your fault."

"You can kill a bug. Man up, dude."

Flying back to New York after being in Austin is like being thrown into a pneumatic tube — an airless shuttling, inexorable. No matter how often Eric said, "It'll be nice to see the cats, won't it?" I could not be cheered. Homard à l'Américaine awaited.

I didn't know why I was doing this, I really didn't. I didn't want to kill lobsters. Hell, I didn't want to cook at all. The bleaders would be disappointed, sure, but they'd get over it. I was used to disappointing people. Besides, how had I become so absurdly arrogant as to think that anything I wrote about Julia Child and French cooking on a blog mattered two shits to *anybody?*

Come on, Julie. You're a vapid secretary with a butter fetish, and that's all.

But I couldn't quit. I couldn't quit because if I wasn't cooking, I wouldn't be the creator of the Julie/Julia Project anymore. I'd just have my job, and my husband, and my cats. I'd be just the person I was before. Without the Project I was nothing but a secretary on a road to nowhere, drifting toward frosted hair and menthol addiction. And I'd never live up to the name I'd been born with, the name I shared with Julia.

Funnily enough, if it weren't for being a secretary I might

never have gotten out of this funk. Because I would never have had the opportunity to field this phone call:

"Hi, I own a business downtown and I wonder if I qualify for business assistance."

"Well, I can try to help. Where are you located?" I actually had nothing to do with business assistance, but once you started forwarding some person to another department, that person often got shunted around for half an hour, and as often as not wound up back at your phone, none the wiser and pissed to the eyeballs. So it was the unofficial position of the personal assistants to answer all questions they got, even if they had no clue what they were talking about.

"My business is in the seaport, and many of my clients used to work in the towers —"

"The seaport is in the designated Area 1, so you should qualify for full benefits. What you need to do is call —"

"Can I be honest with you?" The woman on the other end of the line had a deep, gravelly voice; she sounded like she'd just finished laughing about something. I was intrigued; *can I be honest with you?* is not a question you get a lot when you work for a government agency.

"Uh, sure."

"I own a dungeon. It's the only dungeon in lower Manhattan. We've gotten the NYPD's Good Housekeeping Seal of Approval."

"The police give out seals of approval?"

"The chief of police told his men, you know, 'If you want to go to an S and M dungeon, this is the one to go to' . . ."

I was still sort of just sitting there gaping into my headset when the woman confessed that it wasn't so much that she *needed* assistance, business was quite good, actually, but she really did want to expand, and her accountant suggested she should give us a call —

"That is so *awesome.*" It came out a little belatedly, and rather without the husky cool detachment I might have wished for.

"I know!"

I suppose a breathless *awesome* was by far a better response than she expected to get in calling a government agency for assistance. It must have taken some guts to call; what if she'd gotten Natalie, the loon with the What-Would-Jesus-Do bracelet? Then again, I guess it takes guts to open an S&M dungeon in lower Manhattan.

We spent a few minutes chatting about the vagaries of the polymorphously perverse lifestyle, culminating in her anecdote — probably the one she keeps for cocktail parties — about the client who once a week comes in with three pairs of clogs and a Riverdance tape: "He lies on the floor naked while we clog dance for him. I can't clog dance, and I'm an overweight black woman. I look *ridiculous*. But this is my life, what can I say?" She erupted in a peal of laughter, and I felt a pang of envy. It's not that I think clog dancing naked for financial analysts is really my bag. But I can't imagine loving my job. I never have.

Nate popped by my cubicle, as he was wont to do, just as I was hanging up. "Look at Miss Pink Cheeks! You got a secret admirer?"

"What?" I touched my face, felt the heat of a blush. "Oh, no — it's nothing. What's up?"

"Just wanted to say congratulations on the article."

"What article?"

"Didn't you see it? *Christian Science Monitor.* Kimmy pulled it up doing her Nexus search this morning." He handed me a xeroxed page: holy crap. I hadn't even thought about that reporter since he came to eat Boeuf Bourguignon with us. "Looks like your cooking thing is really turning into something."

Nate was grinning down at me. Press always got him a little high. "One thing, though. There's not really any need to mention where you work, is there? I mean, it's not part of the story, right?"

"Um. I guess not. Sorry."

"No problem. Just for next time." He gave me a wink and turned to go. "Oh, and hey. I checked out your Web site. Very funny."

"Oh. Um. Thanks."

Okay. That made me nervous.

My final victim was another Chinatown denizen. He was spryer than his predecessors, flailing around in his bag for the entire subway ride. Because shivving a dead lobster in the back would be no challenge at all.

I put him in the freezer for a while when I got home, to try to numb him, maybe make it go a little easier, but is there such a thing as an easy vivisection, really? After half an hour or so, while Eric retreated to the living room and cranked up the volume on the TV, I took the lobster out of the freezer and laid him on the cutting board.

JC writes: "Split the lobsters in two lengthwise. Remove stomach sacks (in the head) and intestinal tubes. Reserve coral and green matter. Remove claws and joints and crack them. Separate tails from chests."

"Well, gosh, Julia, you make it sound *easy.*"

The poor guy just sat there, waving his claws and antennae gently, while I stood over him, my largest knife poised at the juncture of chest and tail. I took a deep breath, let it out.

It's like shooting an old, dying dog in the back of the skull — you've got to be strong, for the animal's sake.

"Oh, you've shot a lot of dogs in your time, have you?"

Go ahead.

"All right, all right. Okay. One. Two. *Three.*"

I pressed down, making an incision in the shell where Julia said I could quickly sever the spinal cord.

The thing began to flail.

"He doesn't seem to think this is particularly painless, Julia."

Chop it in two. Quickly. Start at the head.

I quickly placed the tip of my knife between its eyes and, muttering "I'm sorry I'm sorry I'm sorry," plunged.

Oh God. Oh God.

Clear blood leaked off the edges of the cutting board onto the floor as the lobster continued to flail vigorously, despite the fact that its head was now chopped neatly in two. The muscles in its chest gripped at the blade, so that the knife's hilt trembled in my hand. I sawed away at the thing, managing to get about halfway through before I had to leave the room for a bit to clear my head.

But I think perhaps I'm approaching a Zenlike serenity when it comes to crustacean murder, because when I reentered the kitchen to the sight of the giant thing pinned to the cutting board with a huge knife, still squirming, instead of being horrified by man's inhumanity to lobster, I just giggled. It really was pretty amusing when you thought about it.

Laughter through nausea is my favorite emotion, and after that, things got easier. In not too much time I had the thing cut into four pieces, plus detached claws. I cleaned out the intestines and "green matter," which looked more like an organ when it was unsteamed. The pieces of the thing kept twitching throughout, even keeping on awhile after I threw them into hot oil.

My final victim was sautéed with carrots, onions, shallots, and garlic, doused with cognac, lit on fire, then baked in an oven with vermouth, tomato, parsley, and tarragon, and served atop rice. I arranged the rice into a ring on a plate, as Julia asked. I've committed brutal murder for the woman, why not make a rice ring? I piled the lobster pieces in the middle and ladled the sauce over. "Dinner's served."

Eric overcame his momentary horror at being presented with a heap of mutilated lobster and dug in. "I suppose it's no worse to eat an animal you killed yourself instead of one they kill in the factory. Maybe it's better."

"It's true." I took a bite of lobster meat with rice. It was quite tasty. "Arguing the morality of slaughter will send you into a tail-spin of self-loathing every time."

"Unless you're a vegan."

"Uh-huh. But then you're a vegan, and you don't count. Hey, have you read about how they slaughter chickens? See, they hang them upside down on this conveyor belt with their little feet clamped in manacles, and —"

"Julie, I'm eating here."

"Or what about pigs? And pigs are way smart."

"*But* —" Eric jabbed his fork in the air rhetorically. "Does the intelligence of the creature have any bearing on its right and desire to live?" Eric had already finished his first serving of Homard à l'Américaine and was reaching for his second.

"George Bush would say no."

"So, the question is, is George Bush a vegan?"

"No, the question is — wait, am I turning into George Bush? Oh God!"

"I think we're getting a little confused. Let's just eat."

"Oh, hey, I just remembered — I forgot to tell you about this *crazy* call I got at work today."

So sometimes I'm irritated by my husband, and sometimes I'm frustrated. But I can think of two times right off the top of my head when it's particularly good to be married. The first is when you need help with killing the lobsters. The second is when you've got an inspirational story to relate regarding a large African American woman who runs an S&M dungeon. I told it to him as we sopped up the last of the buttery lobster juice with some hunks of French bread.

"That's *great*."

"I know, I *know!*" I knew of no one else I could have told who would have understood the joy this story brought me.

"It just makes you happy, thinking about the *possibilities* out there."

He didn't mean the possibilities of getting naked ladies to clog dance for him, or at least he didn't *only* mean that. He meant that sometimes you get a glimpse into a life that you never thought of before. There are hidden trap doors all over the place, and suddenly you see one, and the next thing you know you're flogging grateful businessmen or chopping lobsters in half, and the world's just so much *bigger* than you thought it was.

So that night I made my New Year's resolution, better late than never: To Get Over My Damned Self. If I was going to follow Julia down this rabbit hole, I was going to enjoy it, by God — exhaustion, crustacean murder, and all. Because not everybody gets a rabbit hole. I was one lucky bastard, when you came down to it.

January 1946
Bucks County, PA

When he got to the bit about Bartleman in her letter, Paul choked on his wine chuckling, thinking without too much regret that perhaps he had been a corrupting influence on little Julie, after all. He'd not been sure it was right to tell her about the astrologer's predictions — he knew she was in love with him, and Bartleman didn't seem to think the two of them had much of a future. He'd thought she might be hurt. But he should have known. Julie wasn't about to let herself get deflated by some honey with a star chart and a few solemn intonations.

Charlie's wife, Freddie, called up. "Paul? We've got dinner on!"

"I'll be right down — just finishing reading a letter!"

Sometimes Paul wondered if he was leading the poor girl on — for a girl was how he thought of Julie still. An unsophisticated, charming, excitable girl. Paul had never before allowed himself to become involved with someone so unformed, so unsure of herself. Still, it was a fact that Paul missed her far more than he'd imagined he would when he left China.

In Julie's letter, she boldly asked him to come out to visit her in Pasadena. And after dinner that night, a lovely roast lamb, he sat down and wrote a letter to tell her that he would. He didn't know yet that he'd decided to marry her, but he had.

The Proof Is
in the Plumbing

There are many ways of arriving at plain boiled or steamed rice, and most cooks choose one which best suits their temperaments. We find the following to be a foolproof system.

— *Mastering the Art of French Cooking*, Vol. 1

L et me say first that I'm fully aware that simply copping to the fact that I possess a half bath is liable to completely obliterate any chance I ever had for sympathy among my fellow non-hideously-rich New Yorkers. (My mother would call it a "powder room," but use that term in a room of frustrated apartment dwellers and see who gets lynched.)

Also, to be fair to the vile black shit that began spewing from the sink in the half bath one Monday in February, it really was just the capper on an independently miserable day. It started with the leftover Charlotte Malakoff au Chocolat I'd made over the weekend. I'd even made my own ladyfingers to put in it, because Julia warns that store-bought ladyfingers will "debase an otherwise remarkable dessert." *Debase.* Jesus, Julia, no pressure or anything. So I made my own, which was a trial in itself, then soaked them in Grand Marnier and tried to line the charlotte mold with them. (Who could possibly guess a year ago that I would be the kind of person to own a charlotte mold?) But they just sagged down until they were bent over at the waist like sad little swooning ladies. Well, the finished product came out looking like an as-is discounted Baskin-Robbins cake. And maybe it was debased by the crappy ladyfingers — I wouldn't know, being rather the debased sort myself — but it was chocolatey and sweet and creamy and cold. Pretty damned good, actually. Good enough that I didn't want it sitting around in my refrigerator to tempt me. So early in the morning of this very bad day I wrapped up the leftover Charlotte Malakoff in waxed paper, set it in a ceramic soufflé dish, and put the dish in a big H&M shopping bag. Just as I was finishing up this operation, the radio news reported that one of the two subway lines out of my station was not going into Manhattan due to track damage. Staff meeting at nine o'clock, of course.

You can probably guess how this ends, right? As I climbed out of the Cortlandt Street stop across from the office, late and sweaty and hurrying, yes of course the bottom of the bag gave way abruptly, and of course my Charlotte Malakoff tumbled to the pavement, and of course my ceramic soufflé dish shattered. Of course a freezing rain that stuck in icy clumps in the Mongolian wool of my coat collar was coming down very, very hard. I picked up my waxed paper–covered Charlotte Malakoff and the pieces of my soufflé dish and rushed into the building, face hot with humiliation. And after I got up to the office and left the heaped remains of charlotte out on the counter of the staff kitchen with a note saying "Please Enjoy!" I had to go to the six Democrats in the office and tell them they might want to take a pass since there might be ceramic shards or antifreeze in it.

Then there was work, which of course is quite bad enough in

itself. I signed a confidentiality agreement when I took this job, so I can't go into details, but I think the fact that bureaucrats are assholes is rather a matter of public record, isn't it? It's probably also not top-secret information that dashing back and forth to the community printer down the hall to print out dais cards for the bureaucrats who decided at the very last minute to join the memorial committee meeting when they heard the governor's people were going to be there is all kinds of annoying. Nor that doing this while at the same time trying to point out to the conscientious but non-English-speaking delivery guy from the caterer where to put the sandwich assortment and cookie plate and coffee urns is even worse.

Then the Turkish grocery near my office was out of the mussels I would need to make the Moules à la Provencale that were next up, and if God wanted me to wander around Chinatown in February he'd have let that hormonal syndrome of mine go ahead and grow me an even layer of blubber and a thick waterproof pelt, like a seal, instead of just unruly eyebrows, Fu Manchu whiskers, and unsightly bulges of butter fat. And who wanted to eat mussels anyway, which I don't even like, when it was about thirty degrees below zero in our apartment? And when I made it home, mussel-less, Eric was watching the *NewsHour* instead of washing the dishes that were overflowing in the kitchen sink and spread over the floor.

"It's not my fault," he protested moodily before I even started sighing and stomping around. "The sink isn't draining right. We need to get some Drano."

I kicked off my awful shoes and retreated to the half bath, perhaps to powder my nose.

The sound that came out of my mouth when I stepped into the room cannot be exactly reproduced in print, but it went something like:

"AihohmafugP AewwkrieeeeeeshitEw. Ew. Ew!!!"

The vile black shit wasn't actual shit. It was something far more disturbing. Bits of rice and parsley drifted about in it, and floating puddles of what I can only imagine was melted butter.

A gimlet is, to my mind, the ideal cocktail, exquisitely civilized and not at all girly, even if it is served in a chilled martini glass and gleams with a pearlescent hint of chartreuse. Philip Marlowe drank gimlets, after all. Gimlets originally were made of a one-to-one ratio of gin to Rose's lime juice. This was back when gin was made in bathtubs. Most bars now mix it 4:1, which is still convulsively limey, in the Powell opinion. No, it is best for beginners not to mess about with bars at all. Mix yourself one at home instead, with just the barest smidge of Rose's, well chilled. Eric and I make ours with vodka instead of gin, which many would consider heresy, but we consider perfect. The one he mixed for me after I finished howling wordlessly at the sink in the half bath was a quintessence of a gimlet, enough to make up for any number of unwashed dishes and *NewsHours*. If Daisy Buchanan's laugh is the sound of money, then a gimlet, well executed, is the color of it. It is just the thing when you are feeling impoverished, financially or spiritually.

Like, for instance, when the sink in your half bath is spewing vile black shit.

Neither Eric nor I was sufficiently steeled (nor, soon enough, sufficiently sober) to handle plumbing problems that evening; instead, we awoke early the next morning. After Eric made a run to Queensborough Plaza for Dunkin' Donuts coffee and supplies in the bone-chilling predawn hours, we spent the morning excavating the sink out from under the dishes and, with the aid of four bottles of Drano, coaxing the pipes to take their effluents back to wherever they had come from. Consumed with such, I didn't manage until that evening to get online to post about my plumbing situation and make excuses for not cooking the previous night. Isabel, though, kept things entertaining in my absence by writing in the comment box the most beautiful single paragraph about Julia Child I have ever read:

> God, Julia Child is definitely the all-time coolest person in the world. I just caught her show on TV — I turned it on just as Julia leaned gamely onto her knuckles like some otherworldly primate god of kitchens and good humor, and told the lady she was cooking with, who I didn't recognize, "I haven't had cobbler in a coon's age!" I think it was cobbler, anyway. They'd also made delicious-looking gingerbread, so maybe it was the gingerbread she hadn't had in so very, very long.

"Julia leaned gamely onto her knuckles like some otherworldly primate god of kitchens and good humor." I think that if I live to be ninety-one, I may never come up with a sentence more ravishingly true than that one. And Isabel doesn't even care all that much about Julia Child. She wrote it because she knew how very much *I* loved Julia Child. I felt an utterly unexpected prickle of teary gratitude. I couldn't write something ravishing and true about, say, Richard Hell for her. I knew I couldn't.

That night, after a dinner of Suprêmes de Volaille aux Champignons and Fonds d'Artichauts à la Crème — creamy, as the title would suggest, but not difficult; I had by this time become quite adept at the mutilation of artichokes — I finished my extralong post detailing our eating experience and plumbing woes, then opened up *MtAoFC* to see what was on for tomorrow's dinner. And that was when I realized something wonderful.

"Eric, come look!"

Eric was up past his elbows in the dishes he'd not been able to get to the previous night; he poked his head out of the kitchen with a quizzical look. I waved him over. "Come here!"

He came to where I sat at my desk and peered over my shoulder at the book I was holding open for him.

"Mouclades. Yeah?"

I turned the pages, then turned them back again.

"Mouclades, chapter six, mouclades, chapter — oh! You're finished with chapter five? Finished with fish?"

I grinned up at him. "Mouclades is the last." I giggled giddily. That was four chapters down — soups, eggs, poultry, and now fish. I'd decided at some point to skip the recipe variations, and the fish sauces all appeared elsewhere in the book, so I really was finished with fish. Yes, those were the shortest chapters, and the simplest, but still, it was evident — progress was being made. I was making my way through *Mastering the Art of French Cooking*. I *was* Mastering the Art of French Cooking! "Let's get us some mussels!"

The next night Eric and I stood over the sink shucking the mussels from their shells, after I'd steamed them in vermouth flavored with curry, thyme, fennel seed, and garlic. The kitchen smelled divine, the mussels were plump and pink and ruffled as tiny vulvas, or perhaps that comparison was just a reflection of my jaunty mood. The next morning I would inform my bleaders that another chapter had been completed, that 268 recipes had been made, that Julie Powell was well on her way to completing her insane assignment. "Just go ahead and schedule that triple bypass surgery and the stay in the mental hospital. I'm a-comin'!" I crowed to the husband at my side, whom I loved so intensely at that moment I couldn't shuck straight. When, later, the butter sauce for the mussels began inexplicably to separate, and I hovered delicately over the pot, gingerly adding dashes of ice water, stirring in butter that wanted nothing more than to come out again, Eric stood beside me. I was Tom Cruise hovering with a bead of sweat. I was Harrison Ford in a battered fedora, weighing a bag full of sand in my hands — and Eric understood. He was my *partner.* It occurred to me, as I beat my rebellious sauce into submission, that my husband was doing more than just enduring this crazy thing I'd gotten myself into, doing more than being supportive. I realized this was his Project, too. Eric wasn't a cook, and like Isabel, he only cared about JC because I did. And yet, he had become part of this thing. There would be no Project without him, and he would not be the same without the Project. I felt so *married,* all of a sudden, and so happy.

My mood was so fine that even Riz à l'Indienne could not spoil it. To make Riz à l'Indienne, you must sprinkle a cup and a half of rice into *eight quarts* of boiling water — which in this age of environmental crisis can be seen as really very nearly immoral, if you care about that kind of thing. I'm no nut on the subject, but even I blanched as I filled up a stockpot. You boil it for ten minutes, then test it "by biting successive grains of rice." Julia writes that "when a grain is just tender enough to have no hardness at the center but is not yet quite fully cooked, drain the rice into a colander." Normally it would be kind of a hoot thinking of Julia Child picking out individual grains of rice from an enormous pot of boiling water, nibbling each one delicately and peering into its center, but I was too busy doing it myself to be amused. After you've drained the rice, you have to rinse it under hot water, then wrap it in cheesecloth and steam it for half an hour.

Riz à l'Indienne has got to be the single most willfully obtuse recipe in all of *MtAoFC*. Wrangling a recalcitrant butter sauce can be a tricky business, certainly, but it doesn't fill you with the angry sense of futility that consumes you in making Riz à l'Indienne. I guarantee you, you cannot make it without at least once screaming at the open book, as if to Julia's face, "My God, woman — it's rice, for fuck's sake!" Eric, witnessing this, dubbed it "Bitch Rice," in honor of both the trouble it is to make and the obvious hidden nasty streak in anyone who would ask you to do it.

Still, we wound up eating before nine o'clock that night, for the first time in ages. Eric washed all the dishes; I mixed up some gimlets. I still had a glow on from finishing the fish chapter, and the mussels had been a light meal; for once, I didn't feel as if I had swallowed a bag of Quikrete for dinner. I sipped my drink. There was a reality show on TV. A pregnant silence settled over the apartment, as we tried to remember: now, what is it, again, that people do when they aren't cooking?

Eric abruptly stood, his gimlet left undrunk on the coffee table. "I think I'll go shave."

Eric really dislikes shaving. He feels that he doesn't know how to do it properly, and that somehow this reflects badly on his manhood. When I used to visit him in college, I'd leave at the end of the weekend with my face red and tingling from so much contact with his stiff whiskers. Once he graduated he did man up and tackle the problem of shaving seriously. But it remained a trial for him, and maybe it was because of this that *shave* has become one of our married-couple-inside-joke code words. As in "Look, honey, I shaved for you," accompanied by a suggestive wiggling of the eyebrows.

But he didn't come out of the bathroom stroking his smooth chin, with a randy smirk on his face. Instead, I just heard "Oh, *shit!*"

I am by now adept at translating Eric's cursing, and when I heard this one I knew to hop right up off the couch and hustle back to the bathroom. There I found my husband standing in an inch-deep pool of water fed by a vigorous gush from a pipe behind the toilet.

"Oh, shit."

"That's what I said."

I ran to the broom closet for a bucket, but we couldn't wedge the bucket under there, so I then ran to the kitchen for my biggest bowl, and got that under the rushing fountain of water. By this time we were both soaked, and the water had spread far and wide. By the time we'd sopped up the lake, the bowl under the toilet was full, so I ran to the kitchen for my second-biggest bowl and traded them out.

"How do we switch off the water?" howled Eric over the drowning roar of the cataract.

"You're asking me? I thought that's what I kept you around for!"

After groping our boiler for a while to no effect, we headed down into the basement, which I had never before been in. I hesitate to call it a basement, actually. Remember the end of *The Blair Witch Project*, in the house? It's kind of like that, except that if you will recall, that place was relatively uncluttered and those kids never caught sight of actual bones in the beams of their flashlight. And I added the experience of picking my way down there in the pitch black to my reservoir of nightmarish images for no reason, because we still couldn't figure out how to shut the goddamned water off.

And so that night was spent not in clean-shaven connubial bliss, but rather taking shifts sitting on the kitchen floor, bailing water out of stainless steel bowls every seven and a half minutes — I timed the rate of flow, because that's the kind of thing you do at four a.m., sitting on the bathroom floor waiting to bail the next bowl of water from under the catastrophically leaking toilet. Eric did far more than his share of this, staying up until 3:30 a.m., when I woke up and forced him to go back to bed. I used my spare time during my shift to make Mousseline au Chocolat, which is technically a jelling-type recipe, but which, miraculously, turned out just beautifully anyway. (Thank God — I don't think I could have handled another disaster.) I chilled it and served it the next night, in the coffee cups with the Raphael cherubs on them that we bought in a cheap souvenir shop outside the Sistine Chapel during our honeymoon, after a long, long walk, which we then used to drink wine with the cheese we had for lunch, on a green square, as we did every day during our honeymoon. And eating it that night reminded us that there was such a thing as fun, which was a good thing to remember right then.

So that turned out fine, and I'm not going to blame the chill in our relations that winter on pipes that spout leaks of biblical proportions.

No, I'm going to blame the chill in our relations on pipes that freeze solid for four days straight.

> . . . I'm thinking a line of high-design furniture just for sex. Chair and sofas with ergonomic, adjustable supports for coitus, but that actually LOOK REALLY GOOD. I've made some drawings, as soon as I can scan them I'll send them along. Maybe your mom can give me some tips on how I can go about getting them fabricated. . . . I've even come up with a name: Schtuppenhaus!

The nice thing about having a friend who is crazier than you are is that she bolsters your belief in your own sanity. How could I worry too much about the wisdom of cooking my way through *MtAoFC* for no particular reason when Isabel was concocting a business plan for midcentury-style fuck-furniture, and asking my mom to be a consultant?

I have known Isabel since the first grade. We used to choreograph dance routines to Cyndi Lauper tunes — she let me in on what "She Bop" was about. When I began telling my friends and family I was going to do this project, exactly two people didn't respond with some variation of "Why in God's name would you want to do that?" — my husband, and Isabel. She is a good friend to me.

I, on the other hand, am *not* a good friend. Isabel has worked to keep in touch, though we have not lived in the same city since we graduated from high school. She has remembered my birthdays, she has bought me presents for Christmas, she has offered to cut my hair. She has adored my boyfriends, and listened excitedly as I blathered on about them. I, on the other hand, have visited cities she's been living in and not called. I couldn't tell you her birthday on a bet, and for Christmas I give her random doodads I pick up at the checkout counter at Barnes & Noble on Christmas Eve. I have never really gotten to know her boyfriends, but I have often wanted to shake her by the shoulders and shout, "Oh for Christ's sake, Isabel, shut up for a minute!"

But even though I'm not a good friend, I do love Isabel. And so I was overjoyed when Martin came on the scene. Martin was taciturn, and a little odd — a photographer and a painter, or so said Isabel, though I never saw his work. He was slightly stooped, in the way of tall, thin men, and especially tall, thin, shy men. But his rare smiles were open and sweet. And he didn't have to say anything to reveal that he *got* Isabel — who is, to say the least, not an easy person to get — that he saw all the stuff that lay just beyond the squealing and the queer subculture obsessions. He just had to look at her.

They were married on her rich uncle's lawn. She had luscious flowers and vertiginously sloppy and delicious bride's and groom's cakes baked by her friend Ursula. She wore a burgundy velvet gown that showcased her considerable décolletage and made her skin look creamy pale. She'd done her hair herself, as always, but for once she kept it simple and forewent the marcel waves and beehive do. Martin wore some strange velvet sport coat he'd found in a thrift store, in the same color as Isabel's dress — he was all elbows and knees, a glowing scarecrow. Isabel's friend Mindy read something or other about marriage being like a base camp, and I read a Philip Levine poem about cunnilingus. It was all very, very Isabel.

Now, as I've made clear, I'm no stickler for the sanctity of wedding vows; I figure each to his own, you know? But sometimes there's an exception. Because sometimes you just get a feeling when you watch someone you love fall in love — maybe especially someone who is sad, or difficult, or just for some reason an uncomfortable fit with the rest of the world. A feeling of relief, really, as if you can let go of that load you'd never actually realized you were carrying. That's what I felt as I watched Isabel marry Martin — "Well, there's that taken care of, anyway." Two people who might so easily have never found one another at all, had. It seemed a precious, and fragile, thing.

And then three years later, Isabel threw it all away.

Yesterday I talked to Jude on the phone for the first time. I don't get so wound up about British accents; in fact, usually I think they are rather off-putting, but on him it's just perfect.

Have you ever watched a friend make the single wrongest choice she could possibly make? All the time she's looking back at you, beaming, happier than she's ever been, surer than she's ever been, and you're watching her foot about to fall onto nothing, onto air, and there's nothing you can do to warn her off the cliff's edge. You can't say to her, "My God, Isabel, don't screw over Martin, who loves you, for some English punk guitarist you met on the *Internet!*"

Thanks for the Bitch Rice post, by the way. You had to do it, for all of us who never, ever will. And I hope your plumbing's back in order, and that you called your landlord. You do know your mom's checking in on you through the blog, don't you? If you don't call the landlord she might KILL you.

Because Isabel was the only one who didn't say you were nuts when you told her you were going to cook your way through *MtAoFC*, and that this was how you were going to save your soul. She believed in you, and now she needs you to believe in her. What do you say? How do you stop her without losing her?

In the next weeks, I kept doing the Bitch Rice. I didn't have to — I'd done the recipe, there was a small check mark by Riz à l'Indienne in the book — no reason at this point I couldn't just throw some Uncle Ben's into boiling water and have done with it. But I was intrigued. Bitch Rice was so needlessly baroque, so stubbornly nitpicky. Every time I turned to the vegetable chapter — in *MtAoFC,* rice resides among the vegetables, which I for some reason find endlessly amusing — it was there, staring me in the face. "Why?" I asked myself every time I came upon it. "Why, Julia? What's so great about Bitch Rice?"

I will say that one problem Riz à l'Indienne does dispense with is overcooking. No matter how distracted you get by gimlets or cooking fiascoes, Riz à l'Indienne won't be ruined. Perhaps Julia, an isolated cooking dervish up in her garret kitchen during those early Paris days, her husband snapping pictures of her and sticking his fingers in the sauce, just needed to remove one item from her list of anxieties. But was it worth it? Is overdone rice so bad, really?

Bitch Rice produced an astonishing amount of chatter on the blog, and turned up a type I had never known existed:

> Don't waste time on this nonsense. A Japanese rice cooker is what you need — stat! No more overdone rice, no more sticking, and NO MORE BITCH RICE. If Julia Child had been given access to a rice cooker when she was writing MtAoFC, she'd have SWORN by it! She has never been wimpy about using good equipment. Love, Chris.

Chris, as it turns out, was a passionate Rice Cooker Advocate. And she was not alone. Rice cookers, according to this startlingly vocal population, were the *bomb*. Lives have been changed because of rice cookers. Apparently.

This outpouring in turn provoked a heated response from another equally vocal contingent, lamenting the gadget addiction and bone-laziness of the rice-cookerists, citing them as a sad example of the insatiable materialism of the contemporary age.

"Bah, just another space-hogging appliance," huffed StoveLover. "Don't give in, Julie!"

I was beset on both sides, being urged alternately to Get a Rice Cooker Right NOW, and to Look Away from the Little Red Blinking Rice Cooker Light. The whole thing rather flummoxed those few of us without a firm opinion on the matter, who were left to think to ourselves what on earth the big deal was. As Heathcliff wrote in, "I've made a hell of a lot of rice and I've never even considered the issue. Is this a New York thing? It's only RICE."

Maybe I worry too much, but all the rice Sturm und Drang obscurely concerned me. Why were all these people riled up about rice cookers, and why could I not find it in my heart to give a good goddamn? Was I missing out on a key issue of my generation? Perhaps it was sort of like being the marrying kind — Heathcliff and I just didn't have it in our genetic makeup to care about rice.

Okay. Maybe I worry too much.

Isabel, as usual, came up with a contribution to the Rice Cooker Debate both imminently diplomatic and irretrievably odd:

> I think perhaps there's a slightly removed parallel universe that we can all gaze back and forth across, in which rice cooks without hitch and easier for some of us in pans, and for others in rice cookers. Across the Rice Veil?

None of us had any idea what she was talking about, of course, but with Isabel the particulars didn't matter so much. We all appreciated the sentiment, and after that the Rice Cooker Debate simmered down, with all concerned agreeing to disagree.

Gimlets are all well and good when your pipes spew vile black shit, and chocolate mousse helps when they leak. But when they quit those things and start freezing solid for days on end instead, something more is called for. Conventional wisdom holds that the remedy for frozen pipes in a Long Island City apartment is a wee heroin habit. But unfortunately I already had a heavy habit for very expensive foodstuffs, which ruled out recreational spending on smack. What I did instead was cook large hunks of meat until I ate myself into a stupor, or ran out of clean pots, whichever came first.

Julia writes that Navarin Printanier, lamb stew with spring vegetables, "is not a seasonal dish anymore thanks to deep freezing," which, when we woke up to a frigid apartment and no water, sounded perhaps more apropos than she had intended. The advantage of Navarin Printanier is that it requires a minimum of dishes, which is pretty much a necessity when your water ceases to run for thirty-six hours, and just maneuvering around your kitchen could land you a place on the Olympic hurdle team.

To make Navarin Printanier, brown in a skillet some lamb stew meat that you've dried with paper towels — I used a mixture of funky vertebrae-like bony bits and boneless shoulder meat — in lard, which is another one of those items that is helpful to have around if you're fresh out of smack. Once the pieces of meat are well browned on all sides, take them out and put them in a casserole, toss them with a tablespoon of sugar, and let them cook over high heat for a minute. This is supposed to caramelize the sugar, which is in turn supposed to make the sauce all brown and yummy. Season with salt and pepper, toss with a few tablespoons of flour, and set the meat, in its casserole, in a 450-degree oven for a few minutes. Take it out, toss it, stick it back in. All this is meant to get the meat all crusty and brown. Turn the heat down to 350.

So now — deglaze the skillet that you browned the lamb in with some beef stock, or, if you happen to be a superhuman hyperfoodie like me, with the lamb stock you just happen to have in the fridge. Pour that over the meat in the casserole. Add peeled, seeded, juiced, and chopped tomatoes to the meat, or, if you're a subpar lazy bastard like me, a few tablespoons of tomato paste. Also some mashed garlic, rosemary, a bay leaf, and most likely some more lamb or beef stock, so the meat's mostly covered. Bring all that to a simmer on the stovetop — and do remember that the casserole has been in the oven and is hot as a motherfucker. I never do remember this, and as a result my forearms (and my belly, after unwisely choosing to cook in a baby-tee) are crisscrossed with shiny burn scars, like an X-Man's special power symbol. When the casserole comes to a simmer, stick it back in the oven for an hour or so.

Eric, who now that washing dishes is not possible has nothing to do with himself but sift through the teetering towers of periodicals piled all about the house — which would be much better employed, in my opinion, as fuel for a nice illegal bonfire — has noticed that the apartment is very cold. It is, in fact, always very cold, something to do with the arctic breezes that blow in through the faulty jalousie windows, which entirely overwhelm the crap baseboard heating we're paying two hundred bucks a month for. But on this afternoon *The New Yorker* is not enough to distract him from the cold. He gets an idea in his head, but you still have much work to do, and besides you haven't bathed in three days, so you put him off by asking him to make you a gimlet.

Chop up some potatoes and carrots and turnips. If you're feeling patient, you can carve the vegetables up into beautiful smooth round shapes. Does it make a difference? I wouldn't know; I'm not patient. Also peel some pearl onions. If you have no water but the melted oily gray snow you scooped up from the sidewalk into your cooler (a cooler that will now have to be disinfected with lye), just so you could flush the toilet, you'll have to peel them the hard way, without parboiling them first. You might need another gimlet for that.

When the lamb's been cooking for an hour, take it out and add the vegetables. Julia wants you to "press the vegetables into the casserole around and between the pieces of lamb." There will be way, way too many vegetables for you to do that effectively, but what the hell, give it a shot. The lamb is going to smell fabulous at that point, which is good, because it makes you forget how much you want to kill yourself.

What also helps with this is cheap-ass Australian wine, so long as you don't mind waking up with a dry mouth at three o'clock in the morning with your last gallon jug of Poland Spring running low, cursing the name shiraz.

However, neither shiraz nor Navarin Printanier will help melt the chill in relations. Eric thought it might. That night in bed he curled around me, kissed my shoulder, and in other ways made it entirely clear that he thought it was time for a thaw. I ignored it for as long as I could, then let out an aggravated sigh.

"What's wrong?"

"What are you trying to do, exactly?"

"It's just — it's so cold in here, I thought we could —"

"What? Have *sex*? Eric! I stink of roasted lamb and three days of body odor! I haven't shaved! I have to get up and go to work tomorrow, and then I have to come back to this SHIT HOLE apartment at the end of the day and COOK some more! I DON'T want to have sex! I may NEVER want to have sex AGAIN!"

Eric turned away from me and curled up on the edge of the mattress, as far away from me as he could get.

"Eric, I'm sorry."

"Forget it."

"I'm *sorry*. I'm just *irritated*, and I'm so *tired* —"

"I said *forget it*, okay? Let's just go to sleep."

Okay. That didn't go well.

If you think about it, it's a miracle Julia ever got married. Can you imagine trying to live in the same house with that kind of energy, forever? Isabel is rather the same — enthusiastically clay-like, eager to be molded by new experiences, phobic about casting her lot with any one destiny. It's an enviable perspective, but it'll run you ragged if you have to keep up with her all the time.

Jude had been writing more poems for Isabel — and not exactly violets-are-blue stuff either. These overheated missives Isabel promptly shared not only with her entire e-mail list, but with Martin as well. "Well, I just think they're *brilliant*, don't you?" Martin, Isabel reported, had had no reaction.

The mind reels.

Her next e-mail to me on the subject was the one I had been waiting for, and dreading:

> I really, really like Jude, and I can't wait to meet him, but this ISN'T just ABOUT Jude, and it ISN'T just about being BORED or something. And so I think I've nearly almost decided that regardless of how it works out with Jude, I'm going to ask Martin for a divorce.

As I'd feared, the great abyss was opening up under Isabel's feet, while I just mm-hmed away.

I got one last e-mail from her the morning she got on the plane to fly to England. She'd told Martin where she was going and why. He was heartbroken, of course. He asked if she'd go to counseling with him to try to save the marriage, but she refused. "I don't want to save the marriage," she told him. "I don't want to be married to you anymore." I'm sure she said this very kindly. Isabel is a kind person. But the cruelty of it took my breath away and left me with an icy spot in my chest, a fear that wasn't just for her. Isabel said she had to be cruel to rescue her life. I understood rescuing your life, and how much you might be willing to sacrifice to do it. But I thought of Eric and me, twisted away from each other in our double bed at night, exhausted and cold and smelling of too much French food, and I wondered if it was

worth it. I wondered if, in fact, rescuing our lives was really what
we were doing.

Our beloved former mayor Rudolph Giuliani once maintained
that the progress of civilization is all about keeping excrement off
the walls. It is an interesting point, but I must respectfully differ.
As far as civilization goes, it's all about the running water. When
ours returned at 8:30 on Tuesday morning, after an eighty-four-
hour absence, Eric and I felt like humans again. And it wasn't just
for the sake of a long, hot, thawing shower that we called in sick
that day.

As for the Bitch Rice, I wound up abandoning it without coming to a definitive opinion on its merits. I didn't go out and buy
myself a rice cooker, either. Not that I have anything against
them. I just didn't want to go to Chinatown. I had some bad as-
sociations there. At this point I'm like the Switzerland of rice —
not going to make any firm stands on the matter, but for the moment boiling Uncle Ben's in a pot is good enough for me.

On the day that Isabel got on a plane to England for her week's
worth of monkey sex with some Brit punk she'd never met, I
found myself thinking about her odd theory of the Rice Veil.
And I began to get what she was saying. Within this world maybe
there are divides that, once crossed, separate people from one another, as surely as if they were in different universes. Once someone begins to use a Japanese rice cooker, perhaps she can never
go back. But perhaps this barrier she has passed through is trans-
parent; perhaps she can look back at her former companions in
the shadowy world of Those Who Cook Their Rice in Pots with
bemusement and contempt. For a while, Isabel and I were together on this side — not of the Rice Veil but of another curtain.
Then in her search to save herself, Isabel, either inadvertently or
in resolute decision, crossed over. For a while — maybe as I
screeched at Eric that night after too many waterless days, too

much cold, too much cooking — I looked across and saw that I might follow her. Then morning came, the water came on, I made love to my husband who is also my partner, and the curtain closed, with Isabel forever on the other side. Maybe that's what Isabel meant by a veil.

Or maybe I just worry too much.

Warning

Do not attempt any dessert calling for a mold lined with ladyfingers unless you have ladyfingers of premium quality — dry and tender, not spongy and limp. Inferior ladyfingers, unfortunately the only kind usually available in bakeries, will debase an otherwise remarkable dessert.

— *Mastering the Art of French Cooking,* Vol. 1

HELL AND DAMNATION, is all I can say. WHY DID WE EVER DECIDE TO DO THIS ANYWAY?

— *Letter from Julia Child to Simone Beck,*
July 14, 1958

Sweet Smell of Failure

T he Project is over. We can't do this anymore."

I looked down at the floor, at the spattering of half-crushed cauliflower and mangled watercress there. I looked at the food mill falling in crumpled, bright pieces from my fingers, limply resting on my splayed thighs. I looked up into my husband's face, his eyes dark and stern.

"You . . . think?"

The Project is over.

I thought I had never heard words so beautiful in all my life.

It had started out okay, if any scenario involving going to work on a Sunday to do data entry can be considered "okay."

Imagine voting in an election. Only imagine that when you step into the booth, instead of a butterfly ballot or a Diebold black box computer, and a series of simple choices to make — Yes or No on Proposition 12; Democrat, Libertarian, or Pure Evil — you find a cheerful, shiny brochure with "We Want To

Hear From You!" splashed across its cover. Imagine opening it and seeing inside a series of questions, designed to get at the nuances of your positions on a variety of issues: the soundness of architectural schemes, the philosophical underpinnings of memorial design, the social implications of various economic initiatives. Imagine that below each of these questions are several ruled lines for you to fill in as you wish, and that you have been handed a nice blue ballpoint pen, with my government agency's logo printed on it, that's yours to keep.

Sounds nice, doesn't it? Makes you feel a part of the democratic process, doesn't it? Makes you feel like your thoughts are valuable.

Yeah, well. Now take an extra moment to imagine what happens to all those carefully considered words. Imagine them being painfully deciphered — a lot of you have really shitty handwriting — and entered — not scanned in but typed, letter by letter, with every single typo intact — into an enormous computer program. By young and underpaid women, because in addition to passing out Kleenex and hugging strangers, another thing that male recent Ivy League graduates don't like to do is data entry. That's thirty *thousand* of these brochures, we're talking. Throw in a constantly crashing server and the fact that they don't turn on the heat in the office on the weekends, and you've got the makings of a twenty-first-century Triangle Shirtwaist fire disaster.

I took comfort in the fact that at least I wasn't the one responsible for designing a program capable of incorporating such helpful comments as "Please make five towers each a different color, white, black, brown, yellow, and red, to represent all the races of those who died," and "ALL This Shit *SUCK!!!!*" into a cohesive analysis appropriate for distribution at board meetings.

So anyway, I did my share of data entry for the day and headed home, stopping by the grocery store for supplies for that night's dinner. I was making plain broiled chicken with Sauce Diable and Chou-Fleur en Verdure (puree of cauliflower and watercress with cream). Sauce Diable is an enrichment of Sauce Ragoût, a classic brown sauce, a sauce to make one feel virtuous and steady and French. The cauliflower and watercress puree, too, had the whiff of authenticity, I thought. So anticipation had me feeling warm and happy. I got off the subway in Queens that afternoon at a stop I usually don't, an elevated station, and as I stood there a moment on the platform, taking in the unusually warm day, the tender blue sky, the skyline of Manhattan stretching out before me, I thought, "See, New York ain't so bad."

Ha.

Sauce Ragoût must cook for at least two hours, so I started with it as soon as I got home. Since I had no spare chicken carcasses lying about, I'd picked up some chicken wings and gizzards with which to enrich the sauce. I began by browning them, with some chopped carrot and onion, in butter and lard. Only I put too many chicken parts in the pot at once, so they didn't brown very well. I was only able to get them sort of stiff and yellow before I took them out and made a lightly browned roux with some flour and the fat in the pot before pouring in several cups of boiling beef broth, some vermouth, and a bit of tomato paste. I put the chicken back in, along with thyme, a bay leaf, and a few sprigs of parsley. I was now going to just let that simmer for a good long while. Smelled great. No problem.

Next up, ladyfingers, for the Charlotte Malakoff aux Fraises. I'd made ladyfingers before; I'd made a Malakoff before. I couldn't imagine that this would give me too much trouble. I serenely measured out my powdered sugar, my granulated sugar, my cake flour, sifted. I separated my three eggs; I buttered and floured my cookie sheets.

"You must be particularly careful to obtain a batter which will hold its shape," JC writes. "This means expert beating and folding." So there's a trick to it; it's all right, I'm a tricky girl. And I'd done this before, it was a snap. I beat the granulated sugar into the egg yolks, then added vanilla. I beat the egg whites until stiff with a pinch of salt and a bit more sugar. Then I scooped a quarter of the egg whites on top of the egg yolks, and sifted a quarter of the flour on top of that. One quarter at a time, I folded the ingredients together with a light hand, so the batter wouldn't deflate, then spooned it all into a pastry bag.

I began squooshing out lines of ladyfinger batter onto the cookie sheet. Now, pastry bags and I don't really get along, and this batter was quite sticky, so at first I thought I was just experiencing the initial bumps of a rapid learning curve. But soon it became obvious that something was seriously wrong. The batter just puddled out over the cookie sheets, and though the recipe was supposed to make twenty-four ladyfingers, I only ended up with maybe fifteen. The whole "expert beating and folding" thing had clearly not happened.

I was beginning to get a very bad feeling about this, but what was there to do but carry on? I sprinkled on a thick layer of powdered sugar. JC said I could remove the excess by turning the pans upside down and tapping them gently, that the ladyfingers would stay in place.

You know the old joke? "Guy walks into a doctor's office with a duck stuck to his head. Doctor asks, 'What can I do for you?' Duck says, "Get this guy off my ass!'" This was like that. Tap the upside-down cookie sheets, and half the ladyfingers fall off, but the excess powdered sugar sticks like a charm. Just the opposite of what I was expecting, see? Ba-DUM-bump.

I stuck the sad remains of my broken ladyfingers in the oven. When I checked them twelve minutes later they were, to my utter lack of surprise, a mess. The powdered sugar had caramelized and blackened into a sucking tar pit in which my ladyfingers languished like so many sunk mastadons.

That would have been enough to call a halt to the whole Malakoff fiasco right there if only Eric, cheery fucking Eric, had not chosen that moment to grow a work ethic on my behalf. "I'll bet they'll still work. Sure they will! Don't give up!"

Oh, *fine.*

So I pried off a few of the cookies, even managing not to break a few of them, and set them on a rack to cool. I hulled some strawberries and mixed up the orange liqueur and water I was supposed to dip the ladyfingers in before lining the soufflé mold with them.

Lining the soufflé mold involved cutting the ladyfingers into small puzzle pieces so they'd fit precisely inside the bottom and sides. It was entirely obvious that I didn't have enough ladyfingers, but I tried anyway. I dipped the carefully trimmed ladyfinger-puzzle-pieces in the orange liqueur mixture, then pressed the resulting disintegrating sugary clay up against the sides of the mold.

It was getting late; the Sauce Ragoût would be done soon, and I hadn't even started on the cauliflower and watercress puree. I put a pot on to boil. I trimmed my cauliflower and my watercress.

Back to the Malakoff recipe I flipped.

The Malakoff required half a pound of unsalted butter. I did not have half a pound of unsalted butter. I did not have half a pound of any kind of butter at all.

Balls to *this.*

The hulled strawberries went back into the fridge; ditto, the soufflé mold with ladyfinger mush. I threw the cauliflower into the pot of boiling water, then, after a few minutes, the watercress. Drained it all as soon as the cauliflower was tender.

There were so many dishes in the sink. So very, very many dishes. My husband had done nothing else for nearly six months but wash dishes. Just as I had done nothing but screw up my ladyfingers.

How had it gotten to be nearly ten o'clock at night? I was so tired. The next day's data entry loomed in my increasingly fretful mind. I dug my food mill out from the pile of sticky appliances erupting out of the pantry. It had been a Christmas present from my mother-in-law; I'd never used it before. How was I supposed to put the damned thing together, anyway? Oh, there we are.

I put the cauliflower and watercress in the mill, over a bowl, and began to crank.

No. No. This was wrong.

I dumped the cauliflower and watercress out into another bowl, now just another dirty dish. I tried again to put the food mill together. No. No. Can't make it fit. Just. Can't. Make it. Fit.

You can insert the hideous collapse here. You've heard them before. Suffice it to say, this was worse. The granddaddy. The Krakatoa. The End of the Fucking World.

In the blogverse, an ominous silence. Crickets. Then:

> . . . So what happened?! Oh God, the suspense is killing me!

Slowly, the faithful gathered in vigil.

> Julie? Are you there? You're not going to quit, are you? It can only get better from here. And think of the dark void that would overcome our world if you quit now. — Chris

> None of the rest of us out here are ever going to make 1/8 the recipes in any cookbook in our whole lifetimes. We love the Project, but my God! What about one dish a day? Like peas on Tuesday, chicken on Wednesday, ladyfingers on Saturday? It doesn't have to be all or nothing is what I am saying. Just do your best. We are all behind you — and you, too, Eric! — Pinky

> Take two weeks and stay far from the kitchen. Do dishes for Eric. Eat takeout. This isn't a quest for self-improvement; it's a death march. — HandyGirl5

> . . . Can you give yourself an extension? . . .

. . . Can you take a vacation? . . .

. . . Take care of yourself . . .

If only you wouldn't use f*** so much — it adds nothing.
— Clarence

Is it love, or is it Memorex? I don't know — the World Wide Web
is a tricky animal. All I know for sure is that Sauce Ragoût can
keep for a day very easily. Which is why I was able to wait until
the next day to strain it and cook it down with some vermouth and
a generous amount of pepper to make a luscious Sauce Diable to
go over my broiled chicken.

Oh, and I also know that when you've gotten a night of sleep,
no matter how tear-stained, and then some bolstering from
people who love you — or "love" you, or whatever — even if
they're people you've never met, sometimes the end of the world
doesn't seem like that anymore. Like the end, I mean. Which is
why the next night I was able to puree my cauliflower and watercress with the potato ricer instead of a food mill, make up a
béchamel sauce with all the élan of someone born with the stuff
coursing through her veins, and bake it all up with some cream
and cheese into an insanely delicious white-and-green-and-
golden mush that went with my chicken and Sauce Diable just
perfectly.

End of the Fucking World? No *problem.*

HOORAY — I never had a doubt. In fact, I wanted to say I was
ASHAMED of all those people yesterday, telling you to take a
break. To imply you're made of anything less than the steeliest
stuff is just a travesty! I was going to say, no! no! Don't listen
to them! Soldier on! For that is the kind of stuff you're made
of, soldier stuff (I'm starting to make myself laugh, here). But

seriously — people need to understand that since there's only a handful of people who could, physically and mentally, even ATTEMPT what you're doing, that means you HAVE to do it. The romance of the death march should be an obvious thing to your faithful readers, and the great thing is that you won't die at the end (knock wood . . .). Hugs and Puppies, Isabel.

What she said . . . — Henry

So the next thing that happened started with some hot sauce.

The delivery guy left them downstairs in the diner; Papa Johnny, who owned the place — everybody literally calls him Papa Johnny, it's adorable — waved me down as I was coming home from work. "I got for you," he called, beckoning me inside. He pointed at two boxes on the counter, one a little bigger than a shoebox, the other bigger than a hatbox and very light. "For you."

I carried them upstairs and ripped them open right away. In one box: an enormous bag of authentic Texas-style tostito chips, cushioned by great quantities of Styrofoam peanuts. In the other: three jars of Religious Experience. Medium, Hot, and "The Wrath."

Dear Julie,

I hope you don't mind me sending this along. You mentioned that Religious Experience is your favorite brand of hot sauce, and I figured this might come in handy the next time your food mill flies into a rage.

Best Wishes,

A Fan from Texas

I suppose I could have wasted time worrying about how easily a random person had tracked down my home address. I suppose I could have been creeped out. But I'm telling you, Religious Experience hot sauce is *the best*.

When I mentioned this unexpected manna from heaven on the blog, a few other people began to get ideas.

From Oregon I got a picture book with food made up to look like cute animals and a Phillip Pullman novel.

From Louisiana I got filé powder and a Ziploc bag full of dried rosemary from a fan's garden.

From LA I got a bar of Scharffen Berger chocolate, some ancho mustard, and a messenger bag that was made especially for the cast and crew of *Laurel Canyon,* a movie I love because — seriously? — girl-on-girl action just doesn't get any better than Fran-McDormand-on-Kate-Beckinsale.

At about this time I was heavily into legs of lamb. Now, legs of lamb are not cheap, unless you're in New Zealand, which we most emphatically were not. Eric's and my bank account was feeling the strain. Which is when Isabel got the idea for the donation button.

A donation button is a link on a blog or a Web site that will take you directly to Paypal or one of the other online money transfer sites, where you can easily and safely donate any amount of money you wish to the person on whose Web site the donation button lives. Isabel's notion was that should I make this option available, hundreds of dollars would immediately be mine for the taking, and my financial troubles would be put at an end. I thought Isabel was crackers.

But as it turns out, many more people wanted to give me money than wanted to give me Religious Experience hot sauce. Within hours after I managed to get the button up and running, cash started trickling in. Five dollars here, ten there, a buck fifty, twenty bucks. Again, I found this slightly creepy, because it's hard not to imagine that Osama bin Laden might have made his first million just this way. I did not make a million. But soon enough, I had a nice little lamb discretionary fund. For which thank God, because it would have been such a shame to waste my rent money on roast lamb Marinade au Laurier.

Six cups of red wine, a cup and a half of red wine vinegar, half a cup of olive oil, thirty-five bay leaves, salt, and peppercorns. Lay the lamb roast in it, cover, don't forget to turn it now and again — and marinate for four to five days.

At room temperature.

We asked four different women over to share our putrefied lamb feast. That all four of them were called away at the last moment by entirely legitimate circumstances is one of the more compelling pieces of evidence I've run into that there is a just and protective God watching over us. Well, them anyway.

Over the course of the evening, the lamb, in its stages of preparation, was compared variously by my husband and me to an alien stillbirth and a piece of mystery meat found hanging in the cellar of an aristocrat's abandoned palace by rabid French revolutionaries. In a way, this lamb marinated in red wine and bay leaves is quintessential French cookery: take some scary-ass piece of flesh and mess with it until it tastes good. I mean, except for the tasting good part. That part didn't quite work out so well. Eric sensed a hint of Welch's grape juice, Julie a whiff of sour milk; I suppose we can be thankful we did not end the evening retching into the toilet.

Which is all to say, thank God for bleaders who make sure I don't pay for the lamb I destroy.

Hello, Everyone.

I'd just like to say how much I appreciate all the support you've been giving Julie these last six months. I didn't know why she started doing this. She's always been crazy. But she's lucky to have friends like all of you, and because of you all, I can now see she's doing the right thing.

Thank you,

Julie's mom

PS — Clarence, who fucking cares what you think, anyway.

September 1946
Bucks County, PA

"When I came to I was covered in blood. Poor Paulski was white as a sheet; he thought he'd lost his wife before he'd managed to get her."

"Now, this was yesterday? Julia, you could have postponed the ceremony a day or two, surely."

She just shook her head, grinning. "He kept trying to hold a cloth to my head, but all I could think of was my shoes. When I was thrown out of the car they'd been knocked clean off — and believe me, when you've got feet the size of mine, you don't take the loss of a pair of shoes lightly. 'Don't worry about me, Paul,' I shouted. 'Find my alligator pumps!'"

Paul watched her; surrounded by her friends and his, she was dressed in a brown-checked summer suit that made her legs seem to go on forever. She still had a bandage over her eye, but she somehow made it look just jaunty. She was radiant.

"Well, brother, you finally went ahead and did it, and about time, too." Charlie clapped him on the shoulder. He'd brought him another glass of champagne, though he didn't remember drinking the first one. "It's a good thing you didn't manage to kill her first."

"Yes, it is. Do you know, I feel downright giddy. Can't tell if it's the champagne, getting married, or averting death."

"A bit of all three, I imagine."

The cane he'd been given at the hospital kept getting hung up on the fieldstones of his brother's back patio, but it didn't matter; he felt like he could do an Irish jig. Julie had Fanny in stitches; even Julie's sourpuss of a father was cracking a smile. "Look at her, Charlie. Just think I almost passed her up."

"Aaah, don't worry about that. Just be glad you eventually got it through your thick old skull."

Paul caught Julie's eye, and she gifted him with a broad, glorious smile. "I'll drink to that."

Flaming Crepes!

I t began around the first of April — a throbbing in my head and in the lower depths of my belly, not so much painful as just implacable. Also familiar. The more immediate problems of shopping and cooking, the less ambiguous objectives of the Project, had drowned out this older, more intangible ticking for a while. But as that dreaded zero-bedecked day drew close, my biological clock would no longer be ignored.

"Maybe we should have a baby."

"What? You want a baby? Now?"

We were eating Wolfman Jack Burgers, which was what Eric always made for Eric's Spicy Thursday. The institution of Eric's Spicy Thursday was conceived as a respite from the rigors and creaminess of *MtAoFC*. After all, Eric and I are Texans, and we had never gone so long with so few jalapenos. Wolfman Jack Burgers are the invention of a particularly fantastic burger joint in Austin called Hut's. Eric made a version of them with green chiles, Monterey Jack cheese, sour cream, bacon, and mayonnaise. Once, long before the Project, Eric fed a Wolfman Jack

Burger to a friend of his from college who had not eaten meat in three years. His friend vomited for two days straight, which is the kind of thing that happens to you when you do something stupid like not eating meat. Anyway, we were enjoying them.

"Well, someday. And you know what all the doctors say. It might not be so easy for me."

"I know. But now? We don't have any money. You're doing the Project, and —"

"You do realize I'm going to turn thirty in two weeks, right? Do you know how much harder it gets to get pregnant after thirty?"

"No. How much?"

"I don't know. Harder. And I have a stupid *syndrome.*" I lifted my plate off my lap and took it to the kitchen. "Do we have any more burgers?"

"The patties are in the oven. Well, I think we should wait until the Project's over to talk about it."

"Right. We'll just keep waiting and waiting and waiting, while my *syndrome* makes me fat and hairy and disgusting, and then I'll just *die.* Can we get a dog, at least?"

"A *dog?* How are we going to take care of a dog? We can hardly take care of ourselves! Julie, this is not what Spicy Thursday is for. You're supposed to be relaxing."

"But how *can* I relax? I can literally *hear* the ticking."

"You need to calm down."

Calm down. As *if.*

When I told Eric the next night that I was making crepes for the first time in my life, to serve atop a dish of creamed spinach, he'd promptly made himself a cheese and mayonnaise sandwich, predicting a midnight dinner. But it was, shockingly, a snap. The crepe batter is just eggs, milk, water, salt, flour, and melted butter, all thrown into a blender together. Including melting the butter without aid of a microwave, the whole process takes approximately four minutes. And if you ignore JC's direction to let the batter sit for two hours — which, needless to say, I did — the actual cooking isn't much more demanding. Or wasn't that first time, anyway. I got the skillet good and hot, wiped it down with a piece of bacon, poured in some crepe batter, and rotated the skillet around until the batter coated the bottom. I took a spatula and slipped it around the edges to loosen the crepe — and up it came! I attempted flipping it with my fingers. It tore, but I was not discouraged— "The first crepe is a trial one," says Julia. I wiped down the skillet with the bacon again, again poured in some batter, a bit more than last time. Again swirled the pan around briefly, loosened the rapidly browning crepe with the spatula. Flipped it over with my fingers.

"*Voila!* Crepe! I'm the king of the world!"

It was too easy to even talk about. By the time I got to my fourth crepe, I was flipping them over like I'd been born to it. And that night, I didn't think about turning thirty or my syndrome at all.

Nothing's that easy, though. I should have known.

The next week was crepe hell. I made sweet crepes and savory crepes, crepes with beaten egg white and crepes with yeast, crepes *farcies* and *roulées* and *flambées*. And over and over again, the crepes stuck. They burned, they shredded. When they did survive the skillet, they came out in the shapes of all the beasts of the forest.

One night Eric went out of town for a conference, and I invited Gwen and Sally over for a girls' crepe night. I should have known that the stars were aligned against me when, while making the crepe batter, the blender — which I have to set on top of the trashcan to use because of this whole big thing with inconveniently placed plugs and my blender's three-pronged pluggedness — hemorrhaged milk and water, making a total mess, and this after I had only just barely managed to make the apartment halfway presentable. But I've never been much good at heeding omens.

I cooked up some spinach and whipped up some Mornay sauce for the filling for the Gâteau de Crêpes — all seemed to be going fine. Sally arrived bearing Milky Way ice cream. While she walked around trying not to notice the piles of dirty clothes, thick layers of dust, and odor of stale kitty litter, I mashed up a cup of cream cheese in a bowl with salt, pepper, and an egg. Gwen showed up next and immediately got to work, as Gwen is apt to do, on the cocktails, while I minced a cup of mushrooms and sautéed them with some shallots in butter and oil. This got dumped into the cream-cheese mixture. All of this occurred without crisis, which is not to say it occurred *quickly*. It was nearly ten when I started actually making the crepes.

I heated the skillet; I rubbed it with a piece of bacon; I poured in batter; I rotated the pan to spread the batter around.

The crepe stuck to the skillet like it had been superglued.

Okay, okay. The first crepe is a trial one. Just start over.

I scraped the stuff out of the pan, washed it, reheated it, rubbed it with bacon, poured in the batter.

Which stuck like glue again.

If it had been just Eric around, I'm sure I would have collapsed into an angry obscenity-laced psychotic state — I suppose it's a good thing that I can be so myself around him. But I had to pretend to be a sane person in front of my friends, so I just gritted my teeth and started over *again*. For the third time, I did exactly the same thing, poured the batter into the hot pan — and lo and behold, it worked like a charm! In less than a minute I had a lovely browned crepe.

So after that I'm in the zone for a while, helped along by the vodka tonics and Marlboro Lights. I get probably four done without incident before the crepes start sticking again. Then I have to go through the whole scrape-and-wash deal a couple more times before I get going again.

Sally can stay up all night if one of her wide variety of Davids is involved, but the prospect of doing so in order to eat food with three kinds of cheese in it had by this point gotten her looking a little peaked. She was trying to be brave about it. I was supposed to make twenty-four crepes, but when I had sixteen by eleven o'clock, I decided to have pity on all of us and make do with what I had.

The Gâteau de Crêpes wound up beautifully, actually. I layered the crepes alternately with the spinach and the mushroom-and-cream-cheese stuff, spooned Mornay sauce over all of it, and re-heated the whole mess in the oven for a bit. While Mornay sauce makes for an odd British-looking beigy-ness, once the Gâteau was cut it was gorgeous, what with all the lines of green and gold and white. It was just too bad everyone was nearly asleep by the time that happened.

So it wasn't that the crepes never turned out; it was just that they turned out so *unpredictably*. Sometimes they would stick, sometimes they wouldn't. Three crepes might be the work of three minutes, the fourth another half hour. I started having anxious dreams about them. In one the entire staff of my office was having dinner together, along with my family and Buffy the Vampire Slayer. While I met with Mr. Kline and Nate and Buffy about a plan to fight the minions downstairs in the lobby, there to destroy the world, my mother was left to make crepe after crepe in the staff kitchen, hundreds and hundreds of them, until she was buried amid the piles of golden, feathery pancakes.

And as the week progressed the throbbing of my biological clock syncopated with my crepe anxiety until they formed one jazz rhythm. Because what if I got to the age of thirty without having learned to make a crepe? What would have been the point of this whole exercise then?

Next Spicy Thursday Eric decided to mix it up a bit. I was going to be quite late coming home from work, because of a press conference being held by my government agency, and Eric figured that since I seemed so anxious about things, perhaps he could ease my mind on one issue, at least, and get one of the *MtAoFC* recipes out of the way.

For his first Project cooking foray, my husband chose to make Foie de Veau Sauté avec Sauce Crème à la Moutarde and Épinards Gratinés au Fromage — that is, sautéed calf's liver with cream and mustard sauce and spinach gratinéed with cheese. He looked the recipes over and figured they couldn't be too hard — he estimated that it would take about forty minutes for him to complete both dishes. After work he went to an Eastern European butcher shop in Astoria and picked up the liver. Delayed though he was by the eight firemen in front of him, who would not stop razzing the butcher — *Where'd you go to butcher school? Hey, watch it, we don't like fingers in our meat. Don't listen to him, fingers have protein!* — still he made it home by a little after seven, in time to catch *BBC World News* with Mishal Husain (the world's sexiest news anchor, in Eric's opinion). There was no hurry with the food — I wouldn't be back home until 9:30 at the earliest. He figured he would start cooking at 8:30 and have everything done when I walked in the door. So he puttered around the house, reading periodicals and picking up dirty socks and such, until 8:40. He cleaned the spinach, and by 9:15 had begun to sauté it. But something didn't feel right. It dawned on him that he'd picked up the recipe in the middle, that he was supposed to boil the spinach and chop it before sautéing it. He frantically pulled the spinach out of the skillet and set some water to boil, just lighting the flame under it as I walked through the door, back from work, not much surprised by Eric's predicament.

By 10:30 or so the spinach had been boiled, drained, chopped, and sautéed. Eric added some cream and Swiss cheese to the mix, poured the spinach into a baking dish and sprinkled it with two tablespoons of bread crumbs and some more cheese. This went into the oven for half an hour. He moved on to the liver, seasoning the slices with salt and pepper, dredging them in flour, then tossing them into a hot pan to sauté in butter and oil. They were done in an instant, before Eric had quite gotten his mind around the idea that he had to make a sauce for it. His head was beginning to spin. He added cream to the pan and let it simmer a good minute or so before rereading the recipe and realizing he was meant to reduce a cup of beef broth in there first. It wasn't until then that I began to hear "Damn! Damn!"s emanating from the kitchen.

"It's okay," I called in, prone on the couch and very nearly comatose. "It'll be fine." I had no idea what he'd done wrong, and did not care. I just wanted dinner and bed.

At eleven o'clock he decided there was nothing more to be done to the sauce. He took it off the heat, stirred in some butter and some mustard, and called it liver sauce.

We ate our liver and spinach while watching the right honorable gentlemen of the British House of Commons yelling at each other about the Iraq invasion on C-SPAN. And it was damned good. It was good because it was liver and spinach with cheese, but mostly it was good because I didn't have to make it. Sometimes I want to beat Eric's head repeatedly against a sharp rock, but other times he knows just the right thing to do to make me forget about turning thirty — lull me into a comatose state on the couch with British news shows, then dose me with offal.

I am feeling much the failure these days. It is not turning thirty so much as it is the eventual turning forty, the fear that I will go another decade without doing a goddamned thing worth doing. What do I have to show for the last one, after all? A husband — a divine husband, it must be said, which would be a significant accomplishment if not for the fact that by all rights he ought to divorce me — and the Julie/Julia Project.

One thing about blogging is that it gives you a blank check for whining. When Eric simply couldn't stand another moment of it, I could take my drone to cyberspace. There I could always find a sympathetic ear.

> If you think you're old at 30, just wait until you're 70 like I am — HOW DID I GET THIS OLD? But I love every minute, especially my wonderful friends who go back to grade school days!! My husband is a treasure, too — a perfect man in all respects — so you and I are very lucky "girls," Julie. And I know you'll think I'm really weird, but I loved turning 40 and 50 and 60 and 70 because I have been able to keep learning and doing all sorts of interesting things. The older I get, the more I can get away with, too. . . . I wish I could live long enough to read all the books you will write. Love, GrannyKitty

See? They loved me out here! They just wanted me to be happy, and to blog and blog and blog. They understood my pain!

> Whenever I get in an age-related funk, a good friend always reminds me, "THESE are the good old days." He is right, in ten years I will probably look back and think my life is just hunky-dory right now. Thirty was wonderful; my husband was a great man (he died ten years ago), I had options, job possibilities, etc. I am looking forward to fifty, who knows. Good luck, Julie, with pulling yourself out of your funk. . . . — Cindy

Gosh. I suppose Cindy had a point. Things *could* be worse, I guess. . . .

> Julie, on my 30th birthday I was living in a homeless shelter. I made a homemade pizza for the other residents. That was my 30th. All I had to show for my life was that I didn't have kids

and hadn't dragged them through the hell my life had become.

Ten years later, I had several years as a journalist/editor under my belt, and my family (who I'd avoided like the plague 10
years earlier) threw me a surprise birthday party.

No matter how crappy it seems now ... it gets better.
Somehow, it always gets better. Hang in there, kid. — Chris

Great. So now I'm a fat failure of a thirty-year-old *and* a pa-
thetically self-involved twit. Maybe this online whining isn't such
a great deal after all.

The other right thing that Eric did was shell out a hundred bucks
for tickets to a staged reading of *Salomé,* which we went to see
the night before my birthday.

Now, I understand that most people would consider it an act of
unconscionable cruelty to force one's wife to trek out on a cold
and damp April night to watch a reading of possibly the least suc-
cessful play in history. That's because most people are not recovering theater geeks whose idea of a good time is watching Al
Pacino flouncing about on a stage playing Herod, King of the
Jews, as Jerry Stiller. Also, it's because most people have not discovered the paragon that is David Strathairn.

The best job I ever had was actually an internship at a nonprofit
theater organization that paid fifty bucks a week. One of the things
that was so very good about it was that I was always getting free
tickets, because Theater Is Dead, except for the occasional hit musical version of *My Two Dads* or whatever, so butts in seats are a real
commodity. Nine times out of ten the plays were crap, but I look
back on them with fondness, and sometimes even glean advantage
from them, as in: "Oh my God! That red-headed guy from the pre-
maturely canceled Joss Whedon outer space–western series was in

that godawful thing we saw at the Belasco with Kristen Cheno-
weth that was open for about a week and a half!"

Now it's eight years later. There are no free tickets anymore,
and in addition to being married and thirty and a secretary at a
government agency and engaged in an entirely senseless and
probably emotionally damaging quest to cook every recipe in a
forty-year-old cookbook, I also have not been to a play in ages.

The other great thing about this internship, by the way, was
that I got to meet famous people — well, famous-for-a-theater-
geek people, anyway. Once, I was stage-managing a big-deal play
reading, and the guy directing managed to snag David Strathairn,
an actor I'd seen in several high-minded independent films, as well
as in *The Firm,* as Tom Cruise's brother, and in *Dolores Claiborne,*
as the father who makes his daughter give him a hand job on a
ferry. I'd only been in New York for a month or two, so I didn't
know from celebrities. All I knew was that I would be spending
two days in the same room with a wonderful, somewhat famous
actor, and that after the reading a party was planned, to which
everyone had been asked to bring "a little something."

It was my first — though not my last — genuine attempt at
star fucking, and I was at a disadvantage. I was neither bleached
and waxed and giggly, nor thin and well put together in the manner of a William Morris personal assistant. I did know I'd have to
forgo my overalls and Ecuadoran wool sweaters — all that awful
college stuff I hadn't yet had the sense to get rid of — for sleek
professional wear, dark, respectable, but slightly clingy stuff that
doesn't suggest sex until you've already got him thinking that
way. What I didn't know was that that stuff made me look kind
of like a William Morris personal assistant — probably the last
sort of person David wanted to see one more of, but oh well.

I played it cool. I handed out scripts and took notes and sat at
the table with all the actors, listening to them rehearse. I spoke
only rarely, when I was sure I had something subtly amusing and
self-evidently intelligent to say, and then I used a voice under-

stated but clear, maybe just a bit smoky. Also, I stared. And I'm not going to apologize for it, either. There was no horseshit, no looking away and tittering, not me, boy. I was bold. I let him have it — all the power of my quiet but searing sexuality, right between the eyes. I stared when he was rehearsing, and when he was taking a break from rehearsing. I stared when I handed him his sides, and I stared, most of all, when I had to pass him in the conveniently narrow halls of the old church the theater organization was housed in.

So okay. David Strathairn is a fabulously talented and gorgeous minor movie star, he probably gets this kind of thing all the time. There are lots of starey-eyed sluts in the world, and many of them are shaped more like Gwyneth Paltrow than I am. But I had something those other girls didn't have. I had Spiced Pecan Cake with Pecan Icing.

I got my recipe for Spiced Pecan Cake with Pecan Icing from the great Paul Prudhomme, so of course it is divine and lust-inducing. First you coarsely chop pecans for the cake batter. (At the time of this incident I owned nothing approximating a nut chopper, and so accomplished this step with a large rubber mallet.) Roast them on a baking sheet for ten minutes. Sprinkle with a mixture of melted butter, brown sugar, cinnamon, and nutmeg. Roast another ten minutes. Add vanilla, creating a pleasant hiss and whoosh of sweet-smelling steam. Roast for a final five minutes. Chop pecans for the icing, finely this time. It goes on like this.

(Yes, it is a royal pain in the neck. But there is something intensely erotic in making elaborate, nearly impossible food for someone you'd like to have sex with.)

(In my experience.)

(Okay, I'll be honest — I detect more than a whiff of masochism here. I'm not entirely comfortable with this revelation about my character, but there it is.)

I finished the sucker a little after two a.m., was in bed by two-thirty. I drifted off in an exhausted, sugary sweat, the taste of icing still on my lips. Just what I'd taste when David, after one bite, took me in his arms and kissed me with all the consuming passion that Spiced Pecan Cake with Pecan Icing can kindle in a man's soul.

When I awoke, I clothed myself in a freshly pressed, black Banana Republic suit with a draping, mannish cut of the sort that would hang so much more beguilingly off the frame of someone shaped like Gwyneth Paltrow. My statuesque three layers of cake wore only a gauzy layer of plastic wrap.

The day passed in an anxious blur — in my memory it's as if I stepped straight off the subway into the shabby library where the postreading party was in full swing.

David was sipping from a plastic cup of cheap red wine and surveying the buffet table. I held my breath as his knife hovered a moment over the store-bought apple pies and pans of Duncan Hines brownies before plunging deep into the center of my Spiced Pecan Cake with Pecan Icing. I stood at a discreet distance near the far corner of the table, nearly panting as he cut a thick slice, lifted it onto a plate, and sank a plastic fork through the voluptuous layer of icing to the moist cake beneath.

His eyes grew wide as he slid the cake into his mouth, then narrowed to slits as he swallowed. He moaned, softly. *"Delicious*. . . . Julie, where did you *get* this?"

It was the first time he had spoken my name.

"I made it," I replied, simply.

Our eyes locked. And he saw that this Spiced Pecan Cake with Pecan Icing could be a mere taste of ecstasy to come. In that moment, David Strathairn fell in love with me, a little.

But David Strathairn is a fine, upright man, a man who loves his wife, a man who would never take advantage of the young and innocent girl he (quite mistakenly) took me for. So no, he did not take me into his arms and cover my face with tiny angel kisses. He did not press me down onto the table laden with crappy merlot and celery sticks, did not slide those long, strong fingers under my Banana Republic suit and blouse to the soft, sweet flesh at the base of my spine. Instead, he whispered, in a voice grown husky under the weight of suppressed desires, "This. Is. *Wonderful.*"

And took another bite of cake.

I have never hidden from Eric the culinary pass I made at David Strathairn, and he, to his everlasting credit, has managed — for the most part, anyway — not to resent me for it. He even knew that when I was so near the end of my rope, what with the frozen pipes and the dozen leg-of-lamb recipes awaiting me and the horrid job and, most of all, the whole turning-thirty thing, I just needed an emergency Strathairn shot. So he got us the tickets (even though Al Pacino was one arrogant son of a bitch to charge fifty bucks for tickets to a *reading,* for God's sake, and one that would almost certainly suck) just because David Strathairn was in it and his wife was in love with David Strathairn. Which is why Eric is the most generous and selfless husband a woman could have.

Getting to watch Marisa Tomei do the dance of the seven veils did make it all go down easier for him.

I blame Eric. It was only because of him that I started cooking in the first place — I was a picky kid, but he was the most mysterious and beautiful boy in school, and I would cook anything to impress him, no matter how weird. It didn't take long for things to get twisted.

Quail in Rose Petal Sauce was the first really bad sign.

It was the summer before I went off to college, Eric and I had just started dating, and the biggest terror of my life was that as soon as I headed up to the Northeast for school, he'd get snapped up by some cute blonde model-looking girl — actually, I was pretty sure one particular blonde already had her eye on him. On one of our dates we went to see *Like Water for Chocolate,* which when you're under the age of twenty and madly in lust can be a fairly persuasive film. I had already read the book, and after we'd gotten out of the theater and I jumped him in the parking lot, and after he drove me home and I practically swallowed the poor boy before finally getting ahold of myself and saying good night, I went back to my room and, entirely unable to sleep, pulled it down off the shelf.

The book *Like Water for Chocolate* is interspersed with recipes that I at that time had no way of knowing were largely literary, i.e., fictional. As I flipped idly through the volume, it came to me: I'll make quail in rose petal sauce! That's it! He won't be able to keep his hands off me, and he'll never think about that blonde again!

The hormones had me addled, I guess.

I used roses from a bin at the 7-Eleven and papaya instead of pitaya. When I tasted the sauce, it seemed pretty inedible to me, but I figured I was so picky I might be totally wrong, so I called my brother in to give a second opinion. The look on his face was enough to make me burst spontaneously into tears. But Eric couldn't keep his hands off me that night, even if I did taste like pizza instead of delectable game birds, and it turned out he never really did think too much about that blonde.

In coming years there were further disasters as well as, eventually, some modest successes. My first gumbo was aborted after a plastic spoon died in the roux, and the barbecued pastrami didn't work out so well, but by the time I graduated from college I could turn out a mean chicken-fried steak.

Somewhere along the way, I discovered that in the physical act of cooking, especially something complex or plain old hard to handle, dwelled unsuspected reservoirs of arousal both gastronomic and sexual. If you are not one of us, the culinarily depraved, there is no way to explain what's so darkly enticing about eviscerating beef marrowbones, chopping up lobster, baking a three-layer pecan cake, and doing it for someone else, offering someone hard-won gustatory delights in order to win pleasures of another sort. Everyone knows there are foods that are sexy to eat. What they don't talk about so much is foods that are sexy to make. But I'll take a wrestling bout with recalcitrant brioche dough over being fed a perfect strawberry any day, foreplay-wise.

(Julia too started learning to cook because of a man — Paul Child was quite a gourmand when she met him, and she didn't know a thing about food. For a while the war flung them together, but then of course the war ended. Maybe Julia was afraid she couldn't keep him, and that's why she began cooking him all sorts of crazy things. I'm particularly impressed by her attempt at calves' brains in red wine sauce. She had no idea what she was doing, of course, and apparently it turned out just awful — nasty pale shreds in a purplish, lumpy sauce. He married her anyway. I say "anyway," but I'd bet a dollar he married her *because* she was the sort of woman to try to seduce him with brains, however badly prepared — *because* she was willing to risk repulsing him to win him. How utterly illogical of her, and yet how utterly right.)

In honor of his performance as John the Baptist in a $50-a-ticket staged reading of Oscar Wilde's *Salomé,* I baked David Strathairn absurdly complicated pecan-cornmeal cookies, the recipe for which I got from Martha Stewart. Unfortunately, Martha's recipes, though suitably complex, fall a tad short if you're looking for aphrodisiac cooking, perhaps only because everything about a Martha recipe, from the font it's printed in to the call for sanding sugar, with appended notes on where to find such a thing, simply *screams* Martha. Wildcat though she may be in bed, for all I know, Martha just isn't someone you necessarily want in your head when you're trying to seduce someone. I would rather have made something from the Book, but Julia isn't much for stalker food — neat nibbles you can leave on a doorstep or send backstage with an usher without risking breakage or messiness. For stalker food, Martha Stewart is the woman to go to.

I can't imagine anyone — a few of the more repressive Islamic societies aside — who would consider baking an act of adultery. Still, for Eric, knowing what he knew of my proclivities, watching me roll out thin layers of cornmeal dough, sprinkle them with chopped pecans, cinnamon, and melted butter, then lay another layer of dough on top, and repeat over and over with infinite patience, must have been a little bit like noticing I'd gotten a bikini wax and a tight red dress the day before leaving for some business convention in Dallas. He didn't do anything but roll his eyes and grumble with careful good humor, but he knew what I was doing. I arranged to meet Eric at the theater after work, then got there early, skipping out on work and rushing off into the chill rain, not because I was doing anything illicit, exactly, but because I didn't want Eric to have to witness me sheepishly slipping the girl in the ticket booth the plate of cookies with the flirtatious note attached, asking if someone could take these backstage for Mr. Strathairn, I was an *acquaintance* of his.

As it turned out, though, all this was a lot of fuss for not much payback. You see, the problem with John the Baptist in *Salomé* is that it's just about the least sexy role in existence. You'd think a part that features being crawled all over by a lithe nymphomaniac would be hot, but the only opportunities David was given were for solemn intoning and hair-gel abuse. It was brutal.

So we were sitting there in the dark watching David intone and Al kvetch and Marisa lithely convulse, and all this excess erotic buzz I'd built up with my cookie baking was spinning around with nowhere to go. My stomach was growling because I hadn't had any dinner yet, and I found my mind wandering. My mind wandered, specifically, to liver.

Now, this is going to be a stretch for some people, but I believe that calves' liver is the single sexiest food that there is. This is a conclusion I've come to relatively recently, because like almost everyone else on the planet, I've spent most of my life hating and despising liver. The reason people despise liver is that to eat it you must submit to it — just like you must submit to a really stratospheric fuck. Remember when you were nineteen and you went at it like it was a sporting event? Well, liver is the opposite of that.

With liver you've got to will yourself to slow down. You've got to give yourself over to everything that's a little repulsive, a little scary, a little just *too much* about it. When you buy it from the butcher, when you cook it in a pan, when you eat it, slowly, you never can get away from the feral fleshiness of it. Liver forces you to access taste buds you didn't know you had, and it's hard to open yourself to it. I got to thinking that it was a shame Eric had served his liver to me on that particular night, when I was too tired to really take it in — it was a waste of its potential.

When the reading ended — finally — the audience, stretching, slightly dazed, started filing out of the theater, but I remained in my seat. Eric stood over me, palpably irritated by the giddiness he felt coming off me in waves. "I guess you want to wait for him to come out?"

But I wasn't listening to him. "Is there a decent grocery store around here, do you think?"

"What?"

"I was just thinking about that liver you made me last week. That was really good."

"Oh yeah?" Eric didn't know where my thoughts were tending, but it was enough that I'd said I liked his cooking. He was sensitive about that. He beamed. "I'm sure we can get some somewhere, if we hurry. It's early yet."

And so we left the theater, stepping back out into a warmer night. The freezing rain had stopped, and suddenly in the air was a softness, as if spring might someday come after all. We walked toward the subway, setting a good pace. As we came alongside a man in a forest-green Polartec jacket, I turned to him, too anxious for some liver to be shy. "Excuse me — do you know —"

It was David Strathairn. He held a pecan cornmeal cookie in one gloved hand, and there were crumbs in his scraggly beard. He had a distracted, faraway look in his eye. "I'm sorry?"

"Oh — Mr. Strathairn — I'm so sorry to bother you. We just saw your show. It was — great."

He waved his cookie dismissively in the air, then took a bite of it. "Oh, thanks." He looked at me, and a curious expression blossomed. "You were asking me something?"

"Oh, just if you knew of a grocery store around here."

"Let's see. . . ." He looked up the street with the hand that held his cookie stretched out before him as if to point. He appeared distracted, though, and kept glancing at me with a searching eye. "Two blocks up and one over, I think."

"Thanks so much. And congratulations."

I took Eric's hand and we walked on. "You should have told him who you were. He clearly recognized you."

I kissed him. "No time. I need me some liver for my birthday."

One very good and simple recipe for calves' liver is Foie de Veau à la Moutarde. Just dredge some thick slices of liver in flour and briefly sauté them in hot butter and oil, just a minute or so on each side. Set the seared slices aside while you beat together three tablespoons of mustard, minced shallots, parsley, garlic, pepper, and the bit of fat from the sauté pan, which makes a sort of creamy paste. Schmear this over the liver slices, then coat the slices in fresh bread crumbs. If you have a husband who is mad for you, you can probably get him to whip you up some good fresh bread crumbs in the Cuisinart. Once the liver is well coated with the crumbs, place it in a baking pan, drizzle it with melted butter, and stick it under the broiler for about a minute a side. That's all there is to it. The crunch of the mustard-spiked crust somehow brings the unctuous smooth richness of the liver into sharp relief. It's like the silky soul of steak. You have to close your eyes, let the meat melt on your tongue, into your corpuscles.

This is the liver I ate on the last night of my twentysomething life. It was a good way to end the decade.

* * *

Someone who doesn't know the first thing about the sexuality of cooking wrote this about English TV cook Nigella Lawson: "Sex and domesticity. This is the inspired coupling that is Nigella's invention, a world far removed from the dithering, high-pitched admonitions of Julia Child."

I read this sentence, which is benighted and offensive to me in about a dozen different ways, in an article from *Vanity Fair*. Because *Vanity Fair* publishes photos of its contributors in the front of the magazine, I know that it was written by a woman with a ropy neck who's had too many glamour treatments, and on the evidence of that sentence alone I would put down good money that she wouldn't know a beef bourguignon if it was dropped on her head.

It was the morning of my thirtieth birthday; I sat on the toilet with a foam rubber dental tray crammed into my mouth, drooling excess tooth-bleach. (It had so far not been the best of mornings.) So at first I thought I might be overreacting, with these unbidden fantasies of dumping large chunks of beef onto some poor journalist. But luckily Isabel reads *Vanity Fair* too, and I got this e-mail later that very morning:

Did you read that shitty little piece on Nigella in VF? Did the whole thing stink vaguely of (1) calling Nigella fat many times, quietly, (2) really, really rotten insinuations created by tabloidic placement of blurbs not actually MADE in the copy, and (3) the vaguest hint of anti-Semitism? Yes, IT DID. AND the JC slam didn't go unnoticed, either. I can't believe the trash. I'm writing a letter. Ms. Ropy-Neck WISHES she could get half the nooky and general joy in life that Nigella clearly gets.

Amen, thought I. And I thought that Nigella and Julia, Isabel and I knew what sex was really about. We knew sex was about playing with your food and fucking up the sauce from time to time. Sex was about the Spiced Pecan Cake with Pecan Icing. Sex was about learning to stop worrying and love the liver.

One of my favorite JC stories comes from a letter her husband Paul wrote to his brother, Charlie. He tells of sitting in their kitchen in Paris while she boiled cannelloni. She reached *into the boiling water* — he mentions this astounding feat only in passing, as if it were the most natural thing in the world for his wife to boil herself — and said with a yelp as she pulled out the pasta, "Wow! These damn things are as hot as a stiff cock."*

I am no Julia Child, though, and my fingers are not asbestos. This I learned when I tried on my thirtieth birthday, not very optimistically, to regain the title of Crepe Queen.

When Julia makes crepes on her television shows, she just flings them up into the air with a sharp pull on the skillet, not unlike the maneuver she uses to roll omelets. I had just assumed that this was a lunatic notion. But after half an hour of shrieking and cursing, scraping up stuck crepes and tossing them in the trash, I stood before my stove, sucking on my fingertips, and thought, *Well, why not?* What could happen, right?

"Eric! Oh my God, Eric! Come quick!"

Eric had gotten used to hiding out during crepe-making sessions, and he came around the corner into the kitchen only reluctantly, sure he was about to be sucked into a fit of pique. "Yes, honey?"

"Watch *this!*"

And so Eric stood by my side as with one decisive gesture I flipped my perfect golden crepe *into midair and back into the skillet*.

"Holy shit, Julie!"

"I know!" I slid the crepe onto a plate, poured out another ladleful of batter.

"That's amazing!"

---

*Excerpted from a letter from Paul Child to his brother, Charles, 1949.

I jerked the skillet's handle, and again, the perfect crepe flipped. "I am a *goddess!*"

"You sure are."

"You ain't seen nothing yet." I slid the last crepe out of the pan and poured in some cognac and Grand Marnier. I let it heat up for a minute, then poured it atop my beautiful crepes and, with my NASCAR Bic lighter, set them aflame, then crowed, shaking my hand to extinguish a singed hair or two.

My husband cooed as he dug into his plate of delicious flambéed crepes. If there's a sexier sound on this planet than the person you're in love with cooing over the crepes you made for him, I don't know what it is. And that blows Botox and ropy necks all to hell.

November 1948
Le Havre, France

She blew a lazy cloud of cigarette smoke that melted into the mist off the water. "Well, it seemed like a good idea at the time."

"It was a good idea. I mean, it is." He paced the pier fretfully, staring up at the belly of the ship as if he could lift his car out of it through sheer force of will. "But it's been nearly two hours. You'd have thought, after all that infernal paperwork —"

"Paul, I was teasing you. Of course it was a good idea. We couldn't leave the Flash! Take it easy. Look, it's barely dawn. We have plenty of time. And it's simply beautiful right here."

Paul gave his wife a sour sideways look. "You must be the first person in history to call Le Havre beautiful."

Julie grinned. "So what if I am? I'm in France for the first time. I'm happy! And no manner of gloom-and-doom out of you is going to change that." She stood and laced her hand in his. He had long ago gotten used to how she towered over him; it made him feel powerful, her height, like one half of a very dynamic duo indeed.

"Look — there she is!" He pointed as the Buick was at last lifted out of the hold by an enormous crane. It swung slightly in its cradle of chains and rubber, the morning light glittering on the drops of condensation scattered across its cobalt skin. It alit on the pier with a gentle bump, and the dockworkers scurried to free it.

"Now, you see there? Can you tell me that isn't beautiful?"

"It's beautiful. Now let's get going. We've got a lot of miles before Paris."

"We are going to eat, aren't we? I could eat a horse!"

When he kissed her, his lips made a playful smacking noise, and he laughed. He was finally going to be showing his France to Julie.

mèère*Julie Powell*

"Darling, when have I ever starved you? There's a wonderful place in Rouen, we'll stop there. You are going to eat a real sole meunière, with real Dover sole, and I guarantee you, your life is going to change!" He came around to the passenger door and opened it for her.

"Oh, that's all right, I don't expect a fish to change my life, so long as it changes this growl in my stomach." She climbed in, folding up her legs with the insectile grace of someone used to fitting into spaces too small for her. She rolled down the window and stuck her elbow over the edge, giving the old Buick the kind of hearty pat you'd give to a favorite horse. "Hah hah!" she cried, as Paul got in and started the ignition. "We're off!"

Time to Move
to Weehawken

I'm going to bring on a nuclear attack at Times Square with these goddamned shoes, I swear. They're the shoes I was wearing on September 11, and I had to stand in line at a Payless on Sixth Avenue for a good part of an hour to buy some Keds knockoffs so my feet wouldn't be bloody stumps by the time I got back to Brooklyn. They're the shoes with which I trashed the office of the gynecologist who had the misfortune to be the third medical professional in a month to tell me I was pushing thirty and had a syndrome and needed to get knocked up quick if I was going to do it at all. And now this.

One of the few nice things I can say about my cubicle is that it's near a large window, which is why I didn't notice at first. I was in the middle of performing a spot-on (if I do say so myself) impersonation of a powerful and contemptible person — whose name I can't mention because my government agency would sue me — for the amusement of my few Democrat colleagues, when Nate called to us from down the hall. "Hey! Have you got power down there?" I glanced down at my screen, which was dark, and the phone, which for the first time ever was not blinking at all.

"No. Wow."

Next thing we knew we were all grabbing the flashlights our government agency had given each of us, being rounded up and sent toddling off down pitch-dark halls to the stairwells. We New Yorkers are getting to be hardened evacuation veterans, let me tell you. We laughed and gossiped and speculated idly about terrorist actions as we trundled in a galumphing sort of spiral down the stairs.

Then again, maybe we're not such experts as all that, because down on the sidewalks a gentle sort of chaos reigned; we knew the whole nearest-exit routine backward and forward, but that congregation point part had eluded us. Other buildings had evacuated too — it looked like electricity was out for a few blocks all around. There was no smoke, no sirens, no wounded people. People milled about, looking a little warm but not too astonished, trying to get through to people on their cell phones and BlackBerries.

Some of us from the office — maybe two dozen all told — hung out across the street, under a sculpture in the shape of a giant red cube with a hole through the middle of it, for twenty minutes or so. Brad from the development department started up a list of people accounted for, though that was a bit of a lost cause. One might consider this the responsibility not of Brad from development but of the president of the government agency. Mr. Kline, though, didn't make it as far as the congregation point. Instead he hopped into a livery cab, pulling along his favorite program manager, who is twenty years old and gets paid one dollar a year for *tax purposes* because his father contributed like umpteen *million* dollars to the New York Republican party. According to later rumor, this program manager then swept our beloved president up to his father's home on Park Avenue to safely spend the night. That's what our president was doing while his colleagues stood stranded under a piece of bad corporate sculpture, and I'm so getting sued for this, but you know what? Screw 'em if they can't take a joke.

And to be fair, there wasn't a hell of a lot our president could have done, anyway, except demonstrate that he gave a shit about the fact that his secretaries were going to have to walk to the outer boroughs in excruciating shoes. I stood around awhile avoiding the obvious fact of this trek as my colleagues peeled off in pairs and trios. All the good-looking, supercilious Harvard grad junior planners of course had cute tiny apartments in the East Village and could easily amble back on home. Brad and Kimmy were headed up Broadway to the Queensboro Bridge to Queens. I knew I should probably go with them, but I couldn't bear it. So I stood around alone with a few thousand strangers, thinking about my feet.

(Also — and I didn't mention this before because it's rather embarrassing — but under my too-tight dress I was also wearing an extremely binding corset/girdle sort of a thing. I had bought it in college for — God, this part is *really* embarrassing — a musical theater troupe I was in, because we were performing — this is *mortifying* — "Like a Virgin." So it's a "Like a Virgin" kind of a corset, a black lace bullet-bra thing. I used to wear it because it was kind of sexy in a silly sort of a way, and as a theater geek semireformed I was into the retro bullet-boob look. Since the Project, though, I've been wearing it because it's the only way I can squeeze into a lot of my clothes.)

I guess sometimes sheer discomfort and sartorial dread are the mothers of invention, because as I stood there staring disconsolately at the cute bows on my excruciating navy blue faille pumps, my brain began to churn, winching up some bit of deeply buried information.

F . . . it's F something . . . eff eff eff . . . ffffee . . . FERRY!!! There's a FERRY here somewhere, I'm SURE of it!

And so there is — ferry service directly from South Street

Seaport in lower Manhattan to Hunter's Point in Long Island City, a mere dozen blocks from our apartment. It's a ten-minute ride, quite pleasant really, especially on a breezy summer evening when all the lights have gone out in New York, and a strange gloaming hush has fallen over the city.

Really, it was only the three-hour wait in an unrelenting press of angry Queensers that made me wonder about the five dollars they charged me for the trip.

The posted charge was $3.50, but that's not what the woman at the entrance ramp stuffing bills into a plastic I Heart NY bag said. A good day for the ferry business, apparently. Or maybe just for one woman with an I Heart NY bag, some brass cojones, and a dream. On the other hand, maybe the extra buck fifty was for the entertainment — sort of a waterside musical chairs sort of a thing. For three hours, a diminutive Latina woman stood on a bench like a camp director, with her hands cupped around her mouth, yelling things like:

"Queens!!! Queens, slip SIX!"

"Everybody going to Queens, Slip TWO, slip TWO!"

"Slip TWELVE. Queens, slip TWELVE!"

We'd obediently shuffle back and forth from one slip to another, secretaries of every color and creed, shoulder to shoulder, our shoes in our hands, at least one of us gasping in a stupid too-tight corset, and just when we'd gotten to whatever slip the small Latina woman had just called out, a boat would arrive — bound for Weehawken. Big bald burly security men would appear out of nowhere, screaming, "Move back! Move *back!*" and Queensers would part like a howling Red Sea before a neat file of Wall Street analysts and soccer moms. Why did this woman do this to us? Because watching thousands of exhausted working-class people lumbering around like confused cattle is fun, I guess.

The Weehawken ferry arrived, I kid you not, every five minutes. I timed it. It's the kind of thing you do while you're being herded about by a suddenly empowered ferry toll collector for three hours. The population of Weehawken Township, as of the 2000 census, is 13,501. This means, by my calculations, that every man, woman, and child of Weehawken was in lower Manhattan on August 14 — twice.

All kidding aside. I've no ambitions to the office of Homeland Security, believe me. But Mr. Secretary, sir? It seems to me that perhaps it might have occurred to someone sometime during the past two years that ferries might come in awfully useful in Manhattan for evacuation in the event of, I don't know, a *nuclear explosion* or something. Are bullhorns such a strain on the nation's security budget? Have they just decided that everyone who doesn't have a livery cab waiting for them at the time is expendable?

One sort of fun thing did happen, though. We were being pushed back in a crush to make way for another load of fleeing Weehawken citizens — I think it was at Slip Five. There were, of course, plenty of reasons in this situation why someone might be saying "excuse me" over and over, so it did not at first occur to me that the woman a few bodies over to my left might be saying it to me. But she kept on saying it, with increasing urgency, until I looked up. She was looking right at me, but I couldn't figure out what I could be doing to attract her attention — I was too far away from her to be stepping on her foot.

"Um, yes?"

"Are you Julie Powell? Of the Julie/Julia Project? I saw your picture in *Newsday*."

(I know, I know, I didn't mention that I had my picture in *Newsday*. It's just such an awkward thing to bring up. How does one broach the subject of being photographed cooking dinner in one's crappy Long Island City apartment, without sounding like a vain, pretentious jerk? Anyway, it was no big deal, really. Sort of a fluke.)

"Oh. Yes, I'm Julie. Hi!"

"I just wanted to say I'm a big fan. And I live in Long Island

City too!" The girl was young, pretty, probably had a much better job than I did. She seemed nice.

"Oh, thanks! Thank you."

All the secretaries around us were beginning to take notice of this conversation; they peered at me curiously. My goodness — I was a celebrity! It felt great. Unfortunately, I didn't have anything else to say. I just nodded some more and grinned vacuously, and the next time we got ushered to another slip, I unobtrusively shifted to another part of the crowd. I'd be a really terrible famous person.

But so that was nice. Creepy, but nice. And the ferry ride itself was, once it finally happened, most pleasant. I sat while around me people took pictures with their digital cameras and pointed and just stared at the uncharacteristic quiet beauty of both shores. Getting off the train at Hunter's Point, I caught a ride home from a man who was offering rides to people going in the direction of Astoria, which was so generous and thoughtful that I almost forgot about the woman with the I Heart NY bag taking the opportunity of a state of emergency to shaft a bunch of secretaries. We drove down Jackson Avenue with the nice man, his pretty dark-haired girlfriend — whose mother was stuck underground in the subway, can you *imagine?* — and a seventy-year-old woman with bottle-job red hair and a thick Queens accent who probably sent me a memorial design at some point, who was saying she'd heard the blackout had affected the whole eastern seaboard, and was certain it must be terrorists. The man dropped me off right in front of the apartment.

The usually barren streets of Long Island City were teeming with people, all trudging with the discouraged air of folks who have miles to go before they sleep. Inside the apartment, a reddish afternoon dusk reigned. Eric's boss was sitting on our sofa, flipping through a magazine. He wasn't going to be making it to Westchester that night.

Shoes were kicked off into the closet, dress — after a sticky moment or two when it seemed Eric would not be able to work the zipper — was peeled off. Stupid bullet-bra corset was painfully unhooked and thrown in the damned trash. Stockings were balled up and stuffed into the sock drawer, and a pair of shorts and T-shirt donned. I was smelly and hot and hungry, and I thought I'd never felt so profoundly comfortable in my life.

I have always loved a disaster. When Hurricane Agnes blew into Brooklyn, I bought canned goods and bottled water and went down to the boardwalk to watch the ecstatic waves crash up over the railings while everybody hooted in glee but for the Orthodox Jewish family, who bent devoutly over their small leather books, rocking on their heels in prayer. Although I hate winter, I love the first big blizzard of the year — love dashing about town before the storm clouds, stocking up on groceries and booze, sharing delightfully apprehensive exchanges with shopkeepers about the latest news on the Weather Channel. If the big storm hits during Christmas that year, while we're visiting family in Texas, I feel an obscure pang of regret at missing it.

I even, God forgive me, felt something of this anxious excitement on September 11, as I wandered midtown in my cheap Keds knockoffs looking for a place to donate my O negative blood. When the wolves stormed the city, I thought, set on ravaging the women getting their nails done at the Korean manicurists, the confused businessmen carrying their jackets over one arm, trying their cell phones again and again and again, the strong-willed among us would have to prove our mettle. I felt ready for it that day. I even relished the thought. It's no wonder they dubbed it the Department of *Homeland* Security — disasters bring out our innate affection for all that Wagnerian hero crap.

I entered the murky kitchen to feed my spouse and his colleague, feeling keenly my duties as a good helpmeet. (Disasters always make me feel a bit old-fashioned and Donna Reed-y. Expressions like *helpmeet* just pop into my head spontaneously.) My job was to provide sustenance for my husband and unexpected guest, without benefit of trifling modernities like light. Eric's job was to bring home the bacon, and in an amazing display of clear-headedness in the midst of emergency, he'd done just that. He came up behind me in the kitchen with a flashlight and whispered, "I got chicken livers. And eggplant."

"Does your boss like chicken livers?"

"Who knows? Doesn't matter. The main thing is, he probably doesn't want to eat at eleven at night."

"Well, I'd better get on my stick, then."

(I never say things like "get on my stick" except during states of emergency.)

Eric kissed me, in a very "you-and-me-against-the-world" sort of way that sent a tingle up my spine, and made me think for a moment of the baby booms traditionally recorded nine months after major blackouts. Then he went to dig out every candle in the house. I had just about figured out how to balance the flashlight under my chin so I could cook when Eric's boss poked his head into the kitchen. "Julie? Someone's outside for you."

As I stepped into the living room, I heard it. "Julie! *Julie!* JULIE!" Peeking down through the jalousie windows, I saw on the sidewalk none other than Brad and Kimmy, staring up at us exhausted. Kimmy held her own excruciating high heels in her hands — her feet were bare, her stockings run to ribbons. They had just finished walking from our office, across the Queensboro Bridge.

Brad took over candle-lighting while Eric got out the large bottle of vodka he had, in his infinite wisdom, picked up on the way home. I, meanwhile, flinchingly lit the stove with my NASCAR lighter. When it didn't blow up in my face and instead spurted into reassuring blue flame, I knew we were over the hump. These are the times when we aficionados of the gas stove know we are on the side of God. I jammed the flashlight under my chin and Eric arranged candles stuck in *mise-en-place* bowls and teacup saucers all around me, until I felt I was embarking on a shamanic rite of hospitality, which I guess I was. I sautéed some rice in butter — I would have thrown some onions in there if I could have retrieved them from the refrigerator's darkened depths — and poured in some chicken broth for it to cook in. When it was done I scooped it into a savarin pan I'd smeared with butter — I am now a person who, in a state of emergency, can always find her savarin pan. This I set into my widest pot, which was filled with about an inch of water. I let it simmer on the stove for ten minutes for a blackout-style Riz en Couronne — a rice ring, of all the silly things to make during a blackout. I was meant to bake it in the oven, but the oven gas proved trickier to light than the stovetop. I sautéed the chicken livers in some butter and cooked down an impromptu sauce with vermouth and broth. Eric helped with frying up some eggplant.

We were just serving plates when again we heard the call: "Julie! Ju-leeeeee!" Down on the street was Gwen, a bit drunk and a bit hungry and a bit worse for wear, having hiked across the Queensboro Bridge after a spontaneous celebration of the blackout and possible end of the world at her office.

Long Island City was in a festival mood that night. In our apartment, dinner was supremely candlelit. My mother had sent us some iridescent lilac sheers to hang on the walls of our dining nook, and they shimmered in the flickering light. We all looked very beautiful and mysterious and satisfied. Kimmy and I bitched mightily about our secretarial jobs, to great hilarity, while Brad and Gwen got surprisingly cozy at the other end of the table. Dinner was a mite sparse for six, but that just added to the apocalyptic funhouse feeling of the night, especially when Eric wandered out into the dark, hectic streets and bought us all some cones from the Good Humor man. It was a good night for Good Humor men — eleven at night and the streets were still full of people walking, walking, who could tell how far they had yet to go. But we were home.

Kimmy managed to get through on her cell to her boyfriend

and got him to come pick her up and take her home. Eric's boss bunked down on the couch while the rest of us stayed huddled around the dinner table a bit longer. Once we'd gotten lightly lit, I managed to pull Gwen to one side to ask her about her married friend, Mitch. (For some reason, I got the feeling it would be better not to ask her in front of Brad — there seemed to be some possibility there.)

"Ah. He got cold feet about cheating on his wife, the loser."

"Sorry."

"You know what? I deserve better than occasional fantastic sex. I deserve frequent fantastic sex. Screw him."

After the dishes were cleared away, we moved the table to one side so Brad and Gwen could crash on the flokati rug in the dining nook. We took to our bed, feeling very cozy and communal, like a bunch of Neanderthals retiring to their cave after a good mastadon feast. Brad and Gwen slept so well that night that they didn't even wake up when the fuzzy lamp directly over their heads came blazing on, along with the clock radio, at 4:30 in the morning. (Gwen swears up and down that nothing happened, but I still hold out some hope. Brad would be great for her.)

Sometimes, there is nothing better than being a nonessential employee. On the radio the next morning, Bloomberg asked us, for the good of the city, to "stay in, relax, don't overexert yourself." Eric's boss's wife came down from Westchester to pick him up, and they gave Brad and Gwen rides home. Eric and I washed the dishes together. I can tell you right now that having no light beats having no water any day of the week.

I heard about the subway passengers being stranded and all I could think was "I hope Julie had to work late. I hope and pray Julie had to work late." Guess I'm a nicer person than I thought, 'cause I'm willing to forgo a REALLY interesting entry in favor of NOT having Julie trapped in an un-air-conditioned subway for HOURS.

I know, I know. My first thought too, after hearing that the power outage wasn't an act of terrorism, was "Oh, God. Julie is caught in that mess." It was pretty much like "Oh, God, my sister is caught in that mess," except my sister lives in Washington, not New York. Actually, after reading you daily almost from the beginning, you are a bigger part of my life than my sister, who never writes.

You're a better person than I, because my first thought was just "How will Julie cook?" Thank God for gas stoves. And then when I saw all the people walking home on the news, I worried again. So, also, thank God for the profiteering ferry woman. Good luck, Julie!

"Poor Julie!" I wondered. "How will she ever do it?" With a flashlight under her chin of course!!! You're a freakin' Indiana Jones of the kitchen with a balloon whip on your belt!

It is a comfort to have friends, maybe especially friends you will never meet. Think about it this way: as I awaited a ferry amid thousands of other disheveled Queens secretaries, a woman named Chris in Minnesota was thinking not, "Oh, poor New Yorkers!" but "Oh, poor Julie!" As I cooked chicken livers with a flashlight under my chin, some guy down in Shreveport was trying to remember if Julie had a gas or electric stove. Around the country, a small scattering of people who had never been to the city, who had never met me, who had never cooked French food in their life, heard about the blackout and thought about me. That's sort of incredible, isn't it? Aside from its being an ego-boost, I mean. Because people who would have looked at this as a disaster happening to other people were suddenly looking at it as a disaster happening to one of their own, to a friend. I don't mean this to be arrogance; in fact, I don't think it has a whole lot to do with me one way or the other. I think what it means is, people want to care about people. People look after one another, given the chance.

I don't know if I really believe this, but on the day after the blackout I sure did. And I figure, maybe just believing in goodness generates a tiny bit of the stuff, so that by being so foolish as to believe in our better natures, if just for a day, we actually contribute to the sum total of generosity in the universe.

That's naive, isn't it? Dammit, I *hate* it when I do that.

The next night we ate pasta with a creamy sauce into which I stirred JC's recipe for canned onions. "All the brands of canned 'small boiled onions' we have tried have tasted, to us, rather unpleasantly sweetish and overacidulated," JC writes. "However they are so useful in an emergency that we offer the following treatment which improves them considerably."

I figured the day after a major blackout was as good a day as any for emergency canned onions. It was hard to imagine, though, just what kind of emergency JC was talking about here. Let's see: a situation in which there are no fresh onions to be had, but an abundance of canned ones (leaving aside for the moment that in 2003, finding canned onions is a feat unto itself). The onions must be drained, boiled, drained again, then simmered for fifteen minutes with broth and an herb bouquet, so we're not talking about an emergency in which speedy onions are of the essence, nor of an emergency in which you are stranded on a desert island with nothing *but* canned onions to eat (unless maybe your first-aid kit has a spice rack). Add it all up and I don't know what you've got, but I suspect it's an emergency during which you'd have bigger problems than whether your onions tasted "overacidulated."

A bleader wrote in on this conundrum:

I wonder if WWII was the sort of emergency Julia was thinking of: decimated crops, sporadic food supplies for years on end, and everyone relying on their canned goods for the duration. . . . We live in much more pampered times: I point to the scarcity of canned onions as proof.

The point is an excellent one, though I still dearly hope JC was never actually in a position to be forced to such measures. Julia and Paul were living in Cambridge when the grandmamma of New York blackouts hit, in '77, so she didn't have to cook through that one. But surely even Cambridge gets blackouts. I wonder if she ever made pasta sauce with canned onions during a blackout. Somehow I doubt it. Maybe she iced a cake with Crème au Beurre, Ménagère, then took Paul by the hand and climbed back into bed for the rest of the day. That seems a better bet. After all, Julia has always had a knack for divining the truly essential.

May 1949
Paris, France

When he walked through the door at midday, she gave a great whoop and flung herself into his arms. "I got the most interesting sausage at Les Halles this morning. I've never seen anything quite like it." She took his hand and began to drag him off to their little dining room.

"Hold on, hold on — let me get my coat off!" She greeted him every day just this way, raucous and delighted. It was one of the joys of his day, coming home to her at lunchtime, but sometimes he felt a tiny, insistent prick of guilt, as if he were imprisoning an ebullient golden retriever, who nevertheless always greeted him with simple love and gratitude when she was freed again.

On the table were two plates, slices of a dark, smoked sausage spiked with large nubs of fat, a loaf of bread, and some good runny cheese. For someone who'd known nothing of food until just the last few years, Julie had an unerring and adventurous sense of taste. He pulled out a chair, reached for the bread, tore off a hunk.

Julie sat down across from him and began to nibble on a bit of sausage. "So, it seems it was a false alarm. Just stomach fatigue, as you said. Between the lovemaking and the food, I imagine every woman who comes to Paris winds up thinking she's pregnant at one time or another."

Paul put down his knife and leveled a gaze at his wife. They had discussed the possibility of children, of course, in a noncommittal sort of way. To tell the truth, he was not delirious at the prospect, but when she'd voiced her suspicions to him last week, he'd made up his mind that he'd settle himself well to it, for her sake. "Are you all right?"

She wrinkled her nose at him and smiled. "Oh, sure. I wonder if maybe I'm not cut out for children anyway."

He felt a stab of guilt. "Julie, it's not as if we won't have other—"

She waved her hand at him with a gaiety so convincing he'd almost have thought it genuine. "Of course, of course! And I'm so enjoying myself, it would seem a shame to spoil all the fun with a little brat just now. It's only—" For just a moment she looked wistful. "It's only, I wish I had something to apply myself to during the days. I can't spend my whole life tottering about the markets, can I?"

Paul cut a wedge of cheese and smeared it onto some bread. "I've been thinking just the same thing. Perhaps you should join a women's group of some sort, or take a class. Something to occupy your mind. It must be dull stuck up here all day alone."

"Oh, I do an all right job keeping myself entertained, I guess!" She leaned her chin on her hand. "Still, you know, I think you're right. I need to come up with a good project for myself. That's what I need."

When he had finished his lunch, she walked him to the door. He kissed her good-bye, and when he looked up at her wide face, he saw a gleam in her eye that he recognized. It was a gleam one had to be wary of, he knew, one that could bring about some unexpected developments. "Don't get into too much trouble, now."

"Oh, I won't. Not too much."

"Only in America"

H i, Julie, this is Karen from CBS? We'd like to do a story about your project."

"Umm . . . Okay." Usually, I don't answer the telephone at home, certainly not when I'm in the middle of writing my blog entry for the day. Usually, it's no one I want to talk to. But this morning, for some reason, I did. Call it a hunch.

"What we'd do first is send a cameraman to meet you at work. He'd film you at your office, then follow you as you go shopping, and he'd take the subway home with you. The rest of the team would meet you there, and you would just cook as you normally do while we filmed you. How's Tuesday?"

So. Here I was writing my blog, when I get a phone call from a major media outlet concerning their desire to do a piece about me and my blog. Which phone call I immediately proceeded to write about in my blog.

This was when it occurred to me that things were starting to get a little meta.

* * *

Evil baby genius Nate was the guy I'd have to talk to before bringing into the office a network cameraman, even (especially) one
who wasn't going to be filming him, so I went down to his office
and knocked on the door. His cell phone was affixed to the side of
his face, as usual, but he waved me in.

"So the governor *is* set for 3:15, yeah? And Bloomberg's at 3:45.
Simone says Giuliani wants in on it now. . . . Yeah. I'll tell 'em.
Yeah." He chortled a bit. "Yeah. See ya down there.

"What's goin' on?"

This to me, I think. You can never quite tell for sure when he's
talking to you — he seems like the kind of guy who might have
a phone implanted in his inner ear.

"Hey, so there's a CBS cameraman coming in on Tuesday —"

"Julie, you know all interview requests for Bonnie have to go
through me — Gabe will have a shit fit." (In the whole office,
only Nate called Mr. Kline by his first name.)

"No — it's not — it's for — well, for me, actually."

"You're kidding. This for that cooking thing?"

"Yeah."

Nate's face opened into a slightly predatory smile. "Well, that's
great! When did you say he wanted to come? After work hours,
right?"

"Yeah. Tuesday."

"That's fine. Just don't let him film anything he shouldn't. You
know, the proposals."

"Right. Of course."

"Or any documents, or anything on your computer."

"Sure."

"Or the front desk, or our company logo anywhere. And
don't mention the organization. And all that 'government drone'
stuff? That's fine on your Web site — funny, funny stuff, Julie, seriously — but you might want to tone that down a little. 'Kay?"

"Um. Okay. Thanks." I started to go.

"Oh, and Julie? Try not to let Mr. Kline see the camera guy. You know how he is. He might get curious about the whole 'blog' thing." He actually made quotation marks with his fingers when he said it. Well, it is sort of a silly word, I guess.

Every time I go to Dean & DeLuca, a.k.a. Grocery of the Anti-Christ, I swear *"Never again!"* Often I swear this aloud, while in the store, slicing through moneyed idiots as if they were swaths of artisanal Belgian grain, as they wait in line for the $150 caviar, or pick up their plastic trays of sushi, or exclaim over all the varieties of green tea, or buy their coffee and croissants, which to do at Dean & DeDevil is just asinine.

After I've gotten good and enraged, maybe I'll head up to Astor Wines and Spirits — where I'll buy three bottles of wine, might as well since I'm there — and then to the Duane Reade for shampoo and conditioner and toothpaste, before going to Petco and picking up a twenty-two-pound bag of dry cat food, two dozen cans of wet cat food, a fifteen-pound carton of kitty litter, and four mice for my pet snake, Zuzu, to eat. Then on the way out, rolling my unwieldy cart — one of those basket things that crazy old New York ladies have, which I bought my first year in New York before I realized they were only for crazy old ladies, but don't mind using now that I'm resigned to being a crazy old lady myself — I'll go through the Union Square Greenmarket, where I'll spy a bin of enormous dogwood boughs. And because Eric and I had dogwood blossoms on our wedding cake, I will decide that it's only fitting and proper that I buy one.

It will only be while descending into the subway with my canned and bagged cat food, kitty litter, three bottles of wine, six veal scallops, four mice, shampoo, conditioner, toothpaste, and bough of dogwood blossoms as tall as I am, all wedged into a crazy-lady rolling basket, that I'll realize this was probably not a good idea. Hopefully the people I slap in the face with dogwood branches will be tourists, and too cowed by the Metropolitan Transit System to try to punch me.

This, of course, is *precisely* why the CBS cameraman wants to follow me on a shopping expedition.

When the cameraman calls up from the lobby at five-thirty on Tuesday afternoon, I'm ready to go except for the Very Important contracts Legal has sent down the hall for Bonnie to sign, which I haven't been able to give to her because she's been in a Very Important meeting for the last two and a half hours. He comes up and films me writing out phone messages while we wait. At 5:40 I'm just getting ready to log off my computer when Bonnie comes out of the conference room. "Where are the contracts?"

"Here you go," I say, handing them to her in professional secretary fashion. The CBS cameraman films me doing it. Bonnie glances at him bemusedly — she's been given the bare details as to what's going on here, but clearly cannot quite fathom it.

"Where's the cover letter? Legal was drafting a cover letter."

This is the first I've ever heard about this. "Shit."

Bonnie glares at the cameraman. "Maybe you should turn that off for a few minutes."

So the CBS cameraman doesn't get to film me running down the hall to Legal, who are now in a Very Important meeting all their own, or shaking some intern by the shoulder to get across how very much I need him to get that letter for me *now,* or finding out I need to have three copies of the contracts, not just two, or screaming obscenities at the Xerox machine which has decided to run out of toner, or muttering under my breath fearsome threats entailing the tossing of vice presidents out of twentieth-story windows into big gaping holes bristling with rebar and bulldozers. Which is a shame, that he couldn't film it, since these were really the only exciting things that happened that night.

I can only assume I've been blessed by the attention of CBS because I'm a foulmouthed hysteric with misanthropic tendencies for whom things are constantly going terribly, terribly wrong. So it's a bloody shame that once the contract debacle is solved and the camera goes back on, suddenly all is smooth sailing. The weather is unawful, the sidewalks clear of surly commuters. The Turkish grocery has everything I need, even the very fancy eight-bucks-a-pound Danish butter. (JC is, as a general rule, not very demanding as to ingredients. It's one of the reasons I was first drawn to her. So when she specifies "best-quality" butter, I think she must mean it.) The resulting bag of groceries is not heavy. The subway station is not crammed, and a train comes right away. People move out of our path as the cameraman follows me about, filming over my shoulder or rushing ahead to catch me coming around the corner. One guy on the train tries to chat me up, no doubt under the impression that I'm somebody of consequence, what with the attendant cameraman and all.

At home, Eric and I get wired with mikes and, with the camera reverently rolling, we sip wine and chop shallots and stir things on stoves, and pretend there isn't a camera in our faces. Suddenly I sprout a civil tongue, without even trying. I am serene; I cook with a minimum of fuss. I make shrimp in a Beurre Blanc, which is essentially three-quarters of a pound of melted Danish butter with some crustaceans stirred into it, and some asparagus with Sauce Moutarde, and it kicks ass. I feel like a celebrity chef; I feel like I'm lying. I'm tempted to invent a disaster, fake a grease fire or something. But they all seem sufficiently impressed/horrified by the three-quarters of a pound of butter, so I guess it's all right.

The news crew — "news" crew, I should say, because who are we kidding? This isn't exactly the siege of Mazar-al-Sharif here — consisted of four people: a cameraman, a sound man, a producer, and a correspondent named Mika. They were planning to come to the apartment three nights in a row, to shoot. That's like fifteen hours or something, which struck me as bizarre and sort of unfair. I mean, here was CBS pouring untold fortunes into a five-minute spot about a thirty-year-old secretary from Queens cooking French food. Meanwhile, I can't get the accounting department to approve a ten-dollar plate of stale cookies for the cultural committee meeting. Anyway. The first two nights of filming went just fine, though they were oddly exhausting, but then on the third day there was an explosion at Yale, and the cameraman had to go cover that. They weren't able to come back until the next week. The next Tuesday, actually. The Tuesday of — and here I begin to ululate in despair — the *very final episode of* Buffy the Vampire Slayer *EVER*.

In between which time, I managed to catch a cold, or it might have been SARS, in fact.

It occurs to me that I've never adequately explained my devotion to *Buffy the Vampire Slayer*. This is partly because I hesitate to put into words an emotion so delicate and precious, and partly because I have just a bit of residual shame at being obsessed with anything involving Sarah Michelle Gellar. *Buffy the Vampire Slayer* is — for those of you who've spent the last ten years living under a rock where the public schools ban Harry Potter books for promoting sorcery — a television show, known to its devout followers simply as *Buffy*. It is about a high school girl who is the Vampire Slayer, the one girl in all the world (well, sort of, things get a little complicated on *Buffy*) who can fight the forces of darkness — the Chosen One. Well, I guess that's what you'd call the premise. It's *about* the agonies of growing up, the importance of friendship in a harsh world, personal responsibility, love, sex, death — and kicking evil ass, of course. In all this it's not so unlike the Bible, except with stunt doubles and better jokes. Those of you who are offended by this can take some comfort in knowing that I am *far* from the first person to have made this observation. Also like the Bible, *Buffy* got a little bloated and Revelations-y toward the end, and between that and the Project I'd not been watching quite as faithfully as I might have in the last few months. But still — this was *it*. The *end*. You don't skip out on

Revelations, no matter how kind of weird and lame it is. Or maybe you do. But not the last episode of *Buffy.*

Except I did. While Eric sat around with the "news" crew watching this historic event (the producer was a fan, too), I slaved away in a hot kitchen, under the watchful eye of a time-lapse camera. I'm not bitter, of course — even I wouldn't go so far as to get pissy that I couldn't watch a TV show, even possibly the *most important fantasy martial arts romantic television dramedy in entertainment history,* because I'm too busy being filmed for a national news spot. No, I staunchly made my *Fricadelles de Veau à la Niçoise,* while hacking up large wads of the vile stuff that had filled my lungs over the previous weekend — all alone. At the end I am always alone. In every generation there is a Chosen One.

Fricadelles de Veau à la Niçoise is ground veal with tomatoes, onions, garlic, and, most important, salt pork. The mixture is formed into patties, dredged in flour, and fried in a quite hot skillet with butter and oil. Then, when the patties are cooked, you throw in some beef stock to deglaze the pan, stir in some butter, and call it done. The kitchen slayer also made Épinards Etuvés au Beurre, or spinach braised in butter, and Tomates Grillées au Four, which are baked, not grilled, and egg noodles.

I even plated it all oh-so-prettily, which caused Eric to mutter, out of camera range — though not out of mike range, we're never out of mike range, we're like reality-show contestants who are always bugged, even when they're going to the bathroom or escaping to the woods for lewd trysts — "It's a Potemkin Julie/Julia Project." Because Julie doesn't use fancy plates and serve things at the table. It was as if the mike snaking down between my boobs under my shirt was in fact a direct line to some frosty cool fount of Martha Stewartness — it was kind of freaking me out.

First the correspondent interviewed me. We perched together on the dining room table, a plate and my worn and battered *MtAoFC* arranged carefully between us, and between hacking fits

I tried to deliver witty sound bites. Then I served Eric and myself in our very cute but tiny dining room while the cameraman and sound man and producer all huddled around and shone bright lights on us, and the correspondent sat down with us to eat — or pretend to eat because the correspondent was a vegetarian, which I guess is the kind of thing correspondents tend to be. After the shooting was done I managed to get the rest of the "news" crew to sit down and eat. The sound guy, whose wife was not only a vegetarian but a *vegan,* for God's sake, nearly went into a swoon. He couldn't stop talking about how the tomatoes in the veal patties made them taste so good. I didn't have the heart to tell him that veal patties with *pork fat* are what really take the cake. And the producer filled me in on what I'd missed on *Buffy,* and the camera guy — who was embedded in Iraq before he got embedded in Long Island City, and so was a for-real news cameraman, not just a "news" one — told good embedding stories.

You know how you'll see some movie star getting interviewed on E!, and she'll chirp something about how "surreal" celebrity is, and you'll think to yourself, "Oh, *please,* give me a *break*"? Well, I don't know what it's like to have reporters digging through your garbage and designers begging you to wear their million-dollar earrings at the Oscars. But cooking a dinner in a crappy outer-borough kitchen with a film crew hovering over you, and ending the night by eating veal-and-salt-pork patties and talking Iraq and vampire-slaying with said film crew — and then, a week later, seeing the whole experience chopped down into a four-minute segment introduced on the *CBS Evening News* by Dan Rather, who then signs off, when it is over, by intoning, mysteriously, "Only in America" — is, indeed, surreal.

Okay, it's August. In the wake of the CBS segment I've been interviewed by *Newsweek,* the *Los Angeles Times,* and half a dozen public radio stations scattered across the US and, for some reason, Australia. I've got thirteen days and twenty-two recipes to go. I'm a little panicked. Bleaders are posting things like "COOK, YOU MAGGOT, COOK!!! Either cook or DROP! Give me 25 in 12! COOK, you worthless little PANSY! COOOOOOK!" They mean it in the best possible way, of course. I'm really not sleeping well, and when I do, I dream. In one of these, I have a very bedraggled pigeon that I've captured off the street and brought up to the office. I am keeping it in an empty Xerox paper box. Julia has ordered me to kill and butcher the thing for my evening supper, but I don't have the heart — and figure it's too dirty to eat anyway — so I furtively release it in the hallway and then pretend I have no idea where it went.

And then last night Eric almost divorced me over some spoiled Sauce Tartare.

It was going to be so easy. Just roast beef sandwiches with some salad out of a bag and Bouchées Parmentier au Fromage, or potato cheese sticks. I got home ready to whip the stuff up and move on to more important things, like drinking and playing Civilization and falling asleep really early.

The difference between Sauce Tartare and regular mayonnaise is that the base is not raw egg yolks, but hard-boiled ones. Mush up the yolks of three hard-boiled eggs with mustard and salt until they make a smooth paste. Beat in a cup of oil, in a thin stream. Okay, now. Julia says, "This sauce cannot be made in an electric blender; it becomes so stiff the machine clogs." So I got out my biggest wire whisk and a cup of a mixture of olive and peanut oil (because using all olive oil makes for a very olive-oily mayonnaise, which is not bad, but sometimes you want a change), and started beating. I poured the oil in very slowly, stopping occasionally while continuing to beat to make sure the oil got absorbed. I was doing everything right. But after I'd poured in half a cup or so the oil stopped cooperating.

Julia says:

You will never have trouble with freshly made mayonnaise if you have beaten the egg yolks thoroughly in a warmed bowl before adding the oil, if the oil has been added in droplets until the sauce has commenced to thicken, and if you have not exceeded the maximum proportions of ¼ cup of oil per egg yolk. . . .

But no. Because I did all of that. I did; I know I did. I ran my eyes over the instructions again, desperately. Yes. I did everything — everything *except* . . . "Is this all because I didn't heat the bowl? You're telling me it's not working because I didn't heat the goddamned *bowl?!*"

"What's wrong? Who's telling you?" Eric peeked into the kitchen with that now familiar expression of uncertain solicitude, like the faithful but concerned hound of a serial killer.

"It's August! It's ninety-five degrees in here! How fucking warm do you want it?"

Eric, with the quick reflexes of one accustomed to running for cover, ducked back out of the kitchen again.

Well, I tried Julia's suggestions for fixing it. I warmed a bowl over a pan of simmering water, and beat a little mustard in with a bit of the failed Sauce Tartare. I was supposed to beat until the mustard and the sauce "cream and thicken together."

"This always works," Julia says.

This worked not at all.

Bitch.

This was when I began screeching a bit, not really words, just guttural noises. I knew I was overreacting, but screech I did anyway. As I was screeching, I poured the failed sauce into the blender, because fuck it, right? What could happen?

Not much, as it turned out. I blended and blended and blended, wishing like Dorothy for home that the machine would clog, but the sauce just spun loosely around like so much failed mayonnaise, and separated out as soon as I stopped the blender.

This was when I began throwing things.

Now the thing you have to understand, the thing that makes this whole sad scene both so telling and so very damning, is that I was doing all this even though I knew there'd been a bombing of an American civilian compound in Riyadh. See, Eric has an aunt in Saudi Arabia; he couldn't quite remember what city, though. She works as a nurse in a hospital, teaching nursing to Saudi women. Eric had been glued to the television all evening, but the news was annoyingly saying nothing at all about the bombing. He'd been making calls all evening — to his mom, his brother, his cousins — but disturbingly, no one was picking up. I knew all this, and yet I screamed and sobbed and threw utensils as if Sauce Tartare was the only thing that mattered, as if Sauce Tartare was more important than family, than death, than war.

Eric put up with this for a good long time. But then he couldn't anymore. And he marched back into the kitchen. He grabbed me by the shoulders, he shook me, he shouted, louder than I had ever heard him shout:

"IT'S ONLY MAYONNAISE!!!!!!!"

It would kill me to say that he was right.

I threw away the failed mayonnaise, and made Bouchées Parmentier au Fromage in a deep chill. I boiled three small potatoes and put them through a ricer. The ricer broke, but I did not throw the pieces on the floor. I stirred the riced potatoes in a hot pan to absorb the water. I beat in a cup of flour, a stick of softened butter, an egg, a cup of grated cheese, white pepper, cayenne, nutmeg, and salt. I scooped the stuff up into a pastry bag, and started squeezing out lines onto a cookie sheet. When the pastry bag split down the middle, I didn't scream. Instead I scooped the rest of the potato batter onto the cookie sheet with a spoon, sort of scraping it up into line shapes. I stuck the pan of

Bouchées into the oven. I only cried a little, and quietly, so Eric wouldn't hear. I made sandwiches with sourdough bread, roast beef, lettuce, tomatoes, some really actually quite delicious an- cho chile jalapeno mustard that I'd gotten in a care package from a bleader a month or so ago. When the potato sticks were done I piled them onto plates beside the sandwiches as if they were French fries. Eric took his plate from me without a word.

Eric's mother called as he was biting into his sandwich — she has a gift for that. Turns out Eric's aunt doesn't live in Riyadh. She was okay. I was too much of a brat to live. Well, at least the potato cheese sticks were delicious. Maybe karma loves a good potato cheese stick.

"Is this Julie Powell?"

"Yes?" I said this crisply, assuming *crazy person* since I was, after all, at work.

"It's Amanda Hesser from the *Times*."

It was the second Thursday of the month, board meeting day, so I'd been at work since 7:30 in the morning. I was also having one of those days where I kept getting this faint whiff of a smell some- where on me, but I couldn't find the source — my clothes weren't dirty, my armpits didn't stink, my hair was fine, but somehow I smelled like someone had smeared Burger King special sauce on my bra or something. So I was in a foul mood when the phone rang. Let me tell you, though, getting a call from Amanda Hesser who wants to write a story about you in the Newspaper of Record has a way of improving your frame of mind. True, you will move instantly from surliness to hysteria over the right insouciant wine, but a little hysteria is good for you. (I'm living proof of that.)

I wasn't, by this time, a complete offal amateur. I'd made sev- eral sorts of sweetbreads and actually learned that I rather fa- vored them, except when they smelled like formaldehyde or I overcooked them to squooshy gray hockey pucks.

I'd even cooked brains. This is a funny story, actually, because on the day I was cooking the brains, I was doing an interview with someone for the radio. The guy came to the apartment and talked with me for half an hour while I was preparing for that night's dinner. Everything was fine until the interview ended and the gentleman asked if he could use the facilities before he packed up and left. It was only once he'd gone into the half bath and shut the door that I remembered I had several calves' brains soaking in the sink in there. Poor guy. At least I didn't try to make him eat them.

It isn't so much the taste, with brains, though that's no great shakes. And it isn't the ick factor — the way, when you wash them, you inevitably wind up with bits of brain matter strewn Tarantino-esquely about the sink and your garments, and the weirdo gummy white matter that holds the brain together, which is sort of like fat, I guess, but also looks and feels like something that could very well be called "spongiform." No, the real problem is the philosophical tailspin part. The inconsolable mystery of life, consciousness, the soul. I want a brain to be tightly knit and deeply furrowed, conduited with the circuitous pathways of thought and deep receptacles of memory, but no. It's just this flabby, pale, small organ that disintegrates in your fingers if you let the faucet run too fast. How can this be? How can *we* be?

We'd invited Sally over that night to share our brains prepared two ways — Cervelles en Matelote and Cervelles au Beurre Noir — on the grounds that Sally was the only person I knew who'd ever eaten brains before. Hers had been goat brain curry in Calcutta. Sally was bringing her new sophisticated wine-drinking boyfriend David (the old David, the one with the motorcycle, who couldn't keep his hands off her, was *long* gone), which struck me as either a courageous gesture of faith in their budding relationship or, possibly, an attempt to hit his eject button.

Cervelles en Matelote were brains gently poached in red wine, which red wine was then cooked down and thickened with *beurre manié*, a paste of butter and flour, to make a sauce. For Cervelles au Beurre Noir the brains were sliced and marinated in lemon juice, olive oil, and parsley before being browned in butter and oil and tossed with a Beurre Noir, which is just a stick and a half of butter, clarified and browned to a nut color, with parsley and cooked-down vinegar. Only Eric had bought cilantro instead of parsley, so actually no parsley. I could take the brains in red wine sauce with onions and mushrooms, because it tasted mostly like onions and mushrooms and red wine. The brains just sort of melted away. But the pan-fried brains — I don't know. Almost unbearably rich — and I *like* rich — and with this smackery texture that sort of makes me shudder just thinking about it. Let's just say that the dessert of crepes filled with almond custard and topped with shavings of absurdly expensive Scharffen Berger chocolate represented a *vast* improvement.

So I had the organ meat experience. And while some people might have considered that when they were having a famous food writer from the *New York Times* over for dinner they ought not try to prepare kidneys for the first time in their life, I wasn't too worried. Just like sometimes you have to dye your hair cobalt blue, or wear jeans and beat-up motorcycle boots to your government-wonk job, sometimes you have to put yourself out there without a net. I'd done the brains — I figured if I could manage that, I'd be all right.

So there was this problem with the wine, though. I thought about asking Sally to ask her new boyfriend, but to tell you the truth, I thought her new boyfriend was kind of a tool, and I didn't want to give him the satisfaction of asking him for advice. It occurred to me that Nate, actually, probably *would* know something about wine — he's one of those slightly bacchanalian Republicans, like Rush Limbaugh, who smokes illegal Cuban cigars or indulges in some kind of mildly deviant behavior. But no, I couldn't ask him. He'd be absolutely insufferable about it. He'd pester me until I told him who was coming to dinner, and when he found out it was the *New York Times,* he would think up some way to make a nuisance of himself. But here it was, three o'clock. Amanda Hesser was coming to dinner that night; I needed *someone* to ask for help. Oh, damn.

I reluctantly stuck my head inside the door of Nate's office. He was, oddly, not on the phone. "Do you know anything about wine?"

He flung his feet up on his desk. "Why do you ask, my little government drone?"

I rolled my eyes at him. "I just need a good wine. Something that will go with kidneys."

"You're going to eat *kidneys?* I knew you were a twisted liberal, Powell, but *kidneys?*"

"Oh, come on. Can you help me or not?"

"So this is some kind of special occasion, is it? You having some *bigwig* over for dinner? Hmm? What's this all about?"

"Okay, Nate, it's just that I've got this very intimidating person coming over to dinner, I need to have insouciant perfect wine, I'm freaking out, come *on!*"

"Insouciant, eh? Very intimidating person, eh? Like who? Tell me who. C'mon, Powell, just tell me. Who?"

"I'm not telling, Nate. Help me, don't help me. I don't care." I started to march out of his office again.

"Oh, okay, okay, don't be so *sensitive.* Jeesh, *Democrats.*" Nate took his time, twiddled his thumbs, made me wait for it. This is the kind of stuff Nate loves. "Well, I do like Chateau Greysac Haut Medoc. The Chateau Larose Trintaudon Côtes du Rhone is another savvy choice. And, if you want to be outrageous, I think that BV Coastal Cabernet Sauvignon is one of the great deals out there in big reds."

I'm only paranoid because people are always holding out on me.

So before going home to prepare a dinner of Rognons de Veau

en Casserole, kidneys cooked in butter with mustard and parsley sauce, with sautéed potatoes and braised onions, and Clafouti for dessert, for Amanda Hesser of the *New York Times*, I rushed into Astor Wines and asked the guy for Greysac. It was the easiest wine-shopping experience of my life — no wandering aimlessly in the Burgundy aisle, choosing by Robert Parker points. When I got home I set the bottles on a table near the front door, and god-damned if practically the first thing Amanda said when she walked through the door wasn't, "Oh, Greysac! Where did you get it?"

So I've got to give Nate his due on that one.

Amanda Hesser, food writer for the *New York Times*, is — and this is an extraordinarily unoriginal observation, but nearly im-possible to let go by un-commented-upon, it's like seeing me and not thinking, "Gee, that lady really needs to get some electroly-sis!" — very, very tiny. She's so tiny that you can't understand how she can eat food at all, let alone for a *living*. She's so tiny that it's hard for a big-boned misanthropist, who has nurtured a secret wish all her life to be considered "cute," to not hate her. Though Amanda Hesser is not cute. She's adorable, empirically, but when you're a thirty-year-old secretary who can't really cook, it's not appropriate to call the tiny famous food writer sitting in your kitchen watching you make Rognons de Veau en Casserole "cute." "Intimidating As Shit," more like. Hating Amanda Hesser is something of a cottage industry in certain, admittedly small and perhaps excessively navel-gazing, circles, and it would be an easy enough bandwagon to jump onto. But when she's going to be writing an article about you in the Newspaper of Record, there's really no sense in starting off on the wrong foot. Besides, I was going to be cooking kidneys for the poor woman — the least I could do was give her the benefit of the doubt.

With Amanda and a photographer watching, I browned the kidneys lightly in butter. Back in March I'd made a leg of lamb stuffed with lamb kidneys and rice. Those kidneys, the lamb ones, had been entrancing — dark and firm and smooth, heavy as river stones in the hand, like a sort of idealization of innards. I'd just assumed that that was what kidneys were like. These kidneys, though, the veal ones, were large and messy and many-lobed, striated with white fat and filaments. They spit up a lot of liquid as they cooked. I glanced anxiously at the book — "a little juice from the kidneys will exude and coagulate," Julia wrote.

"Does this look like 'a little juice' to you? It doesn't look like 'a little juice' to me. It looks like a lot."

Amanda shrugged tentatively. "I've never cooked kidneys before." Poor Amanda. Probably she was a little uncomfortable with expressing an opinion on this; probably she wasn't often in a position to interview someone who so clearly knew so embarrassingly much less about these things than she did.

I removed the kidneys to a plate, terrified that I'd either over- or undercooked them. I added shallots and vermouth and lemon juice to the pan and let the liquid boil down, probably a bit too much, actually. I was also blanching pearl onions even tinier than Amanda Hesser, and sautéing some potatoes that Eric had quartered for me. I shuttled back and forth around the kitchen, from pot to pan to Book and back again, in a sort of mild chronic panic, which I tried to cover with continuous but not at all witty patter.

It was about a hundred degrees in the kitchen. Poor Amanda Hesser's forehead was damp with perspiration, but she did not complain. Neither did she physically cringe from touching anything, even though all around me I could see the sticky, dusty, cat-hairy indications of my pathetic housekeeping. She did say, when she spied the pitchy black soles of my bare feet, "You need some chef's clogs. It'll help your back."

The potatoes got a little burned. Amanda Hesser called them "caramelized."

The onions got braised in butter, perhaps a bit too long, and were sort of falling apart. Amanda Hesser called them "glazed."

I finished off the sauce for the kidneys with some mustard and butter, then sliced the kidneys, which were actually a not-too-terrible-looking pink on the inside, and tossed them and some parsley in the sauce. It was too easy to even talk about. Quickly I whipped up the batter for the Clafouti in the blender — milk, sugar, eggs, vanilla, touch of salt, flour. I poured a layer of it into my springform pan and, per Julia's somewhat mystifying directions, heated the pan up for a minute or so on the stovetop so a film set on the bottom before dropping in some cherries Eric had pitted, pouring on the rest of the batter, and sticking it into a 350-degree oven to bake while we ate dinner.

When I'd told my mother that Amanda Hesser was coming over for dinner and that I was going to make her kidneys, she'd said, "But kidneys taste like piss." But these didn't at all. Though the potatoes were burned, the onions were nice. The Greysac was excellent. And it was so much cooler in the dining room that everyone started feeling giddy and joyful. I told Amanda Hesser the story about Poulet à la Broche, how I faked an "oven spit attachment," whatever the hell that is, by sticking a straightened metal clothes hanger through a chicken and then winding the ends of the hanger around the handles of my stockpot and sticking the whole contraption in the oven with the broiler on and the door ajar. In August. Amanda Hesser's eyes went wide in her tiny face. "You really did that?"

I've got to say, it's a nice feeling, impressing Amanda Hesser of the *New York Times*. Even if it is with your idiocy.

The Clafouti was good too, puffy and browned, with the cherries studded jewel-like through it. The no-longer-quite-so-intimidating Amanda Hesser had two slices. I wonder where she puts it?

So what happens when you get an article written about you in the *New York Times*? I'll tell you what happens.

First you'll get a buzzing sensation in your ears when you see your picture, which makes you look fat but no fatter than you are, to be honest. You'll see somebody on the subway reading the Dining section and think, with hysterical, dreadful anticipation, "Oh my God oh my God! I'm going to be recognized!" You won't be, but you'll hold your breath all the way to the office, waiting for it.

At work, you'll keep expecting your coworkers to congratulate you on being so very kick-ass — though because many of them are Republican bureaucrats who don't read the Dining section, you won't get as much of that as you'd have thought. You will waste a good bit of time checking obsessively to see how many people have visited your blog. Very, very many people will have. Many of these people will think you should stop saying f*** so much, which makes the people who've already been reading the blog for a long time plenty pissed. Arguments will break out.

Back in the real world — at some point Nate the evil baby genius will stop by your desk. "Nice article in the *Times*, Jules," he'll say, leaning over you familiarly. Nate respects nothing as much as a mention in the *Times*, except a mention in the *Post* or the *Daily News*. "Was that who the wine was for?"

"Yeah. Thanks for that. It was a hit."

"So you mentioned the job, I notice. Doesn't reflect very well on the organization, when you say you're unsatisfied in your work."

"Jesus, Nate, come *on*. I'm a *secretary*. I'm *supposed* to be unsatisfied. Am I supposed to *lie* to them when they ask? It's not like I called Mr. Kline an asshole or something. Who *gives* a shit?"

Would you have said this to Nate under normal circumstances? Maybe. Or maybe not.

When you get home, you will have fifty-two messages on your answering machine. (Your number is listed; you've never had any reason for it not to be.) In your AOL account, 236 messages. You will think that your ship has come the f*** in.

Had it, though, really? It was hard to say. Everybody's always got their own stuff to attend to, especially the bureaucrats at my office, who care about French food not at all, and in a surprisingly short amount of time things got back to normal. Well, sort of.

A week after the article came out I was in the West Village on my lunch break to pick up some more veal kidneys at my favorite butcher shop. The guy behind the counter said, "Hey, you had that article in the paper last week, right?"

"Oh — yeah?"

"Thanks for mentioning us. We've been getting all kinds of orders for offal this week — I've never seen anything like it."

That was fun.

Even better, though, was when I got back to the office and Bonnie said the president wanted to see me in his office. She looked nervous. "You should just make nice — I think he's pretty upset."

So I walked down the hall to his office, and he pointed to the chair in front of his big desk. "Julie," he said, looking *very* serious with his hands clasped on the desk in front of him, "it seems to me you've got a lot of *anger.*"

It seemed that someone had finally alerted Mr. Kline about the heretical content of my blog. I wonder if it was the thing I wrote about throwing vice presidents out windows that got him worried. "Are you unhappy here?" he asked.

"No! No, sir. I just — well, I *am* a secretary, Mr. Kline. Sometimes it's frustrating."

"You're an asset to the organization, Julie. You just need to try to find a way to channel that negative energy."

"Mm-hm."

Channel that negative energy?! Since when do Republicans talk like that? I thought that was the one thing to admire about Republicans.

So I made nice, I nodded and shuffled and bowed my head like a chastised child. And yet, in my chest I felt a blooming, something that felt like liberty, like happiness. And sitting unspoken in my brain, repeating there endlessly, was one delicious, rebellious, freeing response: *Or what? You'll fire me?*

Maybe my ship was coming the f*** in after all.

By the time you have completed half of this, the carcass frame, dangling legs, wings, and skin will appear to be an unrecognizable mass of confusion and you will wonder how in the world any sense can be made of it all. But just continue cutting against the bone, and not slitting any skin, and all will come out as it should.

— "How to Bone a Duck, Turkey, or Chicken,"
Mastering the Art of French Cooking, Vol. 1

¤¤¤¤¤¤

Simplicity Itself

What kind of Darwinian funhouse trick is this? The blithe happy humans were just enjoying themselves too darn much to make time for procreation, is that it? Is the self-denigration mutation linked irrevocably to a heightened genetic immunity or something?

If you will be so kind as to indulge me in a quick flashback:

The time is crack of dawn, second Tuesday of July, 2003. I am due at my office in an hour for another in an endless series of early-morning meetings, for which I perform the vital duties of dais card setup, last-minute xeroxing, hysterical, high-heeled running up and down of hallways, and purposeful-looking standing around. This is all quite bad enough. But what is worse is that I have spent the previous three hours lying in bed, wide awake and bitch-slapping myself because I'd failed to make apple aspic.

Here I am with just over a month to go, fifty-eight recipes left, and instead of making the apple aspic like a responsible member of society, I wasted the whole night eating mashed potatoes and steamed broccoli and London broil. Yes, I made Champignons Sautés, Sauce Madère. Do you know what Champignons Sautés, Sauce Madère is? It's beef stock simmered with carrots and celery and vermouth and bay leaf and thyme, then thickened with cornstarch; some quartered mushrooms browned in butter; and some Madeira cooked down in the skillet. Combine the brown sauce and the mushrooms and simmer. It's horseshit, is what it is. I should just get that scarlet L branded on my chest now, because I'm a big LOSER. And then there's Eric. "Maybe part of the Project is that you don't finish everything." *Where has he been for the last eleven months? Doesn't he get it? Doesn't he understand that if I don't get through the whole book in a year then this whole thing will have been a waste, that I'm going to spiral into mediocrity and despair and probably wind up on the street trading blow jobs for crack or something? He hates me, anyway. Look at him, curled over on his side of the bed like he doesn't want to so much as touch me. It's because I've got the stink of failure on me. I'm doomed. . . .*

Ah, yes. Nothing like a good night's sleep.

I shower a bit of the failure-stink off me and pull out my Big Important Meeting Suit. I haven't had it on in a while, and so I guess I shouldn't be surprised that I've gotten too busty to wear it. I'm gaining cup sizes like — well, like twenty pounds of butterweight. I'm like the Lara Croft of food, only without the groovy outfits and exotic locales and sex appeal.

Though running late and busting out of the front of my suit and sweating like Nixon before seven in the morning, I hook up my laptop to scrawl out a blog entry and check my mailbox because what can I say? I'm an addict. I've gotten a note from an older gentleman who spent twenty-two years in the military in France, who feels the need to tell me, in no uncertain terms, that he thinks my project is, in essence, an unpatriotic glorification of Charles de Gaulle's 1966 decision to withdraw France from NATO's unified military command structure, and the resulting relocation of NATO headquarters from Paris to Brussels. Christ. As if I don't get enough of this crazy-old-man, "pour-out-your-Bordeaux-and-call-your-fries-'Freedom'" crap at the office.

The thing that makes me wonder if I just don't have a knack for this happiness stuff is that this early-morning meltdown came right on the heels of one of my most impressive accomplishments. For the weekend before, we had had a blowout of tarts, a tart bender, tart madness — even, I dare say, a Tart-a-pa-*looza*, if you will forgive one final usage of the construction before we at last bury that cruelly beaten dead pop-culture horse. Tarte aux Pêches, Tarte aux Limettes, Tarte aux Poires, Tarte aux Cerises. Tarte aux Fromage Frais, both with and without Pruneaux. Tarte au Citron et aux Amandes, Tarte aux Poires à la Bourdaloue, and Tarte aux Fraises, which is not "Tart with Freshes," as the name of the Tarte aux Fromage Frais ("Tart with Fresh Cheese," of course) might suggest, but rather Tart with Strawberries, which was a fine little French lesson. (Why are strawberries, in particular, named for freshness? Why not blackberries? Or, say, river trout? I love playing amateur — not to say totally ignorant — etymologist. . . .)

I made two kinds of pastry in a kitchen so hot that, even with the aid of a food processor, the butter started melting before I could get it incorporated into the dough. Which work resulted in eight tart crusts, perhaps not paragons of the form, but good enough. I made eight fillings for my eight tart crusts. I creamed butter and broke eggs and beat batter until it formed "the ribbon." I poached pears and cherries and plums in red wine. I baked and baked and baked and baked. I washed all the plates and coffee cups that had accrued a sticky black layer of industrial wasteland grit. I think I even washed myself, because we were having people over. And I did all this without throwing a single hysterical fit, while Eric stalked these damned flies that are everywhere all of a sudden, dozens of tiny flies.

A year ago, it was like pulling teeth getting people to come over to our house and eat. Now when I ask, they come. I don't know why. I like to think people want to be involved in my grand social experiment, but I sniff a sense of narcissism there. We had

a full house that night, and no one worried too much about the
heat or eating too much; we laughed a lot and promoted our personal favorite tart. I made them sit down and watch some DVDs
of JC's shows, thinking I think that somehow I could convert
them to the ineffable wisdom and rightness of her. From the polite, slightly mystified looks on their faces, and their occasional
Dan Aykroyd jokes, I inferred that this didn't work — wild-eyed
proselytizing rarely does — so I soon switched JC out for some
more accessible Season 3 *Buffy*.

Eric cheered my accomplishment with a hearty *"That's* the
way we do it in the L.I.C., *bitch!"* And indeed, it was a magnifi-
cent groaning board of tarts, more tarts than an army of *Buffy*
fans could actually eat — though an army of Republican bureaucrats did a pretty good job with the leftovers, even eating what
was left of my Tarte aux Cerises, Flambée that failed to *flambé*
and as a result tasted excessively boozy. (I guess they have to get
their intoxicants wherever they can — who can blame them?)

I'd made eight French tarts, any one of which would have
done me in a year ago. I'd had a dozen people over to my apartment, where a year ago I'd have been lucky to tempt two. Julia
would be proud of me, if she knew. Hell, she *was* proud of me. I
knew this because for nearly eleven months Julia had resided in
my brain, in those drafty, capacious, hopeful apartments where
the ghost of Santa Claus still placidly rattled about, along with
my watchfully dead grandmother, and reincarnation and magic
and everything else that couldn't survive out in the brighter hard
highways of my mean metropolitan mind. She'd ensconced herself in there, so that now, though I couldn't look at her straight
on without her melting away, I believed that she was with me
more than I believed that she wasn't.

But on the morning after I failed to make the goddamned
apple aspic, none of that seemed to matter.

"The End" is a tricky bugger, but if you wanted, you could de-
fine the *beginning* of the end as the point when the protagonist

has to see that her actions mean something, and that if they don't
work out right, she is well and truly fucked. By this definition,
the end was a long time in coming. And it might have started
back in July, with a sleepless night and punishing thoughts about
aspic.

It was August 19, 2003. I had six more days left, and I was making three icings for a single cake to take to my appearance on
CNNfn. (Don't ask why CNNfn was interested in me and my
cakes — I cannot fathom it myself.) I'd figured that since here I
was with exactly one week and twelve recipes to go, three of
which were for icing, I'd go ahead and get all the icing out of the
way at once, and ice a third of the cake with each one, Mercedes-
logo style. It was making me a little crazy, or maybe I was going
nuts because on the morning I was to appear live on national
television, I had come down with a raging case of pinkeye.

I'd made the first icing, Crème au Beurre, Ménagère, which
was a snap, and the second icing, Crème au Beurre, au Sucre Cuit,
which *would* have been a snap, if only I could read. Although, in
my defense, please take a look at these first two instructions:

1. *Cream the butter until it is light and fluffy. Set aside.*
2. *Place the egg yolks in the bowl and beat a few seconds to blend
   thoroughly. Set aside.*

What does that mean to you? To me, it means that what I did,
two times, was: beat the butter until fluffy, then beat in the egg
yolks. And when I moved on to the third step:

3. *Boil the sugar and water in the saucepan, shaking pan frequently, until the sugar has reached the soft ball stage. . . . At
   once beat the boiling syrup in a stream of droplets into the egg
   yolks, using your wire whip.*

Two times I wound up with an egg-yolk-and-fluffy-butter mixture studded and wire whip adorned with marble-sized globules of hardened sugar crystal. At first I blamed that whole "soft ball stage" part, "soft ball stages" being things I've long heard of but never truly believed in, like the Easter Bunny or, more aptly, the bogeyman. It wasn't until the third read-through that I noticed the clue embedded in the Enigma code of the text:

> *... beat the boiling syrup in a stream of droplets into the EGG YOLKS ...*

The egg yolks *and butter,* don't you mean, Julia? See, you say so yourself, in instruction #2: *"Place the egg yolks in the bowl..."* THE bowl, see? As in the bowl sitting here next to me with the beaten butter in it, no? Into which the egg yolks must be beaten. Is my logic not impeccable? Though in truth, "placing" the egg yolks does strike me as somehow the wrong way of putting it ... and look over here to the left, at the list of necessary equipment ... TWO 2½-quart bowls. Not one. One for the butter. One for, just to make sure we're on the same page here, the egg yolks.

Ah.

The third time, the Crème au Beurre, au Sucre Cuit worked like a charm.

So it was 9:45. I'd taken the morning off work to do this, because what were they going to do, fire me? I had to leave by eleven if I was to make my 11:30 makeup call; I'd made two icings with one more to go (plus actually slapping the icing on the cake, of course), and still needed to take a shower, since I thought I probably ought not appear on TV with globs of hardened sugar-lava in my hair, smelling like a dockworker. Plenty of time to check e-mails.

This was when I got Isabel's announcement.

He asked me to MARRY him, and I said YES!

The ink on Isabel's divorce papers was not yet dry.

... He asked me on a bridge overlooking the Weir — you must come and visit us, it's so unbeLIEVably lovely here — because he wanted us to have a place we could always go to remember this and show OUR KIDS, and he gave me a ring he had made for me specially, and we're going to be SO disgusting! Julie, I've got me my fairy-tale ending, and I don't even BELIEVE in those!!!

My thoroughly rational first response was, "Oh, for Christ's sake!"

My second reaction was to turn off the damned computer. There are times with your friends when you just have to put their whole mess out of your mind for a while. This is especially true of Isabel. What the hell was she thinking? She of all people should know that a goddamned marriage proposal — from a goddamned punk guitarist in Bath, no less — wasn't the ending of anything, fairy tale or not. And how was I supposed to deal with her ruining her life when I had to ice a cake and take a shower and go on TV?

It wasn't until midway through my second attempt on icing #3, Crème au Beurre, à l'Anglaise, that I had my third response.

Crème au Beurre, à l'Anglaise is based on Crème Anglaise, which is sort of a building block of French desserts, at least French desserts Julia writes about. So I had already made it a couple of times. I was still nervous, though, because it involves custard, which is in the jelling/thickening family of cooking. It's just egg yolks blended with sugar and beaten together with hot milk, all cooked over very low heat until thick but not curdled. It's then beaten in a bowl, over another bowl that's got ice in it, until it cools nearly to room temperature, at which point you mix in a lot of butter. Which sounds simple, and I'm sure is, if you're really solid on the difference between "thick" and "curdled," but after doing this a dozen times in the last year I still wasn't.

So the first time I didn't cook it long enough, and nothing thickened and it was this whole big thing. It was after I'd thrown the first attempt away and was cooking the custard for the second time — stirring, staring into the pot trying to spot "thick" — that I found myself giggling, thinking about how I was making three cake icings before eleven in the morning, to ice a cake which I would then be taking with me onto a nationally broadcast financial news show. I was doing all of it with pinkeye and was getting out of my secretarial job to do it, which made it both the best day I'd have all week and an ending no one could have invented for my blog, or for me, a year ago. A perfect ending.

A fairy-tale one, even.

And it was only then that I had my third response to Isabel and her e-mail.

What was I, the woman with the plan? It was not exactly as if I told my friends and family, "Hey, I'm going to cook my way through an old French cookbook, and when it's done, I'll have figured out what to do with the rest of my life," and they all just sat back with a sigh of relief, thinking, *Well, I'm so glad Julie has got it all figured out. Sensible girl, that Julie.*

Who was I to judge somebody else's navigation? Was I some kind of existential backseat driver? I mean, who exactly did I think I was, anyway?

I was interviewed on CNNfn by three women anchors, all at once, all of them gobbling up my cake at the same time they were interrogating me, so that I didn't get a single bite myself. It was disconcerting. One of the things they were really curious about was how much weight I'd gained. Which is kind of an insulting thing to be asked about on national television, but understandable, I suppose. It's all about the "French Paradox," that much-publicized puzzle of how French people eat all that fatty food and drink tons of wine, yet still manage to be svelte and sophisticated, not to mention cheese-eating surrender monkeys. Reasonable individuals quite naturally hope there's a way to prove its existence scientifically, to the immense benefit of mankind, while dried-up, self-righteous fascists hope there's a way to disprove its existence, so they can go on feeling superior with their good-war-fighting and/or raw food–eating ways. Everyone's always looking for evidence, and I guess the Project is sort of a naturally occurring laboratory test.

But I would call the results inconclusive at best. Eric hasn't gained anything at all, skinny bastard that he is, but while I have not bloated to a New Yorker's Midwest-airport-nightmare proportions, neither would I call myself either svelte or sophisticated. We both have a persistent corset-shaped ache cinched around our torsos. There have been some other unsuspected side effects, but I'm not sure how they affect the hypothesis — I don't believe the French are known worldwide for letting inch-thick layers of dust accumulate on every surface of their homes. I've also never heard that the French keep fleets of houseflies in their kitchens. And we already were cheese-eating surrender monkeys, so I guess we weren't really the ideal test subjects on that count. Also, the tendency we had to eat four helpings of things and drink, in addition to wine, entirely too many gimlets, may have polluted the results somewhat. Julia had always preached moderation, but if there's one thing this year has proven once and for all, it's that I have no talent at all for that particular virtue. I'm more sympathetic to JC's old runnin' buddy Jacques Pepin on this: "Moderation in all things — including moderation."

And then the CNNfn ladies didn't give me my plate back. Which kind of pissed me off.

On the morning of the Sunday I was to serve the second-to-last meal of the Project, I began with Petits Chaussons au Roquefort, pastry turnovers with Roquefort cheese. The pastry was made the normal way, as I have made it perhaps three dozen times in the last year. The weather had taken a turn for the better, with a small injection of cool in the air, a small extraction of moisture, and this helped the pastry turn out, this penultimate time, perfectly.

While it was resting, I made the filling by mashing together a half pound of Roquefort, a stick of softened butter, two egg yolks, pepper, chives, and, oddly I thought, kirsch. Then I rolled out the dough. Moderate though the day was, preheating the oven had gotten the kitchen a little hot and bothered, so I had to work quickly. I cut the dough out into (roughly) two-and-a-half-inch squares, put a little dollop of filling in the middle, painted the edges with some beaten egg, and sealed them together with my fingers.

There was something about all this familiar work — the kneading and rolling and flouring, the Book beside me, Julia in my head chortling quietly to herself like a roosting pigeon in its cote. Something about all the checks on all these recipes on these 684 yellowed pages — 519 black checks, five left to be made. It made me philosophical — or maybe just hungry. (I'd eaten nothing but what Roquefort filling I could suck off my fingers.) Anyway, as I was stuffing and sealing turnovers, I found myself considering the essential rights of Roquefort filling. I'd brought the filling into being, and now I was seeking to entrap it in a buttery pastry prison, though it was obvious from its evasive behavior that there is nothing Roquefort wants more than to be free. Was this not arrogance? Was it not, in essence, a slave-owning mentality, to be approaching this from the perspective of how best to trap the Roquefort filling, without consideration for the Roquefort's fundamental desire for freedom?

I was getting a little dizzy.

In retrospect, of course, this can be recognized as the first sign of my imminent psychotic break.

I manage to get the turnovers made, though the pastry dough is getting sticky fast. Some of the turnovers are not pretty. I throw them in the oven anyway. My head's spinning, I've got spots before my eyes — except they're not spots. They're flies. Hundreds of them.

They're EVERYWHERE. While the turnovers bake I position myself in the middle of the kitchen like Gary Cooper with a fly-swatter, my body like a coiled spring, ready to kill. But they are too fast for me, and too many. For every fly that falls fluttering to the floor, two more take its place. Discouraged, I turn to the dishes. This, too, is a loser's game because, well, there are so fucking many of them, several days' worth, and the water doesn't want to drain in the sink, probably because of the accumulated sludge down there in the drain catch.

I take out the Roquefort turnovers. They look okay. I stuff one into my mouth, not realizing until I feel a tingling throb that starts in my mouth and travels ahead of the (searingly hot but actually quite delicious) masticated knob of Petits Chaussons au Roquefort down my throat into my stomach that I'm not just hungry, I'm *starving.* Ignoring the blisters rising on the roof of my mouth, I quickly gobble another turnover.

I figure the least I can do while waiting for the sink to finish draining is put away the dry dishes waiting on the dish rack. I start putting up plates and utensils and measuring spoons. The flies seem especially thick in the air around the sink. I notice too a moldy sort of odor, which doesn't particularly surprise me. I peer down into the shallow puddle that's collected in the plastic tray under the dish rack, which can get a little scummy. And it is that. I can't remember the last time I washed it. So I fold up the metal rack and pick up the tray so I can wash it in the bathtub.

As I'm turning to go to the bathroom, a tiny movement catches my eye. I look down at the counter, where the drip pan had been sitting. The origin of the legion of flies becomes nauseatingly clear.

"Aaaaaauuuuggghhhhheeeeeeeeeeeewwwwwwwww!!!!!!!!"

"What?! Jesus, what?" Eric, who's spent the whole morning and into the afternoon cleaning the house, dashes into the kitchen, where he finds me, pale as a ghost, eyes like saucers, the drip pan held out from my body with one hand, pointing with a shaking finger at the counter. "What's the matt — AUGH!"

So what exactly does one do when faced with a thriving colony of maggots under one's dish rack? I mean other than shoot up a quick, grateful missive to the heavens for letting you live in a forward-thinking time and place, in which one's husband cannot lop off one's breasts and nose for a crime called Depraved Domestic Neglect? Martha Stewart doesn't touch upon this quandary, so far as I know, the maggot one, I mean, so we had to sort of make it up as we went along. We began by hopping up and down in frantic disgust. Then we lifted the dishes out of the sink and put them on the floor, gingerly swept the floating, squirming white things off the counter into the sink, threw the sponge in after them, and poured a bottle full of Clorox over the whole mess. Then we took the drip pan from under the dish rack into the bathroom, flung it into the tub, and poured Clorox all over it as well.

After that we pretty much went about our business. Awful as it was, this wasn't quite as traumatic as it might have been for other people because after a year of this, part of you just *assumes* there's gotta be some maggots somewhere around. We did break out into occasional spasmodic shudders, and sometimes threw utensils from our hands in sudden panic upon imagining a creeping, burrowing sensation, especially when in the vicinity of the kitchen sink. We had that much humanity left in us, anyway.

It was two o'clock in the afternoon. Even leaving aside for a moment the insect larvae now bravely facing their hideous fate in a pool of bleach in the sink, the kitchen was absolutely disgusting — dabs of butter stuck to the side of the fridge, various meat juices spattered in violent arcs across the walls, layers of doughy, buttery, dusty, cat-hairy crap on every surface. I would be making the pastry for the Pâté de Canard en Croûte in the food processor, and if Julia didn't like it, well then, balls to *her*. In thirty hours' time this would be over, and she and I could both just go our separate ways.

I threw the flour and salt and sugar into the Cuisinart, plus a half cup of chilled shortening and a cut-up stick of butter, and ran the thing briefly to cut the fat in. Then I added the two eggs and some cold water and combined.

The dough was too dry. It wasn't sticking together. I added some more water. No change. I dumped it onto my marble pastry board, which didn't have maggots on it, but might very well have had trace elements of any number of other repulsive/toxic substances. I added cold water, in drops, then tablespoons, then rivers. The dough was going straight from floury heap to melted-butter puddle. I began to burble — in simple confusion at first, then in increasing desperation, and then at last in incoherent existential rage.

Eric was beside me, peering down at the mess. "Is it too hot in here?"

"Too hot?! Too *hot?!* You *idiot!*" I threw granules of dry dough about in blind fury. "Goddamn this pastry dough. Fuck it! Three hundred and sixty-four days and I can't even make *pastry dough*. This whole thing was fucking POINTLESS!"

Eric said nothing — what was there to say, really? He went back to his vacuuming. As cavernous dry sobs issued from a hopeless hollow in my chest, I threw away the dough and started again. I made it by hand this time. And it was still too goddamned dry. But I squeezed the stuff together until it kind of — really, just barely — stuck together. I twisted it up tight in some plastic wrap.

I had the hiccups. I had to go lie down.

I awoke an hour later. The kitchen — the whole apartment — sparkled. Well, that's not true. But the difference was remarkable. Eric was on the couch reading the *Atlantic,* munching a Roquefort turnover. "You feeling better?" he asked, when I came around the corner into the living room, looking pretty wobbly, I imagine.

"Yeeeaaah." God. Even *I* hate myself when I use that pathetic whine. "Thank you for the house. I love you."

"I love you too."

Dispensing with guilt is a multibillion-dollar industry, but I don't think it's such a bad thing to have, really. Not if you deserve it. Like if on the second-to-last day of a year of torture imposed on the man you love, you scream and throw things and call him an idiot (which isn't true at all), and if instead of slamming the front door in your face and seeking out comfort in the arms of Mishal Husain, he cleans the house while you take a nap. This guilt, mingled as it is with gratitude like a pain and a sudden ineffably sweet recognition of your unbelievable good fortune, is not only good for you; it's also delicious. I straddled him, kissed him, nuzzled down into the crook of his neck, crumpling up his *Atlantic* as I did.

"I *really* love you."

"You love me? Who loves *you?!*"

We just sat like that together for a little bit. I lifted my head off his shoulder, blew some air noisily through my lips.

"So." He gave my rump a brisk pat. "What do we do now?"

The answer was unbearably frightening, except it wasn't, because look who I was sitting on top of. The guy who makes sure none of it is unbearable, not ever. So I took another healthy, strengthening breath, and stood. I said, "Now I will *bone the duck*."

"Ah. Well, good luck with that," Eric replied, before opening up his creased *Atlantic* and hiding himself behind it.

I returned to my newly deloused kitchen. Eric had wiped down the counter and placed the Book squarely in the center of it. The Book's poor spine had cracked several times, and I'd performed some inexact triage with packing tape. In the ensuing months it had gotten grimier and grimier, so that beneath the clear tape was preserved evidence of an earlier, brighter phase in the Book's existence. I riffled through the pages, past check marks and stains and water-rippled pages, others stuck together with who-knows-what, until I got to Pâté de Canard en Croûte — boned stuffed duck baked in a pastry crust.

I'll leave you to contemplate that for a moment. If you have your own copy of *MtAoFC*, open it to page 571. Peruse the recipe — all five pages of it. The drawings, particularly — there are eight of them — are enlightening. Terrifying, but enlightening.

Okay, Julie, you can do this.

"Did you say something, honey? You okay?" Poor Eric. Imagine what it must be like, sitting out there, waiting for the inevitable first whimper of distress, knowing where it will go from there.

"Huh? No, nothing — I'm fine."

The knife drawer slid smoothly on its tracks. I peered in, like a malevolent dentist examining his instruments, before removing the Japanese boning knife I had bought for just this event. It had never before been used; its blade gleamed in the kitchen's gloom (for the fluorescent light in the kitchen, oh best beloved, had declined to come on for the second-to-last day of the Project), and sounded a tiny *snick* as I placed it down beside the cutting board. Next I removed the duck from the fridge, unwrapped it, and cleaned it over the sink — after making extra sure that the sink no longer had either dirty dishes or maggots or Clorox in it, of course — setting aside the neck and excess fat, the liver, the gizzard like two hearts and the heart like half a gizzard. I dried the bird with paper towels and set it on the board, breast down. I took the knife up in my left fist before bending my head to the Book.

You may think that boning a fowl is an impossible feat if you have never seen it done or thought of attempting it.

Another good, cleansing breath.

Although the procedure may take 45 minutes the first time because of fright, it can be accomplished in not much more than 20 on your second or third try.

No fear, Julie. No fear.

The important thing to remember is that the cutting edge of your knife must always face the bone, never the flesh, thus you cannot pierce the skin.

I twisted a kink out of my neck. "Hon? You sure you're okay?" Eric's concerned voice came to me as if from a great distance.
"Hm? Oh — fine, fine."
The knife hung poised over the duck's pale, bumpy flesh.

To begin with, cut a deep slit down the back of the bird from the neck to the tail.

I made the first incision, a deep slice down to the backbone. Slowly, slowly, I began to scrape the meat away from the bone, down one side. When I got to the wing and the leg, I separated the bone at the joint, leaving the leg bone and the two outermost joints of the wing attached to the skin, just as Julia instructed. Then back up along the breastbone I scraped. The Japanese boning knife slid through flesh with terrifying precision.

You must be careful here, as the skin is thin and easily slit.

I slowed my breathing as if trying to go into hibernation. I forced myself to move slowly. Once I'd gotten to the ridged breastbone I stopped, and performed the same operation on the duck's left side.

You will wonder how in the world any sense can be made of it all.

"Did you say something, sweetie?"

"*What?*" The kitchen was still quite hot. I wiped my damp forehead with the back of my hand before touching the tip of my knife to that fragile juncture of cartilage and skin at the breast-bone.

"Nothing. Sorry."

One more careful slit, and I'm done.

Oh.

That was a *breeze.*

The day before, I'd made the pâté my duck-suit was to be stuffed with — it was just ground veal and pork mixed with chopped-up pork fat, onions that had been minced and sautéed in butter and Madeira that'd been cooked down in the same pan, some eggs, salt, pepper, allspice, thyme, and a clove of crushed garlic. Hardly worth mentioning at this late stage in the game. This stuff I mounded up into the duck-suit lying splayed across the cutting board. After that it was just a matter of sewing it up.

When I'd gone out to buy my glittering deadly Japanese bon-ing knife, I'd also picked up some "poultry lacers," which sounded like just the thing for lacing up poultry, don't you think? They even came with twine included. I was a little bit concerned, though. Because these poultry lacer thingies, rather than ending with eyes at their nonbusiness ends, just curled into a biggish loop, maybe a little more than half a dime in diameter, the tail of which did not quite meet the shaft of the needle. (Actually, they looked exactly like the metal things we'd had scattered around the kitchen for years, which we called "skewers" and lost all the time, because they were so small, and lots of times they'd slip through the bars of our dishwashing rack and fall into the stinking muck that was always building up in the drip pan, and you didn't really want to use them after that.) How was I supposed to sew up a duck with something like that?

I've never crocheted before, but I used to watch my granny do it, and I believe the maneuver I was attempting here bore similarities. I looped twine several times through the "eye" of the skewer, stuck the skewer or poultry lacer or whatever through two layers of duck skin, then pulled it all the way through both layers of skin, easing the skin around the open loop at the end, trying as I did so to worry the twine through the holes in both flaps of duck skin before it slipped off the open end of the loop.

This didn't work very well. In fact, it led to a renewal of obscenities, sobs, and pounding of hands on tables.

But then my husband, who's not an idiot at all, had a brilliant notion. For a while he fiddled about with the possibilities of safety pins — Eric's a big fan of safety pins, he always carries one around in his wallet; he claims it's great for picking up chicks — before coming upon the most elegantly simple solution of all: a sewing needle. A really, really big sewing needle. I couldn't imagine how he'd ever found it, or why we had a needle that big in the house in the first place, but I'm not looking a gift horse in the mouth. It worked like a charm, too — too easy to even talk about. Which was good, because it meant I would not have to stab my eyes out with a skewer/poultry lacer.

Once the duck was sewn I bound it tightly with lengths of string until it was basically football shaped, then browned it on all sides in a skillet with oil. While it cooled, I took out the pastry dough — and lo! it had miraculously transformed from a crumbly mess into dough! That I could roll out! This day was just getting better and better. But seriously, for once.

In no time I had the browned duck-suit-pâté-football sealed inside two ovals of pastry. It went so easily I was almost embarrassed. I even cut out little rounds from the leftover pastry, made fan shapes on them with the back of a knife, and used them to disguise the pinched edges of the ovals. More rounds formed a floret shape in the middle, around the hole I poked in the crust to let steam escape. I tell you what: rather than me trying to explain all this, go get your copy of *MtAoFC*, and turn to page 569. See that picture? That is *exactly* what my Pâté de Canard en Croûte looked like.

"Eric Eric Eric! Look!"

He came in and was duly impressed, because how could he not be? It was goddamned *amazing*. "And your Julia impression's definitely improving, by the way," he said.

"What?"

"When you were burbling away, boning the duck? It was really good. You should take that on the road."

Huh. I didn't remember saying a word.

So the ending may be a long time in coming, but that doesn't mean it doesn't have a way of sneaking up on you.

Gwen and Sally came over to celebrate our second-to-last day. We stuck a DVD of Julia's greatest hits on the machine and casually watched it while we waited for the Pâté de Canard en Croûte to cook, eating Roquefort turnovers and drinking sixty-five-dollar champagne — which tasted just like regular champagne, only more expensive. It all felt very celebratory and nice, and if it seemed just a smidge anticlimactic, drinking champagne always serves as a good cure for that.

I really hardly ever pick up the telephone. I thought it was my mom this time. "Julie! Congratulations!"

It wasn't. "Um, thanks."

"Finished the Project, have you?"

"No, actually — not until tomorrow —"

"Oops! Well, congratulations in advance, then."

"Uh — ?"

"Oh, I'm sorry! My name's Nick. I'm a reporter out here in Santa Monica, and I just finished up an interview with Julia for our paper out here."

I was really going to have to get my phone number unlisted.

"I'd like to get your thoughts on some things. Because I asked her about you, and frankly, she was kind of a pill about it. Is this a bad time?"

"Oh. No. It's fine."

When I hung up the phone five minutes later, I felt numb. Eric and Gwen were watching Julia demonstrating how to char the skin of a tomato; I stood for a moment in front of the TV, watching. She looked young, but she must have been at least seventy at the time.

Julia took out a blowtorch and brandished it, and Gwen laughed. The aroma of duck was beginning to seep from the kitchen.

"Who was that on the phone, babe?"

"Julia hates me."

"I'm sorry?"

I sat on the couch beside Eric. Gwen and Sally were staring at me, the television forgotten. "That was a reporter from California. He just interviewed Julia. He asked her about me. She hates me." I giggled, like I do in these situations, breathlessly. "She thinks I'm not respectful or not serious or something."

Sally made an offended noise in her throat. "That's not fair!"

"Do you think I'm not serious? Not *serious?*" I laughed again, but this time there was a tickle in my nose and I squinted at the beginning of a burn behind my eyes.

"Oh, please." Gwen held the bottle of champagne out to me,

and I stopped rolling the glass I had between my palms so she could pour. "Screw her."

Eric put his arm over my shoulder. "What is she, ninety?"

"Ninety-one." I sniffled.

"See? She probably doesn't have the first idea what a blog *is*."

"I don't understand how she could *hate* this." Sally sounded nearly as wounded as I felt. "What's *wrong* with her?"

"I don't know. Maybe she thinks I'm taking advantage or I'm — I'm not —" I was taken surprise by a sudden rush of tears. "I thought I was — I'm sorry if I —"

And then, abruptly, I was wailing. Everyone was shocked into stillness for a fraction of a second, then Eric was pulling me to his chest, and Gwen and Sally were fluttering down on either side of me in that ruffling-feathers way of best friends. As they clucked over me, I cried open-throated, as if my heart would break, my head back so tears ran into my ears, heaving, taking loud, rasping gulps so I could keep going, until after a while it wasn't just about what Julia did or didn't think about me, and it wasn't about dough that was crumbly or aspic that didn't set or a job that didn't make me happy, and then until, eventually, it wasn't even about being sad.

I sobbed and sobbed and sobbed until it turned into a Good Cry — the best cry I'd ever had, in fact, even though this last year I'd had far more than my share. I got snot all over Eric's shirt, and Sally took away my champagne glass to make sure I didn't break it, and Gwen held my hand, and it all felt so good that I began to laugh too, sobbing and giggling, all of it very loudly.

The alarm in the kitchen started to beep, which meant that it was time to take out the Pâté de Canard en Croûte. "I'll get it." Eric left me to the girls, and got up to go to the kitchen.

"So what did you say to the reporter?" asked Sally, as she handed me back my champagne glass, evidently taking from the tittering amid tears that I could now be trusted with it. I lifted the glass to my lips.

"I said, 'Fuck her.'" I crack myself up sometimes, I really do. Sally nimbly managed to avoid the champagne spew, but Gwen caught some friendly fire.

"No, you didn't!" cried Sally.

"No, of course not. I should've though."

The bleeping from the kitchen had stopped. "Hey, Julie?"

"Yeah?" I rolled my eyes, snuffling onto the back of my hand while Gwen dabbed at her shirt. "What's wrong now?"

"You oughta take a look at this."

Gwen and Sally stared at me, and I stared back. "Oh *God*. What is it?"

At that moment Eric came out of the kitchen. He had oven mitts on his hands, and he was carrying a roasting pan before him.

It was my Pâté de Canard en Croûte. And it was *perfect*.

Gwen squealed, Sally clapped her hands. Eric was grinning at me.

"Would you look at that?" I sighed.

"Julie, this is seventy-five percent as good as Julia could do. At *least*."

One more sob/giggle escaped me, but I shook it off. "Okay, then." I waved him back into the kitchen. "Let's crack this mother open."

Julia wanted me to excavate the duck, detruss it, carve it, and return it to the crust. That was simply not going to happen. What I did, while everyone watched with their hearts in their mouths, was carve out a sort of pastry lid, move it carefully to one side, and gingerly reach in with a pair of scissors to cut any strings from around the duck I could get to and pull them out. After that I put the top back on, took my biggest carving knife, the one with which I couldn't make a dent in a marrowbone most of a year ago, and just sliced right through.

It did not taste unlike anything I'd ever eaten, or even better, exactly — it just tasted *more*. More rich and smooth and crispy and buttery and duck-y. Culinary plutonium was what it was, but what a way to go. We all sat around the dinner table, sated and burping, under the fuzzy lilac chandelier Eric had gotten me for Valentine's Day, which looked like a Muppet and which, thanks to CBS, had seen a fifteen minutes of its own. "Well," said Gwen, "if Julia isn't happy with this, then there's just no pleasing the bitch."

Forget Tart-a-palooza . . . *that's* the way we do it in the L.I.C.

Once Sally and Gwen went home and the remaining Pâté de Canard en Croûte, now looking sad and ravaged, was bundled in plastic wrap and stuck in the fridge, Eric and I got into bed. I laid my head on his chest and hitched my leg over his thighs and soon was doing the giggle / cry thing again, only quieter, and heavier on the giggling side of things. "Almost done," said Eric.

"Almost done."

"So what's for dinner tomorrow?"

"Kidneys with beef marrow."

"Mmm, beef marrow."

"Yeah."

"And then, after that —" Eric kissed the top of my head as I snuggled closer — "can we have a dog?"

I did another little giggle / cry. "Sure."

"And lots and lots of salad?"

"*Ohhhh* yeah. And a baby? You know I need to get started with that, Eric, because you know I've got a —"

"A *syndrome.* I know. I'm not worried."

"Why not? Maybe we should be worried."

"Nah." He nipped my shoulder. "If you can do the Project, you can make a kid. No problem."

"Hm. Maybe you're right."

And so we slept — like a pair of duck-football-stuffed babies.

The last day of the Project I took off work — because like I said, what were they going to do? I think I thought I would spend the day serenely preparing the final meal, contemplating the meaning of the year and all the bounteous blessings that had been bestowed upon me. But you know, I've never been much good at contemplation, and serenity, like French cooking, takes more than a year to master. So instead I spent the morning in a bout of severe Civilfixation ("I'm just going to finish taking Rome, and then I'm stopping *for sure. . . .*"), and then had to rush frantically to get errands done. At Ottomanelli's, where I went for my kidneys and marrowbone, the guy behind the counter said, *"Heeeey. How's the cooking? With, whosit, Julia Child?"*

"Good. I'm done with it, actually."

"That's good, that's good. I'm tellin' ya, never saw so many people ordering offal in my life." He held up the marrowbone I had ordered. "Say, you usin' this for enrichment? Because I can cut this in half for you so you can get it out."

Now he tells me.

Eric and I ate our Rognons de Veau à la Bordelaise alone together, with green beans and some sautéed potatoes on a plate decorated with Mayonnaise Collée — that's mayonnaise you put gelatin into, so you can shape it with a pastry bag into squiggles and designs, should you have a mind. I figured I should save at least one catastrophic failure for the end. Waiting on the kitchen counter as we ate our meal was the very last recipe of *MtAoFC* — Reine de Saba. Otherwise known as chocolate cake.

My deadly new Japanese boning knife made cleaning the kidneys much easier — it went right after all those bits of white fat, and the white tubes buried in the muscle. The Reine de Saba went smoothly as well. This was almost a torte, really, with pulverized almonds substituting for a good proportion of the flour. The only trick to it was not to overbake it. JC said that "overcooked, the cake loses its special creamy quality," and I would hate for the final bite of the year to be a cake with no special creaminess, so I was on tenterhooks, I'll admit, but all went according to plan.

The Mayonnaise Collée, well — it's mayonnaise. With gelatin mixed into it. What can you expect? I didn't make it any easier for myself, either. Because here I was, after 365 days, still confusing easy with simple.

"Beating mayonnaise by hand is just too Martha. I'll screw it up, I know I will. The food processor is easier."

Disregarding a year's worth of evidence that I *always* screw up the mayonnaise when I use the food processor — every single time — I dumped the eggs and mustard and salt into the bowl of the Cuisinart and buzzed it, then added the lemon juice, just like Julia told me to. To add the oil I used the cup that slides into the top of the Cuisinart, which it had taken me an embarrassing number of attempts at mayonnaise to realize has a pinprick hole in the bottom of it that is exactly the right diameter for dispensing oil for mayonnaise. Probably, if I still had the manual for the thing, which obviously I don't, I would find that that hole is in fact called the "mayonnaise hole." I poured the oil in there and let it take care of the conscientious drip-drop. This had worked in the past. On this day I wound up with liquid. "God*dammit*," I muttered. However, I heroically did not scream "FUCK IT FUCK IT FUCK IT!" at the top of my lungs. Instead, I started again. This time I would do it by hand. I did not have high hopes.

I beat together the egg yolks, and the mustard and salt. I took the cup out from the top of the Cuisinart and gave it to Eric. "Hold this over the bowl and just let it drip, okay?" So he stood, the oil dripped, and I whisked and whisked and whisked.

I'll be damned if it didn't work like a charm. "Eric?" I said, giving a few last beatings to the beautiful, pale yellow, perfectly thick stuff in the bowl.

"Yes, Julie?"

"Don't let me forget this. If I've learned nothing else here, I've learned that I *can* make mayonnaise by hand."

"*We* can make mayonnaise by hand," he corrected, as he shook out his sore wrist with a wince.

"Right. *We* can."

I stirred into the mayonnaise some gelatin that I'd softened in white wine and vinegar and stock, and then I set it in the fridge to set.

Rognons de Veau à la Bordelaise is simplicity itself to make; no different, essentially, from Poulet Sauté, and no different, especially, from Bifteck Sauté Bercy. In fact, making it that night felt like falling into a time warp — I stood before the stove, melting butter and browning meat and smelling the smells of wine deglazing and shallots softening — but the dishes changed before my eyes, and I heard Julia warbling, "Boeuf Bourguignon is the same as Coq au Vin. You can use *lamb,* you can use *veal,* you can use *pork. . . .*"

I retrieved the split marrowbone from the fridge, where it had been slowly thawing for some hours. Just as the guy at Otto-manelli's had promised, the strip of marrow lifted easily from its bone-furrow in one piece. I diced it and soaked it in hot water a couple of minutes to soften it further, then tossed it into the sauce along with the sliced kidneys, and reheated the pan until everything was warm.

Julia says of Mayonnaise Collée that it "can be squeezed out of a pastry bag to make fancy decorations." Reading that sentence wigged me out like nothing I'd read all year — more than brains, more than cutting lobsters in half, more even than eggs in aspic. I thought of a cake iced with mayonnaise florets, mayonnaise curlicues, "Congratulations, Julie!" written out in big cursive letters. Nineteen-sixty-one was a different country, no doubt about it.

I used Mayonnaise Collée to decorate the plate I'd be serving the potatoes on. As you'll remember, my pastry bag had split apart on the night that Eric almost divorced me over Sauce Tartare, so I jimmied a makeshift one out of a Ziploc bag. With it I made mayonnaise curlicues and mayonnaise florets and, because

"Congratulations, Julie!" seemed a little, well, self-congratulatory, a mayonnaise "Julie/Julia," in cursive letters around the rim of the plate. But, as it turns out, Mayonnaise Collée works significantly better on *cold* dishes. Once I scooped warm potatoes onto the plate, my fancy decorations swiftly melted into undistinguished blobs, and the letters of "Julie/Julia" grew fatter and more vague, and finally completely illegible. I guess I should have thought of that. No matter. Mayonnaise Collée, jelled or not, still tasted delicious on sautéed potatoes.

The Rognons de Veau à la Bordelaise did not taste like piss, no matter what my mother says, because I cleaned them with my deadly boning knife, and because the beef marrow conducted a two-pronged attack with the finishing sprinkling of parsley on any holdout pissiness — extinguishing it between fatty, velvety richness and sharp, fresh greenness. We ate it with a wine that I bought in the city that is cloudy and dark and tastes a little like blood. The lady who sold it to me called it "feral." Like me. For dessert, some creamy smooth Reine de Saba and Season 1, Episode 2 *Buffy*.

And all of a sudden, that was it. For twelve months I had been doing this thing. I had cooked for friends, and for family, and for anchorwomen on CNNfn, and somewhere in there it had gotten a little surreal. But now here we were, back exactly where we started — just Eric, me, and three cats, slightly worse for wear, sitting on a couch in the outer boroughs, eating. *Buffy* was on the TV, and somewhere Julia was chortling — even if she did hate me.

The End

Except of course that then I woke up and had to go to work again. I'd kind of forgotten about that. And although my kidneys had not tasted like piss, I did notice that, the next morning, my piss smelled faintly of kidneys. And I went to work, and it was pretty much the same as it had been before, and here I was just a secretary, albeit a fatter one who had been on CBS and CNNfn.

"Eric, this is weird." I called him between the crazy people, while Bonnie was in a Very Important meeting.

"Yeah, I know."

"I'm at work. It feels sort of like it's not over, and sort of like it never happened."

"Just wait until you cook something without butter, then you'll know it's over."

But then I decided to make a stir-fry for dinner. I'd forgotten what a pain in the ass stir-fries are. There was no butter and no Julia, but we still ate at 10:30 at night, so it still didn't feel over.

That was when we decided that in order to finish it for real we had to do something serious. We had to make a pilgrimage. We would go to the Smithsonian Institution, and we would visit the Julia Child exhibit there. We would see her kitchen, which she had donated to the museum when she went to live in a California retirement community, and which had been moved — lock, stock, and pegboard — from the house she used to share with Paul in Cambridge, Massachusetts, down to DC. We would leave a stick of butter in thanks. For closure, we figured, you couldn't get much better than that.

One thing about Eric is that he really hates to drive. And one thing about me is that I've got a freaky Bermuda Triangle–style disruptive force field centered on my belly button. Just before the occasion of our pilgrimage this force field had eaten up my driver's license. Eric, good citizen that he is, would never let me drive without it, which meant that the only one doing the driving up and down the NYC-DC corridor would be the one of us who really hated to do it. So on the beautiful morning in early September when we collected our rental car and started off, there was that little frisson of resentment brewing from the beginning —

keep in mind, of course, that even in the best of situations, Eric and I are not exactly *Amazing Race* material.

It's wonderful not to be in New York on a beautiful day. It's wonderful to have the wind in your hair. It's wonderful not to be making a shopping list. It's not so wonderful getting into DC with a lousy map and a worse navigator. My big idea was to take the exit for Georgia Avenue and just shoot straight on down to the Mall. As it turns out, it takes approximately fifteen years to do this. When Eric started making audible rumblings about committing hara-kiri on the gear shift, I got my second bright idea, which was to make a right turn somewhere. Which decision sent us careening off like a (very slow) pinball, spinning around traffic circles and screaming like, well, apoplectic New Yorkers, at pedestrians crossing the street so slowly it was like all of Washington DC was either developmentally disabled or on drugs. We might have been lost forever had we not happened upon Pennsylvania Avenue. Talk about something I'd never think I'd be saying during the current administration, but God bless the White House.

Eric had a friend from DC who'd said that parking around the Mall was no problem. This might have been the case on some other day, but it certainly was not on the occasion of the National Association of Negro Women conference and American Black Family Reunion. It was two in the afternoon by this time, and we had eaten nothing all day. We didn't know what time the Smithsonian closed, or where it was, or where we might be able to buy butter, which we had to do before we went to the museum because if we didn't get the butter then the entire point was lost — *and* there were all these goddamned trees everywhere, plus the masses and masses and *masses* of people on the Mall didn't walk any faster than the ones crossing the streets. So we were feeling a little panicky. The reflecting pool had been drained during the construction of the mind-bogglingly hideous World War II memorial, which meant we could just dash straight across it. We wandered and wandered, both warm and astonished, asking cops for directions as we went, dodging children with fried snacks, stopping along the way to buy Eric (a) a Polish sausage, (b) camera batteries, and (c) (once he realized, after he'd thrown away his first set of batteries, which he'd bought about a week before, and put in the second set of batteries, and freaked out because the "no battery" icon was still blinking, except we figured out that that was actually the "no film" icon, and that the first batteries, now in a public garbage can and covered in ketchup and powdered sugar, had been fine all along) film.

The prospects for butter were looking exceedingly grim. The vicinity of the Mall in Washington, for those of you who've never been there, is a good place to go for big gray government buildings, and statues of presidents, and bookstores, but don't try to get any grocery shopping done there. I asked the manager of Harry's restaurant if I could buy a stick of butter off him. The manager wasn't a New Yorker, you could tell because he wasn't an asshole, but he couldn't fix me up because Harry's *uses no butter.* Which freaked me out and made me think that even though the slow-walking populace is very nice, and there are all these trees, I really couldn't live in DC. He did say, though, that I could probably find some at the CVS three blocks down.

Which indeed we did.

Okay. We were ready. It was now 3:30. Eric had eaten his Polish sausage, and we were in possession of both butter and the camera and film we would need to document the drop-off. We got to the Smithsonian and took our place at the end of the line of museumgoers filing through security at the entrance. Now we just had to get the butter inside.

One thing you might not know about me, because it's not something I exactly go around bragging about, is that I'm a total goody-two-shoes. No, that's not quite right, because I'm not all that honest, or courteous — hell, I'm not even clean. I guess what I am is a coward. When I was a kid, I fancied myself a bit like Scarlett O'Hara — brave, resourceful, ruthless, irresistible.

But these days, I mostly just see myself in what Rhett says to her when she tells him she's afraid of going to hell: "You're like a thief who's not at all sorry he stole, but is very, very sorry he got caught." Nothing upsets me more than the prospect of getting caught. And there's not much I won't do to avoid it. Am I proud of offering to hold Eric's carryall while he tied his shoe, then slipping the box of Land O'Lakes into it while his back was turned? Of essentially turning my husband into a butter-mule, so that should the burly guards with billy clubs hanging from their belts, shining their small flashlights into every bag, find the contraband, it would be Eric's ass and not mine? Of course not. I'm ashamed. All I can say in my defense is that the security guards could've cared less about Eric's carryall or his butter, so it all turned out fine. We got through security with no hassle at all, then hoofed it down a long, wide hallway, and in no time at all we were there, at the Julia Child exhibit.

Footage of Julia and interviews with other people about Julia were playing on a continuous loop on a large television in a smallish room. The walls were lined with cases, in which were arrayed strange and wondrous kitchen utensils from Julia's enormous collection — a device called a *manché à gigot* that looked like a really vicious nipple clamp, the very same blowtorch that I'd watched her char a tomato with. Along one wall was laid out all seventeen pages of her French bread recipe from *MtAoFC*, Volume II — if I'd thought that after Pâté de Canard en Croûte nothing could scare me, that recipe would put me right.

And then there was the kitchen, enclosed in glass. Smaller than I'd imagined it, not as many powers of magnitude larger than ours as I had thought. The pegboard, marked with the outlines of all her many, many pots and pans. The beautiful, enormous Garland oven. The burnished maple countertops, built two inches taller than standard. It was the kitchen that Julia had built to fit her, after half a lifetime of squeezing her great big frame into the kitchens of a too-small world. I pressed up against the glass, craning my neck to get a glimpse of every corner and nook. I wished only that I could get in there for a minute, let myself feel dwarfed inside Julia's kitchen.

Three small kids were plopped down on the carpet in front of the TV. Eric and I were waiting for the exhibit to empty out for a bit so I could leave the butter in peace, and after I'd pored over the exhibit I watched the kids watch for a while. They sat Indian-style with their little skulls rolled back on their necks almost onto the slouched humps of their backs, mouths gaping open so they could breathe through them. Mostly they were silent, except for the odd giggle when Julia pitched a rolling pin over her shoulder or something, and when one of them breathed in awed tones, "Julia Child is *crazy.*" For a while I couldn't tell whether it was just the hypnotic pull of television on young minds, but then Alice Waters came on, and the kids were out of there and halfway to the Model Ts quicker than you can say "perfect peach."

We waited a good while longer for folks to clear out, but they never did. Coward or not, I was going to have to bite the bullet.

"Eric, get out your camera and hand me the butter."

"Don't you have the butter?"

"Er . . . no." I bared my teeth in a sheepish grimace and pointed. "It's in there." Eric pulled the Land O'Lakes box out of his bag, gaping in the dawning recognition of my betrayal, but this was no time for arguments. "Now come on, get out your camera. Let's *do* this."

There was no question of where to make the drop-off — at the center of the exhibit, beneath a large black-and-white photo of Julia in a chef's apron and wild seventies polyester shirt, one hip cocked, grinning. There was even a narrow shelf running along under it, as if it really was a shrine, and pilgrims really were expected to leave their offerings there.

I held the box in my hand a moment and looked up at her picture. It was a good picture, an excellent likeness. She looked friendly and strong and hungry, broad of shoulder and face and mind, just like she'd looked as she rattled around in my brainpan every night of the last year. The Julia living in a retirement community in Santa Barbara might think I'm an unserious, foul-mouthed little upstart. Maybe if I met that Julia I wouldn't even like her. But I liked the Julia in my head — the only one I really knew, after all — just fine. And what's more, the Julia in my head liked me just fine too.

"Well, *bon appétit* and all that, Julia. And thanks. Really."

I placed the butter beneath her picture — and then I ran like hell, cackling all the way, Eric on my heels.

And that was it, really. A secretary in Queens risked her marriage and her sanity and her cats' welfare to cook all 524 recipes in *Mastering the Art of French Cooking* — a book that changed the lives of thousands of servantless American cooks — all in one year. The same year she turned thirty. It was the hardest, bravest, best thing a coward like her ever did, and she wouldn't have done it without Julia.

The End

▚▚▚▚▚

June 1949
Paris, France

"Well, Paulski, I've gone and done it."

"Here, lean out the window there so I can get the rooftops behind you. Done what?"

"I've found myself a project." Minette leapt up onto the windowsill against which Julie was leaning; she rubbed the cat's ears and smiled for the camera.

Paul clicked once, wound the film, clicked again. The watery light falling into their apartment that afternoon seemed designed to flatter the soft, broad planes of his wife's face. Picking up the camera always put him in a good mood. "Well, what is it?"

"I'll show you — just stay there one minute." She pushed herself off from the windowsill and clomped off down the hall to their bedroom, Minette skittering along after her. Paul heard her riffling through papers on their messy rolltop desk, and then she was out again. She held a paper in front of her.

"I'm going to be in a class with eleven veterans — the GI Bill is paying for the tuition. I'll be the only woman, so I guess you'd better keep an eye on me!"

Paul took the mimeographed sheet from her, the better to read it. "Cordon Bleu, eh? The culinary school? Going to take a cooking class?"

Julie chortled. "Oh, it's much more than that. This is a professional class, for chefs. When I'm done, I can be a restaurateur, if I want to be. We'll call the place Chez Paulski, what do you say?"

"Sounds fine by me." He returned the application to her, hugged her. When she returned the squeeze, she nearly cracked his ribs.

"I'm going to learn to cook for you, my husband. No — I'm going to master cooking for you. Ha-HAH!"

Paul snapped another picture as his wife lifted the cat high up over her head, much to Minette's consternation. "This might be just the thing for you, Julie, you know that?"

She turned to him, her face suddenly thoughtful. "You know? I think it just might be." She laughed, and he laughed along with her. "Maybe it's a new beginning for the old girl!"

. . . Well, Not Quite

The thing I keep learning about endings is that they aren't a long time coming, and they don't sneak up on you either, because endings just don't happen.

A week before the end of the Project, I bought two bottles of champagne. One of them I popped on the second-to-last night, with Sally and Gwen, for a sort of The End Celebration (Observed). I was going to open the second bottle for The End Celebration (Actual). But then I didn't, because it wasn't really over until the last dish was washed, was it? And we weren't going to wash any dishes that night. And then we hatched the plan to make the Julia Pilgrimage, and that was really The End. Except by that time, there was this book deal possibly going to happen, and once that happened it seemed like a jinx to celebrate until I got paid, or got to quit my secretarial job, or got a dog, or finished the book, or or or . . .

I'm totally lying, of course. Of course we drank the second bottle — what have you read in the last three hundred–odd pages that would lead you to believe I'd let a bottle of champagne just sit in my fridge for an entire year? Nothing, that's what.

Still, the point is a sound one. With a book it's easy — to distinguish, not always to write (as you can see) — but what qualifies as The End when it comes to life?

I've spent the last year preparing for this moment, but for some reason the obvious answer never occurred to me until it was too late.

I was working on the book that Friday morning — I was always working on the book at this point, only to be honest, "freaking out over" would probably be a better term — when the phone rang. I let the answering machine pick up, as usual, and wasn't really paying attention to whoever might be on the other end of the line.

"Julie? Jules? You there? Pick up if you're there."

Everyone knows that dread of the familiar voice on the machine, affectless with suppressed grief. It is the voice you hear on the heels of car accidents and divorces, illness and death. I ran for the phone.

"Mom? What is it?"

"Haven't you heard? Oh, baby, I'm so sorry. . . ." And she began to cry.

Julia Child had died on the eve of her ninety-second birthday, peacefully, in her sleep. My mother called me the moment she'd heard, that morning on the radio while she was on her way to work. She was still in the car, parked in front of her office, sobbing into her cell phone.

"I can't imagine how you must feel," she said. "After all you've been through."

I didn't know Julia Child. I never even met her. She did write a response to a letter I wrote her. "Thank you for your kind note," it read. It was printed on a computer, on official Julia Child stationery. "I am happy to know that I have been such a positive influence on you." I have no idea if she actually wrote it or not. The signature looks real, anyway.

Even if I had known her, there is no tragedy in such a peaceful death, after such a long and rich and generous life. It's the death that all of us wish for — well, either that or finding out you have a terminal brain tumor and going out and assassinating some plutocratic motherfucker who's systematically destroying America's democracy brick by brick, before you get shot down in a rain of glory. Or maybe that's just me.

Not a tragedy — an opportunity for celebration, if anything, of a life lived with supreme, if somewhat klutzy, grace. I knew that immediately. I was very calm, and I didn't feel sad at all, not at first. "Thanks for telling me, Mom."

She sniffled. "Are you going to be all right? Do you need anything? What about your blog? Are you going to write something? Everyone's going to be so *sad*." Her voice cracked again.

"I'll be fine. I'll write a little something this morning. Look on the blog later today, okay?"

I knew I had to write something on my blog, even though I hadn't been writing on it for months and months. I knew people would come looking to see if I had anything to say. I wanted to write Julia the best, funniest, greatest *in memoriam* ever. I got to work on it, and I was on fire, let me tell you. I had funny, touching insights. I was coming off clever and heartfelt and sad and grateful and joyful. I was on a roll.

And then I wrote this sentence: "I have no claim over the woman at all, unless it's the claim one who has nearly drowned has over the person who pulled her out of the ocean."

And I started crying so hard I had to stop writing.

Two years ago, I was a twenty-nine-year-old secretary. Now I am a thirty-one-year-old writer. I get paid very well to sit around in my pajamas and type on my ridiculously fancy iMac, unless I'd rather take a nap. Feel free to hate me — I certainly would.

Eric and I still live in our crappy Long Island City apartment (though if this book sells we'll be out of here like a shot). Now Eric's the one with the crappy job. It's the same job, except actually he's been promoted — but everything's relative, so now his job is the sucky one. But we have a dog now, so that makes Eric's sucky job bearable. His name is Robert and he weighs a hundred and five pounds and likes to lean on people. He's got a chicken-bone addiction, but other than that he's perfect. Soon we're going to start trying to make a baby; if we wind up with a baby human as good as our baby dog, we'll be very lucky people indeed.

Isabel went ahead and married her punk-rock boyfriend. They're living in Bath, and last month they opened their own independent bookstore, and they're going to start trying to get pregnant. They're so happy it's disgusting, just like Isabel predicted they'd be. You can feel free to hate them, too. But if you're ever in Bath you should stop by their store and say hello. Buy my book while you're there.

Gwen is still in the movie business. She comes over to eat all the time. We don't smoke and drink quite as much as we used to, but it's still a great time. A better time, in fact. Sally's doing fabulously, and the guy she's dating is named Simon, which I have to say is a relief. My brother spent the presidential election season out in New Mexico, trying to get John Kerry elected. Now that that's gone to hell, he doesn't know what he's going to do, but if he's got any irrational assassination fantasies, he's keeping them to himself. The government agency I used to work for picked a memorial design for the victims of September 11, 2001. Everyone hates it, but then what did you expect? Personally, I think it's okay. Nate the evil genius got himself married, actually to a really lovely girl.

Overall, life is pretty good. I mean, it's not my own enlightened sheikdom, but it sure doesn't suck.

And it's all because of Julia.

I'm not saying this just because blogging about her was what got me the fifteen minutes of fame I was then able to parlay into what's so far looking like maybe (knock wood) a permanent respite from temp work. (Knock wood one more time on that.) Though it's certainly true that blogging about, say, David Strathairn or Jason Bateman would probably not have gotten me quite the attention (no offense, guys, you know how I adore you. *Call me!*). No, what I really mean is this:

Julia taught me what it takes to find your way in the world. It's not what I thought it was. I thought it was all about — I don't know, confidence or will or luck. Those are all some good things to have, no question. But there's something else, something that these things grow out of.

It's joy.

I know, I know — it's truly an *obnoxious* word, isn't it? Even typing it makes me cringe. I think of either Christmas cards or sixty-something New Agey women in floppy purple hats. And yet it's the best word I can think of for the heady, nearly violent satisfaction to be found in the text of Julia's first book. I read her instructions for making béchamel sauce, and what comes throbbing through is that here is a woman who has found her way.

Julia Child began learning to cook because she wanted to share good food with her husband, because she'd fallen in love with great food late but hard, because she was in Paris, because she didn't know what else to do with herself. She was thirty-seven years old. She'd found love, and it was divine. She'd learned to eat, and that was pretty great, too. But it wasn't enough. She probably thought she'd never find whatever it was that was missing if she hadn't found it by the age of thirty-seven. But then, at a cooking school in Paris, she did.

I didn't understand for a long time, but what attracted me to *MtAoFC* was the deeply buried aroma of hope and discovery of fulfillment in it. I thought I was using the Book to learn to cook

French food, but really I was learning to sniff out the secret doors of possibility.

Sometimes, if you want to be happy, you've got to run away to Bath and marry a punk rocker. Sometimes you've got to dye your hair cobalt blue, or wander remote islands in Sicily, or cook your way through *Mastering the Art of French Cooking* in a year, for no very good reason. Julia taught me that.

In the month or so since Julia died, a lot of people have put forward their two cents on How Julia Changed the World, or What Julia Meant to Me, or, very occasionally, Why Julia's Not All That. These statements tend toward the possessive — "*I* saw Julia in this-and-such restaurant," or "*My* whatever-Julia-dish is *really great*," or "I never really *bought* Julia's opinion on this-or-that. . . ." God knows I'm guilty of the same thing. It seems there's something about Julia that brings out the self-centeredness in others. I'm actually worse than anyone, because I get very defensive when other people talk about her. I tend to believe that they don't understand what's really so special about Julia, that they don't *get* her like I do. How self-centered is that? Especially since as far as I know, Julia left this world thinking I was a useless little uppity bitch.

When you don't believe in heaven, death is about as "The End" as you can get. As lovely as it would be, I just don't believe that Julia's eating *sole meunière* in heaven with Paul. I believe that her body's buried — under a very cool gravestone, as it happens; I'll give you one guess what the epitaph is — and the brain and heart and humor and experience that made that body Julia have been extinguished. All that's left of that is what resides still in all our memories.

But that's a kind of afterlife too, isn't it? And for a woman like Julia it's much for the best. When I was in high school I had a particularly damaging drama teacher. Which is *so* a story for another book, and I'm not going to go into it now except to say this: he's dead now, and he lives on in my memory, but he lives on in my memory as a callous, manipulative, unhappy son of a bitch. That's no way to spend eternity.

But with Julia, it's different. Instead of wandering around some hokey, half-baked heaven, wondering how to obtain real Dover sole, she's rattling around the apartments of my brain, banging away at a good sturdy Garland stove and drinking her wine and having a high old time. She's set in her ways, and she can be mulish, but she doesn't clarify butter anymore because she's decided it's just a nuisance, so she's still learning. And since I've given her a place to crash, she's decided I'm not such an uppity bitch after all, and that in fact I'm a pretty great broad. At least that's what the Julia in my head thinks. There are thousands and thousands of her around, in brains all over the world, but this Julia is *mine*.

Practically every single thing written about Julia since she died has ended the same way — including what I wrote on my own blog that day. It's irresistible. It was her sign-off for forty years. It's on her gravestone, for Christ's sake. But I'm not going to do it. I won't. Because although it is affectionate, it is also, ultimately, meaningless. It doesn't get across all that Julia has meant to me — the Julia still in my head right now, saying it, shrieking like a deranged schoolgirl, "Bon *Aaa* —"

No. Let's just say "The End" and leave it at that.

Oh, and thanks.

Thanks for everything.

ACKNOWLEDGMENTS

Like every other author in existence — and especially every first-time, seriously clueless author — I find that there is simply no end of people to thank. This is my first time with this, and I'm going to forget someone here, so apologies in advance for any pique:

Thanks to —

Eric, of course;

Mom and Dad and brother Jordan;

Hannah, Helen, and Em;

the Two Texans and all their hangers-on;

the six Democrats at my erstwhile government agency — most especially Anita, John, Sharon, and Katie, but also Ben, Peter, Chris, Amy, David, and . . . (Wait. That's more than six, isn't it?);

Elizabeth Gilbert, who saved my ass all the way from Afghanistan, within twenty minutes;

Sarah Chalfant, who saved my ass several more times;

Molly, who reminded me at the last minute of the virtues of inconsistency;

Judy Clain, for believing in me;

Eric Steel, for believing in me some more;

and anyone who ever read my blog, ever ever, but especially all of you who became family to me.

Julie Powell was born and raised in Austin, Texas, where she met her husband, Eric. After a long, long time spent working as a temp, she now writes in her pajamas in Long Island City, Queens, where she shares a "loft" apartment with Eric; their dog, Robert; their cats Maxine, Lumi, and Cooper; and their snake, Zuzu Marlene.